THAT MEAN OLD
YESTERDAY

STACEY PATTON

THAT MEAN OLD YESTERDAY

ATRIA BOOKS

NEW YORK   LONDON   TORONTO   SYDNEY

ATRIA BOOKS

A Division of Simon & Schuster, Inc.
1230 Avenue of the Americas
New York, NY 10020

First Atria Books hardcover edition September 2007

ATRIA BOOKS and colophon are trademarks of Simon & Schuster, Inc.

Epigraph credit: "Still Here," from *Collected Poems of Langston Hughes* by Langston Hughes, © 1994 by The Estate of Langston Hughes. Used by permission of Alfred A. Knopf, a division of Random House, Inc.

Book design by Ellen R. Sasahara

Manufactured in the United States of America

10   9   8   7   6   5   4   3   2   1

Library of Congress Cataloging-in-Publication Data

Patton, Stacey Pamela.
   That mean old yesterday / Stacey Pamela Patton.—1st Atria Books hardcover ed.
      p. cm.
   Includes bibliographical references and index.
   1. Patton, Stacey Pamela—Childhood and youth. 2. Adult child abuse victims—New Jersey—Biography. 3. Adoptees—New Jersey—Biography. 4. Child abuse—New Jersey—Case studies. I. Title.

   HV6626.23.N43P38 200 2007
   362.734092—dc22
   [B]

                                                                                      2006101280

For information regarding special discounts for bulk purchases, please contact Simon & Schuster Special Sales at 1-800-456-6798 or business@simonandschuster.com.

ISBN-13: 978-0-7432-9310-5
ISBN-10:   0-7432-9310-X

For William Tucker, the first black child born in America in 1623. He was the son of Antoney and Isabella, Africans who were sold to the British colony in 1619 as indentured servants.

I've been scared and battered
My hopes the wind done scattered.
Snow has friz me, sun has baked me.
   Looks like between 'em
   They done tried to make me
Stop laughin', stop lovin', stop livin' —
But I don't care!
   I'm still here!

—Langston Hughes

THAT MEAN OLD
YESTERDAY

SCARS

Late November in 1999, on a cold night, I was walking down the street without a jacket and without shoes. I hadn't been robbed. Wasn't homeless. Wasn't schizophrenic. Wasn't high. I just didn't care anymore.

At any second the rain was going to sheet down, and hard because I could hear the fat splats tapping soft and slow at first, and then a little harder and more frequent on the leaves above my head. For a split second, I thought about my socks getting wet. I hated that like I hated wet towels on my bed. So I had to hurry up and do what I intended to do before nature soaked my cotton socks and my anger slipped away. Before my impulse got cold. Before I changed my mind.

I took the heavy black nine-millimeter out of my pocket. Some pusher man named Country sold it to me by the water fountain in the center of Washington Square Park just outside my NYU dorm. Country was originally from N'awth C'alina. He started hustling when he moved to Baltimore. I knew him from "The Cage," the legendary basketball court on West Fourth Street where I was one of three females who consistently played with some of the best male ballers in New York City. Country came up north from time to time to play ball, move packages, and sell weed and guns.

When I told him what I needed, all he said was, "Aight shorty. I gotchu. But if shit go down, you 'on't know a nigga. Understand?" Less than a week later, Country brought me what I asked for. When he put the piece in my hand wrapped in a brown lunch bag, I almost dropped it.

"Shorty, you can't be scared of it," he said as he took a mint-flavored chew stick out of his mouth and pointed it at me. "How you g'on shoot sumpin' if you cain't even hol' on to it? You gots to let yo' anga' help you grip 'dat shit!" He gripped the gun and quickly jerked it three times at an invisible man in front of him just before rushing it back into the bag.

Country gave me detailed instructions on how to use the weapon. He said, "Do the damn thing," then put the chew stick back in his mouth and walked away.

Country didn't know what "the damn thing" was and he didn't seem to care. Maybe making that green *paper* was his only concern. But the fact that he armed me let me know that he understood that life could push a man, a woman, or a child to kill.

Almost a month later, I found myself lying naked on my cold bathroom floor with the lights out. I needed the darkness and the silence. I needed to feel that coolness against my sweaty hot face. I was crying. Shaking. Angry. I had the gun next to my head. I wanted to do it so bad. I wanted to pull the trigger. End the flashbacks. Deaden the voices. Kill the pain. But I couldn't do it. I was afraid of the loud bang. I was afraid of doing it the wrong way. Most of all, I did not want to wreak pain on all those people who loved me. I had to find some way to end my torment without hurting myself and those I loved. There was only one other way I could do that.

Three hours later, I dried my tears off the bathroom floor and my face, got to my feet, and turned on the bathroom light. I put my clothes back on and decided that there was another way, besides killing myself, to find redemption. So there I was—a twenty-one-year-old black female university honor student walking down a suburban street in New Jersey with no jacket and no shoes, with murder on my mind.

I was going to kill my past. I didn't know what else to do with it. Time and time again, I had looked back in search of healing. What I found was pain. Anger. Hatred. Helplessness. Vengeful thoughts and impulses. Now I wanted to do to my past all the wrong it had done to me. But my common sense did not tell me that if I got even, my past would always remain, unchanged.

For a few moments, I sat on the curb in front of that big house on Hilltop Drive listening to the distant roar of traffic from Route 1 and gripping the gun like Country said. And then I told myself what to do.

Take a deep breath.

Get on your feet.

Cross the street.

Walk across the lawn, quick.

Ring the bell.

Wait.

Breathe easy.

Don't let the gun get heavy.

Don't let your palms get sweaty.

Stand up strong.

Tighten your grip on the gun.

Stay angry.

Wait for the big, heavy brown door to open. And while you wait, think about all those years you spent in a child's place—seen and not heard, speaking only when spoken to, answering when called.

Promise not to change your mind.

Promise!

Swear you'll finally make your parents hear you loud and clear with gunshots—one to his forehead and empty the rest all over her body. Don't change your mind. Your problems won't end if you change your mind and let them live. They must pay.

I couldn't decide if I would stay and wait for the police, or if I'd run and get back on the New Jersey Transit train to New York. But I knew that once I rang that doorbell, there'd be no turning back.

Everything about the place was the same. Same cream-colored '73 Cadillac. Same blue '87 Lincoln Town Car. Same miniature wooden African sculptures in the window. Same lace curtains. Same black rubber welcome mat. Same Jesus Loves You sticker on the front door. It had been eight years, and they hadn't changed. The dog must have been dead, though. I didn't hear their big, slobbery pit bull bark or thrash against the brown picket fence.

A surge of blood rushed through my face and the center of my chest just as I rose to my feet and stepped off the curb. I looked down at my weapon again and then stopped dead in my tracks. The air went out of me. My shoulders dropped.

"Ain't this a bitch?" I huffed and looked up at the night sky as if it would carry the echo of my question to some distant place and bring me back the reply, "Yep, a real bitch!"

"Damn," I grumbled.

I had forgotten the clip. Not only did I not have a jacket and shoes, I had no bullets. My mind had been so trapped in the network of memories, anger, and voices telling me to do the damn thing that I forgot to come equipped.

There I was, feeling stupid, defeated, and helpless as I stared at that brown door I had walked through from the time I was five until I turned thirteen. All I could do was get back on the train to New York City with all my monsters still alive while Myrtle and George were safely tucked away, sleeping comfortably inside their cookie-cutter suburban Jersey home. Their God was on their side that night, and they never knew that I attempted to slay my past.

As the train snaked out of the Trenton rail station hours later, I slumped down in my seat and thought about that saying, "Everything happens for a reason." Maybe I was meant to forget that clip. Life would eventually take care of them without me having a hand in the process.

Now, I tried to figure out a good place along the eastern corridor to get rid of the gun. I decided to drop it between the train cars once we got to Newark. No one would ever find it amid all that detritus and despair on the outskirts of the city. When the train reached the New Brunswick stop just alongside Rutgers University, I took my other weapon out of my pocket. I pushed back my left sleeve near my honey-colored wrist and dragged the ball of my ink pen along my skin to write these words:

Wounded eyes
Scabbed fingertips
Cut up soul
Despair on my lips
Bloodied memories
Still, I am stronger than death's gaze

Because love and hope dance in my soul

I will bend my pain and cast it away
I will tear myself from ignorance
I will soar in a sky littered with possibilities
I will live until my breath fails
And when Armageddon is over . . .
I will be that eternal orchid
Blooming through the rubble

Four years later, in the spring of 2003, I find myself in my Brooklyn study, seated at my cluttered steel and glass desk staring at that poem that I eventually transcribed onto paper. I wrote in red ink and labeled it *Untitled*. A green pushpin secures my promise to the wall alongside other items that pay homage to the woman I've become.

My bachelor's degree from NYU is encased in a shiny mahogany-colored frame. Next to it is my 2000 collegiate Pulitzer Prize in Feature Writing from the William Randolph Hearst Foundation. A postcard of the Ponte Vecchio is tacked next to a black-and-white photograph of poet Langston Hughes, broadly smiling with his fedora hat cocked to the side. A photo of me and Hillary Clinton that was taken at the Waldorf Astoria during her Senate campaign sits just above a sketch of six little black boys with faces of old black men. They are the kind of little boys that society would rather throw away. They look as if they're going to end up in prison or an early grave. Maybe. But I feel I know those little boys.

Next to the sketch of the little boys is a framed pamphlet that was printed in 1955 and sold for a nickel. On the cover there is a portrait of a smiling Emmett Louis Till wearing a white shirt and black tie. The pamphlet, written by Louis Burnham who was a civil rights activist, investigated the lynching of Till. Next to Till, are two old wooden signs affixed to the wall with skinny nails. One reads: UNATTENDED CHILDREN WILL BE SOLD AS SLAVES. The other sign reads: COLORED ONLY. Underneath those two signs is an index card with a quote from a book I read by Alan Keyes. I never thought I'd find myself reading anything written by a black Republican. But I was inspired so much by his words that I wrote them on the index card in big red letters. It reads:

Real liberation from racism comes with the realization that what whites think of blacks, or do to blacks, is less important than what we think of, and do for, ourselves.

My eyes catch a photograph of thirty girls in white dresses standing in front of a dormitory on graduation day from the Lawrenceville Prep School, me among them. Taped underneath that photo is a *New York Times* clipping of Senator Daniel Patrick Moynihan's obituary with my words, "Good Riddance Old Man," written in black ink across his photo. Next to Moynihan is an index card with a quote from W.E.B. DuBois: "No people that laughs at itself, and ridicules itself, and wishes to God it was anything other than itself ever wrote its name in history."

Dominating the lower space of the wall is a large drawing of a former slave exhibiting a view of his back and his life story for an artist, printed in *Harpers Weekly Magazine* on July 4, 1863. His back looks like a web of keloids. The caption underneath simply reads: "Scars."

I slowly turn in my chair, listening to the wheels rolling on the wooden floor underneath me. My eyes absorb the powerful colors of the texturized images of pain and dehumanization. History is not simply a dead past. Things that happened hundreds of years ago, hundreds of days ago, or hundreds of split seconds ago influence right now. Slavery still lives through us. The past is immortal.

I read and contemplate the brutality of slavery and its consequences. As a student of history, I write about how the vestiges of that peculiar institution get repeated and readapted and why the images of history on my walls are not just visuals frozen in time. When I look at them, I can hear my ancestors' screams and moans and the smack of the whip, which was the music they heard and anticipated all day long. I see their gyrating bodies and know that they could never make sense of their bondage.

Each time I study the images of those black bodies writhing in pain, blood rises in my cheeks, anger flares behind my eyes and between my ears, and my heartbeat accelerates. I start to breathe differently. I want to cry, but my tear ducts are empty. And then I see my own naked body stretched out on the living room floor waiting for the switch, belt, hanger, or extension cord to cut my skin. In an instant, my clouded brain decides that it is my duty to reach into the pictures and protect my ancestors even though I couldn't protect myself. I think of how my body jerked like a convulsing patient—how I screamed like a maniac. How I had that one thought in my head: *I cannot survive this.* The flashbacks make me want to crack open that bottle of Hennessy one of my writer friends gave me for Christmas.

"Stacey, every writer needs alcohol," she said, holding one hand on top of the cool bottle warming in the palm of my hand. "How else do you think we can write about all we see with our third eye? We are life's articulate stenographers. So take this Hen-Dog so you won't feel all the bullshit," she advised.

My eyes leave the tempting bottle of Hennessy and land on a "runaway" ad published in the *Virginia Gazette* on December 10, 1736. On November 14, a twenty-seven-year-old Negro fellow named Quash ran away from his master's plantation in York Town. He had small eyes and a scar on the right side of his cheek, and he had lost a toe on his right foot. Although the ad didn't specify, he probably got the scar from being whipped and probably got his toe cut off for trying to run away several times. I picture myself that night I ran away. I thought for sure I'd be captured and returned to face more lashings.

In a different image, a slave fastened to the ground is being flogged. A white man raises a whip into the air. I wish I could reach into the picture and stop the whip from landing on the naked back of somebody's great-grandfather. In the background, three male Negroes hang their heads as a Negro woman clutches a willow tree and weeps for the male being whipped.

I blink one time, hard and slow. When my eyes are fully open again, I count eight blacks. Two women are on their knees weeping. Another woman is being dragged by her hair as one of her breasts escapes her dress. A small boy stands naked before his master, who is sitting in a wooden chair wearing a floppy hat and holding a switch. A tall, slender black man walks away with his back and clothes torn and bloodied as a white woman stands behind the master's chair chatting with other whites looking on. The caption reads: "An overseer brings slaves to their master for punishment." I see myself hovered over bushes snapping off switches; picking out a belt from the top drawer in the master bedroom; making that dreaded trip to the kitchen to retrieve the extension cord from the coffee pot. Whatever weapon was requested, I had to get it, bring it back, and be beaten with it.

My eyes dart quickly through the images: diagrams of paddles, whips, shackles, branding irons, switches, and whipping machines. My eyes stop abruptly at *The Flagellation of a Female Sambo Slave.* The woman is hanging from a tree by her wrists with deep lacerations. She is dyed with blood from her neck to her ankles after receiving 200 lashes for refusing to have sex with her overseer. I wince at the sight of her blood dripping from her body.

I don't know which is worse: seeing the images or reading the testimonies. This one makes my head spin every time I read it. I photocopied it and taped it next to another image of a black woman with gashes on her back.

James Clark, a well-known citizen of Clark County, made an assault upon one of his Slave women, for an object which need not be stated. He then ordered her into a corner of the room, and commenced pitching his knife at her, point foremost. *As the knife would enter her flesh, he would compel his victim to draw it forth, and return it to him.* This demoniacal amusement was continued until the poor slave was covered with some fifty bleeding gashes! He also cut off her eyelids!

When my tears turn into two long, salty streaks, my sniffles turn into dry breaths, and my anger at those white people simmers just a bit, I study those images again. But this time I pay special attention to the scars of the slaves. They remind me of my own scars and my own enslavement. I list words in my head to describe them: *permanent marks, wounds, indents, sores, streaks, disfigurements, shadows, burns; emblazoned, small, thick, thin, harsh, curly, wide, long, irregular, staggered, symbols of bravery, racial tattoos,* and *lasting effects of grief.*

Those black bodies were the receptacles of their souls and the casings that endured the ravages of one of America's most inhumane institutions. And their bodies were the records of the brutality of slavery written in their scars. America has never been held accountable for its crimes against black people. The white masters of American slavery left their psychic imprints on the flesh and minds of my ancestors. They were loud, intense, and unforgiving scars.

Three generations later, the woman who was supposed to love and nurture me when she and her husband legally adopted me left those same marks on my body and mind when she whipped me. Our home on Hilltop Drive mirrored a southern plantation. Our relationship was like that of a slave and master. The man I called father and expected to protect me stood by helpless, like a slave himself.

Whipping was something that was designed to distort and destroy black bodies to bring about deference. And out of that legacy, my black mama tried to break, distort, and destroy my spirit to make me obedient. When I look at the pictures on my wall, I try to count my ancestors' scars just as I've tried to do with my own. But there are so many that some overlap each other. When I trace them with my fingers, the memories come back. At times I cry. I feel like a vulnerable little girl again. And other times I think about murdering my past.

My scars are a double punishment. Like the slaves, first I had to live through the trauma that marked me, and now I have to live with the reminder for the rest of my life. My scars are the fleshy braille that narrates the story of my battered childhood and how I escaped it. They are a natural part of my healing process. A few of them hide my pain. Some are more noticeable than others. Time has allowed some of them to fade. Although I have not found some magic technique to return my body and soul to its uninjured state, I have found meaning in my scars, my bondage, and my freedom.

PART I
SLAVERY

ONE

S ome black children living on antebellum plantations often had no idea they were slaves. During their early years, they played not only with other slave children but also white children. They wandered freely and explored the plantations. Sometimes masters, especially if they were the biological fathers of slave children, took young slaves horseback riding, cuddled them, and rewarded them with gifts and other special treatment.

But most slave children did not have such an idyllic beginning. Children were the most vulnerable in the slave community, which was characteristically fraught with violence. White youth, at the urging of adults, often abused their black playmates. Older black children meted out cruelty on the smaller ones. Slave children played games like hide-the-switch. One child would hide a willow switch, and the others would search for it. The lucky one to find it got to whip other children at will, mimicking the behaviors they saw whites mete out to their parents and black parents dish out onto black children.

In addition to many forms of verbal, physical, and psychological abuse, slave children faced the threat of being sold at any time. Children often didn't know their biological parents and could be detached at any time from people who were familiar to them because they or those people were sold and shipped off to other plantations. The births of black children helped replenish a cheap labor force and perpetuate the system. During slavery, black children had economic value even before they were born. As property, they could be used not only for their labor but also as collateral for mortgages, to buy land, and to pay other types of debts. Their bondage also helped define what it meant to be white and free.

Slave children died in droves because they were not properly cared for.

Old women, slightly older siblings, or inexperienced mothers had the impossible task of taking care of a large number of children in the plantation nursery. Like adult slaves, children were fed improperly and suffered many illnesses. Despite all this jeopardy, family, such as it was in plantation society, was an important survival mechanism for slave children. Family served as a comfort and layer of protection, as well as a buffer between the humanity of youngsters and the evils of the peculiar institution.

TWO

The day I was told I was a ward of the State of New Jersey and what kind of family I was in changed my view of life. From that moment forward, I lived in a fictive family that I could be uprooted from at any moment. What I knew then was that I was a little girl named Stacey with a lost past and an unknown identity. And I was scared of what awaited me. From then on, childhood became a tortuous and seemingly never-ending form of bondage, where I was at the whim and mercy of various adults, some of whom had little intrinsic value for my humanity. I spent most of my days willing my feet to grow so I could take that big step toward the other side of freedom. Like America's slave children who had been robbed of childhood, I too would have to grow up before my time.

The big house overlooked a busy highway in East Orange, New Jersey. It was cerulean blue with wide, creaky, and splintered wooden steps and a ramshackle porch that wrapped around the front and left side of the Victorian house. Sometimes Mommy smacked my brothers on the back of their heads for climbing and sliding up and down the long white columns that framed the entrance over the steps.

"What the hell do you think this is? A zoo?" she yelled. "The neighbors will think I got a bunch of wild heathens living here."

My siblings and I buried ourselves under blankets of fallen leaves in autumn. The whole winter, our grass was tinged brown and crunchy under our feet. In spring, scattered dandelions sprang haphazardly out of the ground. We snatched the yellow heads off the stems and pelted each other with them. Mommy blamed us when the grass didn't grow in summer.

"You know why this grass won't grow? Huh?" she yelled, demanding an answer as she held dry needles of grass between her fingers before letting the gentle wind blow them from her hand. We stood there looking stupid. "Because," she paused pointing at our little feet, "ya'll trample on it like little horses all the damn year long!"

The mouth of the matching blue mailbox that stood a few feet from the front porch never closed. Our back yard was shaped like a rectangle. The gated fence surrounding it was crooked in some places and had large gaping holes where we eased through to rescue a ball or Frisbee tossed way over our heads. Our back yard was carpeted with concrete instead of plush grass. Mommy constantly warned us about running around like maniacs.

"Don't come in here cryin' if you bust your head open or scrape your knees," she hollered down from the second floor. "And don't bother King!"

Mommy loved King even though he was grumpy and ugly, and smelled nasty. Like a real king, that german shepherd had his own throne, but it was dirty and smelly. King's throne was adorned with a chew bone he hardly played with, a bowl of water, untouched dried food, pee circles, and what we called doo-doo plops. If one of us got too close, he bared his teeth, growled through his evil smile, and took off chasing the little invader until he bit the bottom of the fleeing butt or an innocent bystander.

Mommy always took sides with King. "He bit you?" she'd say and then make a tsk, tsk, tsk noise with her tongue while shaking her head like she felt sorry for us. "What'd you do to him?" she'd ask sardonically. "You *must* have been teasin' him."

Next door lived a lady who growled and barked louder than our dog. She always complained when she saw me standing alone on the porch.

"See there," she'd say, harrumphing and balling her hands into tight fists against her hips. "She ought to know better than to let you be out here by yourself. Don't she know that's how little girls get snatched up?"

I was clueless. Maybe that was how some grown-ups said hello. I always gave her a big Kool-Aid smile and said, "Hi, Miss Lady," in a chipper voice.

"Hi, Miss *Lady*?" she rolled her neck and glared at me. "It's Ms. So-and-So to you, little girl."

I'd correct myself. The steam would stop shooting out her nose, her arms would relax, she'd look around, and then her voice would get soft. "Aw," she paused. "You don't know no better."

She inched closer to me as her eyes got smaller and her bottom lip dropped. Suddenly her engine of a mouth revved up again.

"Why does she put you in them homely lookin' clothes? Look at them shoes!"

I dropped my eyes down to my feet.

"That shirt is dingy!"

My eyes moved up to my shirt.

"And them pants is high waters!"

My eyes moved back down to my ankles, and I imagined my feet being overtaken by floodwaters, as I stood before her looking helpless and unwanted.

"And . . . look . . . at . . . that . . . head!"

My eyes rolled to the top of my head as I caught a glimpse of a ragged plait escaping from a plastic pink barrette.

"Chile," she sighed. "I ain't neva' knowed no white woman that could tame a black child's head o' hair."

By that point she would reach for a plastic black Goody brand comb she had either hidden in the front pocket of her housedress or anchoring the tightly braided bun in the back of her head.

"Do she even grease your scalp?"

"Grease?" I frowned, looking stupid. Why in the world would Mommy dip her hand into the can of used Crisco to coat my head like she did the cast-iron skillet before frying chicken?

"Lawd have mercy," she sang. "Umph. Don't DYFS [Division of Youth and Family Services] know that a white woman can't raise a black child? How they 'spect her to raise nine of 'em? She got ya'll walkin' 'round here lookin' like a bunch of pickaninnies!"

She pulled my face between her thighs and went to work on my hair. It sounded as if she was raking leaves at first. My yells and ouches were muffled because my face was smothered in her housedress. After a few minutes, the pain eased. I could feel her fingers digging for curls pulling straight down my back as far as they'd go. She'd plait them and take bobby pins out her own hair, grip them momentarily between her front teeth, and then use them to lock them into little buns.

"She don't read the Bible, do she?"

"I dunno, Ms. So-and-So." I shrugged my shoulders wanting to touch my hair, but knowing I'd get my hand tapped if I did.

"Well, if she did, then she'd know that it say a woman's hair is her crown and glory. And that applies to little girls too."

Ms. So-and-So never failed. Every time I saw her she talked about

DYFS, the white woman, my nappy hair, and pickaninnies. I asked Mommy, "What's DYFS? What's a white woman? What's nappy? What's a pickaninny?"

"Don't listen to Ms. So-and-So," Mommy said. "She is forever in other folks' business. Plus, she likes to hear herself talk."

If it wasn't raining or cold, I sat on the porch and waited for Daddy to come home from work. I could spot his tall black figure floating down the street wearing his blue uniform with the daily paper tucked underneath his armpit. He'd be either cracking some nutshell with his teeth or spitting sunflower seeds from his mouth.

"Hey, Daddy," I yelled to him two or three times.

Sometimes he mumbled, "Hey girl." Other times he gave me a cool head nod as his long legs strolled up the steps. Daddy was a mailman. His job was simple: he put things in boxes and closed them up. When he walked inside the big house every day, that's what he did with himself. He washed his face and hands, changed his uniform, fixed his plate, and closed himself off from the world of our house.

When Daddy was in a good mood, he let me sit at the foot of his bed and watch television. "Sit still and don't say nothin'," he said. "One word and you're out."

What would me and the mailman talk about anyway? I remember Daddy as merely the man who slept next to Mommy. I thought that was all daddies were for. He didn't play with us. He didn't say more than a few scolding sentences to us. He didn't cook, clean, or dress us. And he never took us anywhere. For fun, he smoked smelly pipes, drank liquor, and played spades with some of his buddies.

When Daddy fell asleep with the TV watching him, I stood over him and studied every detail of his body. He seemed like a strange black alien. Although his lids were closed, I could still see his sunken eyes rolling in the sockets. When he snored, his nostrils twitched. His lips were the color of portobello mushrooms. I wondered what that bulge was behind his zipper. Why he had hair around his chin. How his feet got so big. His hands lay on his pelvis, and his feet, covered in black polyester old-man socks, pointed toward the ceiling. A coffin would complete this description and story of Daddy because, indeed, he was like a dead man. The only time he came alive was when his thunderous voice yelled, "Shut up!" before putting ice cubes in a mouth that wouldn't stop crying.

I can't remember much about life inside the big house. I don't remember names. Today Mommy is just a white blur in my memory. But I do remember that she could take her teeth out of her mouth and put them back in. Sometimes I saw them soaking in a small glass on the windowsill in the bathroom. I wouldn't go near them because I thought they'd jump out the glass and start yelling at me or bite me.

What else can I remember?

Watching pot pies rise in the oven and going to bed without dinner when I acted up. The time I threw up on my face because I was convinced that if I lay on my back, the vomit wouldn't make it to the top of my throat—but to my surprise, it did. I remember spending afternoons sitting next to the kitchen window peering out like a hungry bird while Mommy watched her stories like *As the World Turns* and *The Guiding Light*. Bumping all the way down to the bottom step on my butt because I was too afraid to walk down. *The Soul Train* after *Josie and the Pussycats* on Saturday mornings. *Fat Albert and the Gang; The Jeffersons; Laverne and Shirley; The Love Boat; WKRP in Cincinnati; Mr. Belvedere; The Facts of Life.* Peanut butter and jelly sandwiches with chocolate milk. Being afraid of the toilet because I believed it swallowed little kids. The time my tooth fell out and I put it under my pillow for the tooth fairy. When I woke up, I found a $50 bill and I ran downstairs to show Mommy my treasure.

"Oh damn." she snatched it out of my hand. "I ain't mean to leave fifty dollars." She reached into her bra and pulled out a dollar bill and handed it to me. And then she put the fifty back in her bra.

I remember the doll I got for my fifth birthday. She was so tall she looked me in my face. She had yellow hair and glass blue eyes that blinked when I shook or tilted her. I remember the one time Mommy hit me. I had tried to mimic my brothers by standing over the toilet to pee. She walked in the bathroom to find the seat, floor, and my pants wet. When she popped me on my backside, that's when I discovered I wasn't a boy and what the bulge was in Daddy's pants. It seemed so much easier to stand than sit, to be a boy than a girl. I thought I had finally realized why boys could run faster, jump further, and had more strength. The source of the power came from the fact that they could stand up and pee. I was so envious of them.

When I lived in the big house, I had no concept of childhood. I didn't know that adults were once kids and that kids became adults. I thought I was destined to be small forever and walk a long, unquestioned path. But one day I began to grow up way before my time.

"Dy-no-mite!" yelled JJ from the show *Good Times*. Mommy and even Daddy joined in on the laughter blaring from the television.

Without looking, her shaky hands searched the small table next to her bed. Her pink fingertips located the glass that always sat next to her glasses, the lamp, and the mail. When she picked up the glass, she looked at it and was disappointed to see that it was empty. Her gritty, bloodshot eyes found me sitting cross-legged on the floor.

"Hey, little girl," she coughed, holding up the glass. "Bring me Mister Walker."

I jumped to my feet, ready to fulfill the task, twisted the cold closet doorknob with both hands, and pulled the door into me. Stepping past high-heeled shoes, stockings, boxes, and a crowd of other bottles, I located Mister Walker. I braced myself and made my hands strong, as I always did, some three or four times a day.

"And don't drop him!" Mommy ordered. "Show Mommy you're a big girl."

I carefully walked Mister Walker over to Mommy's welcoming hands. When she took him from me, I felt like a huge weight had been lifted, but the task was not complete. She put the glass in my hands, and I had to hold it while she poured what she called her "magic juice." If I didn't spill any, which I rarely did, then I felt more like a big girl.

Mommy put Mister Walker's cap back on and told me to put him back in the closet next to Mister Jack Daniels. After closing the closet door, I resumed my spot on the floor and watched her complete her ritual. She moistened her lips and pursed them in anticipation of the cool liquid's approach. When her lips met the rim of the glass, her eyes closed and her cheeks expanded. She held the "magic juice" in her mouth for a few seconds and then swallowed. A look of pain would always cross her face as the liquid rippled down her throat.

"Whew!" she wolfed.

By the time the glass was almost empty, she would start slurring insults and talking mean to me, like always. She admitted she told lies when she drank. But that night she told the truth.

"Ya know suttin', little girl." Her speech was garbled. "Ya know I aint ya' mommy."

I giggled. Sometimes she said the silliest things to make me laugh.

"You hear me," she snapped. "I said I ain't ya' mother."

My heart dropped fast to my private parts. She seemed like she was no longer drunk. Perhaps she needed her magic juice to break the news to me.

"I ain't ya' real mother," she repeated and peered hard at her glass.

I stared at her glass too, confused and still feeling my heart beating in my private parts. "Mommy, what's a real mother?"

She blurted out a laugh. "Don't you git it? Don't call me Mommy anymore! A *real* mommy is somebody who gives birth to a child. You didn't come from my stomach, so you ain't my child and I ain't ya' real mommy."

I had no idea that I came out of a stomach. And if I came out of a stomach, how did I get in there? And how did I get out of there? Wouldn't it hurt to be inside a stomach? I was too big to be crammed into a stomach. Real mother? Was Mommy my mother for play-play?

"You gittin' a new mommy and daddy."

New mommy? New daddy? Nobody asked me if I wanted new parents. Did everybody get new parents at five? Were children like dolls that were replaced with new ones once their parents grew tired of playing house with them? Did they not like me anymore?

"They are real nice folks." The words staggered out of her mouth like drunken soldiers. "They gonna take real good care of you. Give you a much better life than we could ever give you," she said.

A better life? What was that? I had nothing else to compare life in the big house to. I didn't know if life could be better or worse, let alone who could provide it. Either way, the thought of newness and the unknown frightened me and a feeling I never had before rose in me: confusion.

"If you not my Mommy, then who are you?"

"I'm your foster mother," she responded. I heard the glass scrape lightly against the table as she set it down. The mailman was still laughing at JJ, oblivious to the exchange.

"What's a foster mother?"

"It's kind of like a Mommy, but I take care of other people's kids when their real mommy or daddy can't, until they find a good home.

"Where's my real Mommy?"

She breathed hard and sighed slowly, "I don't know."

"She didn't want me?"

Her intoxicated eyes looked deep into mine. "No, baby, I'm sure she wanted you. It wasn't your fault. Sometimes things happen, and parents can't take care of their children. Sometimes they don't have enough money, or they get sick or die."

"My mommy got sick?"

"I don't know," she shook her head.

"My mommy dead?"

"I don't know."

I felt like I had some huge hole in the middle of my body. There was no tooth fairy. No Santa. No Easter Bunny. And the ice cream man didn't come every day. I had gotten over all that bad news. But no real mommy! No daddy! Life was a lie! A trick! All I had trusted and known to be true had crumbled with my foster mother's words.

Who was I? Where did I come from? What was my identity? What was my real name? What was my history? What was truth?

THREE

S lave communities got their start in America during the eighteenth
century. Africans underwent painful reluctant adaptations to the
violent social and cultural processes of their bondage in the New World.
When they arrived in the New World as slaves, they had their bodies and
the contents of their minds, which included memories of their homeland.
But they were often denied the right to own their bodies or even own or
express their own thoughts without consequence. Despite the brutal conditions facing them in the New World, the first generation of slaves were
still able to hold onto scraps of memories that mostly induced a longing
for their previous life.

In response to the demands of their circumstances, African slaves had
to learn new ways of perceiving, believing, acting, and even breathing
because at every turn, their humanity was called into question. Because of
the suffocating environment of the New World, men, women, and children had to suddenly and violently detach themselves from their old culture in order to survive.

Redefining themselves and working out new patterns of life, Africans
became African American slaves—a new people. They tried to fuse
African with African American beliefs, behaviors, and institutions. But for
the most part, they had forced on them a new environment, new language, new names, new culture, and a new white master. Slaves had to recognize their bondage and the overwhelming power of whites. Everywhere
they turned, someone was ready to beat and break them: the master, master's wife, overseer, driver, patrollers, constables, and jailers. And for slave
children, the list also included black adults.

What does a child do to survive bondage? Centuries later, I discovered such reluctant adaptation in me. Perhaps it's a black thing. Maybe it's a universal feature of perpetually oppressed people. Or it could simply be a primal human instinct to save one's own life. I had to quickly learn how to survive within my new world of bondage.

FOUR

The whip symbolizes the subjugation my ancestors lived through and died under. A thick black leather belt hanging on the bathroom doorknob in the hallway of our house symbolized mine. The naked wire hangers in every closet did too. The wooden broomstick resting in the corner by the refrigerator was another one. A handful of freshly pulled, sweet-smelling thorn switches lying on the coffee table in between replicas of Rodin's *The Kiss* and *The Thinker* came in handy as well. I called the extension cord that Myrtle used to whip me "the snake," because it bit and tore open my flesh. High-heeled shoes, combs, brushes, rolled-up newspapers, her hands and her words: they were all weapons.

My foster mother may have been a drunk who said mean things, hollered, and even broke promises. But her tongue was not razor sharp, and she never hit me or the other foster children. So when my new mommy hit me for the first time, I got angry with my foster mother. My foster mother had told me I was going to get a nice new mommy who would take care of me. But that was a lie.

The day I met Myrtle, her soft, warm hands welcomed me into her lap and stroked my hair from time to time as we rode in the back seat of the social worker's car. As her hands clasped around my small middle, I traced the ornate details of her intricately designed rings that adorned two fingers on each hand.

"What's your name?" she asked, as if she hadn't already been told by the social worker.

"Sta-cey," I sang and grinned. My eyes zoomed in closer to my roasted walnut–colored hands pressed against her creamy latte–colored hands.

"Stacey, Stacey, Stacey," the black man sitting in the passenger's seat repeated as he turned his head to look at me. I think he was the first black man ever to speak to me this way. It shocked me at first because I couldn't ever remember my foster father calling me by my name.

"Hi, Mister," I mumbled shyly and tried not to stare at him too long.

"Stacey-Wacey," he played around with my name.

When he showed me his teeth, I noticed there was a huge gap that I swore I could slip my pinky through if I tried. He looked like the type of man girls probably swooned over back in the day. His skin tone was evenly dark, and he had the type of hair that appeared to be conked and Brylcreemed into place every day. But that was just the front view. From the top, it seemed someone had gotten jealous of his beautifully carved hair and taken a circular patch for themselves, leaving him a clean, shiny bald spot. When he took his thick brown-rimmed glasses off to wink at me, I noticed the large half-moon birthmark under his eye that was shaded a sickly green.

"What happened to your eye?" I asked him, assuming it was a scar.

"It's a birthmark," he replied.

"What's a birthmark?"

"Somethin' you're born with," he answered. "I'm sure you got a birthmark."

"I don't have no marks under my eye," I shot back. Everyone chuckled. I wondered why.

"People got birthmarks in different places," Myrtle said. There was silence again as I watched him clean each thick lens of his glasses with a handkerchief that had been hiding in his front shirt pocket with some ink pens. He put one lens at a time between his lips and made a huffing sound. The lenses got cloudy. He then wiped each in circular motions until they were clear again.

"Stacey." He said my name again just as he returned his glasses to his face. "A pretty name for a pretty little girl."

That was the first time I heard anyone call me pretty. Honestly, I wasn't really sure what it meant. But coming from him, it sounded good and made me smile even more.

"What's your name?" I pointed my little finger at him.

"I'm George," he said.

"But I call him G," Myrtle said.

"Just about everybody calls me G," he said.

"Hi, G!" I said in an excited voice as everyone broke into laughter.

I basked in the attention. All eyes on me. My head resting against Myrtle's breasts. Her slight breaths in my ear, her hands on mine. G's questions about things I liked, and his corny jokes made me laugh.

The four of us drove to Quakerbridge Mall located on Route 1 near Princeton. G and Myrtle mostly talked with the white social worker named Evelyn. They all looked so serious but smiled whenever I demanded their attention. I rode a carousel. Begged for toys they happily bought for me. Stuffed myself with pizza, soda, ice cream, and candy.

Just as I finished my treats, I tugged Myrtle's hand and asked, "Can we bring some pizza and ice cream back for my mommy?"

G shot his eyes at Myrtle and Evelyn. Myrtle's face turned gray like she was going to throw up or had diarrhea. Her jaw tensed up. Clearly they didn't know how to handle such a question. So Evelyn came to their rescue.

"Well Stacey," Evelyn let out a long breath. "The ice cream will melt, and the pizza will get cold before we get back. It's a long ride from Trenton back to East Orange."

Evelyn's reasons made perfect sense to me. There was no need for further elaboration. But Myrtle added, "Yeah, I don't think you want your foster mother to eat cold pizza."

G let out a loud fake cough to get her attention. He mumbled something under his breath to her. But it was too late to undo Myrtle's reminder to me that Mommy wasn't my real mommy. At that point, it all came together in my head. I was on a visit with the people who were going to be my new mommy and daddy. Visits were designed to ease the transition between the foster home and a new permanent home. I guess the State of New Jersey figured it would be traumatic to snatch me away from my foster mother and just drop me into a new home without us getting to know each other.

For the next few months, I went on more visits with Myrtle and G, but the type of visits changed over time. They were supervised day visits with Evelyn at first. Then unsupervised day visits. Overnight weekend visits. Week-long visits. And then by August 1983, I had one last weekend visit at my foster home before the woman I had called Mommy for the first five years of my life handed me over to Myrtle and G for good.

My foster mother didn't cry, at least not in front of me. Perhaps today, I'd like to think she cried before facing me for the last time, or maybe she cried when she got back inside. Maybe knowing that she actually shed tears over my departure would make me think that she really did care about me. If she shed tears that day, I'd like to know so I won't think that I was just a monthly check to her.

I didn't cry either. I had no idea what was happening. The social worker told me I wouldn't be living in that house anymore. But I didn't think that I wouldn't see my first mommy ever again. I watched her stand behind the car holding a lumpy green garbage bag with a blank expression on her face. Just before Myrtle and G drove away with me, my foster mother ran up to the car holding the little trash bag, yelling, "Wait! Wait!"

G stepped on the brakes hard and got out of the car. My foster mother told him what was inside the garbage bag: the white doll with glass blue eyes and chopped blonde hair I had gotten for my birthday, three books (*Humpty Dumpty, Mother Goose,* and *The Three Bears*), and some clothes. Even though I had lived in that foster home for the first five years of my life, the few belongings I had didn't show it. As foster kids, we owned next to nothing. We shared everything. I was probably wearing somebody else's socks and panties the day I left. G took the bag from her and dropped it into the trunk. My foster mother opened my door and stuffed a small sheet of paper in my hand. It had numbers on it.

"I want to hear your sweet little voice," she said. "So call me sometimes. You be a good girl. That shouldn't be hard 'cause you are a good little girl." And then she kissed my forehead.

That was the only time I can remember my foster mother ever kissing me. Maybe she did it other times. Perhaps I can remember that kiss only because it was the last time I ever saw her. Had I known that I was never going to see her again, I would have said something instead of giving her a dizzy look. Maybe I would have studied her face a bit longer so that I could remember her features just in case I saw her walking down the street later in life. Although she had a nasty mouth, yelled all the time, and drank too much, my foster mother still gave all the kids who lived in that house a certain measure of love.

As we drove away, I could still hear her voice inside my head—those words she uttered to me the day she told me she wasn't my real mother.

"You got to understand sumpin', little girl." She was about to burp from drinking her magic juice, but she swallowed it back down her throat. "Nothin' is promised to you in this life. Don't nobody owe you anything.

Not even your own mother and father. But you—you are blessed," she said, slicing the air with her shaky finger. "You are five years old, and somebody still wants you. That don't happen too often in this system."

System? What was that?

"Most people want babies," she continued. "They don't want old kids."

Old kids? Kids could be old?

"Old kids come with too much baggage," she said. I could still hear the ice cube slightly clanging against her glass as I remembered what she said to me.

"We're home," G cooed as we pulled into the driveway of the huge white Cape Cod–style house with a large, manicured lawn and shade trees. During the ride from East Orange to that suburban town near Trenton, he peeked through the rearview mirror and kept winking his eye at me.

I rushed out of the car and ran up to the porch. I couldn't wait to get inside and play with all those toys they said were waiting for me. For the first time in my life, I had my own room, toys, clothes, and books. I didn't have to share with other kids or worry about them breaking my stuff. I could say, "*This* is mine. *This* is mine. And *this* is mine."

As I stood on the porch like a little princess, G opened the trunk and took out the lumpy garbage bag. Myrtle walked up to him and snatched it away. He and I watched her, confused, as she walked to the end of the driveway where she dropped the bag.

"What you doin', Myrtle?" G frowned.

"It's garbage." She frowned back at him as she made her way toward the house.

"That's my stuff," I whined, pointing at the bag.

"Honey, you have all new things now," she said. "New clothes. New toys. New home. New mommy. New daddy. A new life," she said tapping a different finger on her hand as if she were counting. "You need to leave your foster home, that garbage on the curb, and your foster mother behind. Forget about it all. Thank God for what you have now."

I wasn't thinking about God. I was worried about something happening to my things.

That night before I went to bed, I lifted the shade covering my window and saw the bag still on the curb. I remember how the moonlight hit the top of the bag. I wanted more than anything else to rescue it. But the next morning, I awoke to the loud roar of a big orange truck. I threw off the sheets and ran over to the window. My heart pounded against my little chest. With my hands over my mouth, I watched the monster-mouthed truck devour my bag and move on to the next house. I wanted to curl up and die.

I stomped down the staircase leading from my playroom to the main hallway. Myrtle was sitting at the kitchen table sipping perked Maxwell House coffee. Her eyes zoomed in on my angry eyes and poked out lips.

"What's your problem?" she growled in a tone of voice I hadn't heard from her before.

"My stuff . . ."

Bang! The back of her hand stopped the rest of the words from coming out my mouth.

When I snapped back to my senses, the mean look on her face along with her hand moving away from my mouth confirmed for me that she had slapped me. My lips heated up and began to throb. My spit tasted like metal. I felt like the world was coming to an end. Why did she hit me? That hurt! Hot, fast, furious tears sprinted down my face. I cried more from shock and disbelief than from the pain.

"Shut up!" she yelled. "This is a new day!" I scanned the room for G, but he was nowhere to be found.

"He ain't here, so stop lookin' for him. This is my house. I pay the cost to be the boss. You ain't got nothin'! You ain't got a good pot to piss in or a bed to push it under. You remember that."

I pressed my lips together to keep any whimper from escaping. I summoned my tear ducts and told them, *not now!* My foster mother had always let me cry. Sometimes I even cried myself to sleep. When I'd awake, she'd say, "Feel better now?" But I instinctively knew that with Myrtle, tears could get me hit again. Her hands had gone from soft, warm, welcoming, and protective to weapons.

"You ain't with your foster *mammy* no more!" she yelled. "You in my house. And I got rules. As long as you under *my* roof, you g'on do what *I* say, or you can let DYFS come get you and take you back to that piss-infested foster home where you came from with all them other little nappy-headed pee rats walkin' around."

At that moment, I didn't think that was such a bad idea. But when I thought about the words she used to describe my former home—

piss-infested and *nappy-headed pee rats*—it made me think that it wasn't such a good place to live. Her home was better.

Then came the rules:

1. Don't get out of bed in the morning until she tells me.
2. Don't let her have to tell me to get out of bed twice.
3. Make my bed up.
4. Don't come downstairs in my pajamas.
5. No stomping.
6. No pouting.
7. No whining.
8. No talking back.
9. Don't question her.
10. No rolling my eyes.
11. No sucking my teeth.
12. Answer "yes" when called. Don't ever say "huh," "yeah," or "what."
13. Call them Mommy and Daddy. Don't ever call them by their first names.
14. Don't ever talk about my foster mother or foster home again.

These were just a few of her rules I had to soak up on the first day. She assured me that if I broke any of them, I would risk getting what she called "a good butt whupping." That day would begin a pattern of searching for her lurking around every door and shadowy corner in every room. Although that initial slap shocked and hurt me, I could never be prepared for what followed: beatings for about any small infraction. I had to make sure I knew where her weapons were at all times. Of all of them, those pretty latte-colored adorned hands became the worst weapons.

I missed my old house. My brothers and sisters. Getting magic juice out the closet for my first mommy, and the world I had come from. The only things I feared then were falling into the toilet and walking down the huge staircase in our hallway. I never feared other people. I didn't know what to think of this new world. Maybe it would be only temporary, just as it had been in my foster home. Perhaps G and Myrtle would keep me for only five years, just as my first mommy had done. And then I'd be put with nicer new people. But meanwhile, I had to adjust to the life I was in.

FIVE

Despite their bondage, slave children had spare time to experience pleasure and play. Play was a means through which they learned the values and social mores of their parents' world.

Like free children, slave children role-played and imitated the behaviors of adults. They wished to be grown-ups. To feel needed. To love. To compete. To express their individuality. To join groups. To express power and control. Through their play, they coped with their fears, relieved anxieties or reflected them, and mastered aspects of their bondage they couldn't realistically change. Play allowed black children a sense of dignity and unique existence. Because they were allowed to participate in pleasurable activities with each other, slave children could withstand their bondage more easily.

Play for me was usually a solitary activity. Otherwise Myrtle supervised how I dressed my Barbie dolls, combed their stringy yellow hair, and organized the furniture in the large dollhouse that sat in the middle of my playroom. I was expected to recreate a world for my dolls that mirrored life in my new home. Sometimes I played bingo and checkers without a partner—never winning or losing. When I got angry, I took it out on my dolls by punching them, breaking their arms and legs, cutting their hair, or writing on their faces. Other times I sat in corners staring at the ceiling while holding myself and rocking back and forth.

When I was allowed to play with other children—usually my adoptive cousins—I was more of a spectator than an active participant in their games. I wasn't accustomed to socializing with other children. Adult conversations were more familiar than kid codes and sayings. I didn't know the popular kids' TV shows because I watched what Myrtle watched. I didn't know the words to singing games or the right body slaps, claps, and taps to ring games. So from a comfortable distance, I watched them simulate the world of the black adults in our family. From the beginning, I began to recognize the patent schism that existed between black children and black adults within the family dynamic.

SIX

Myrtle was my master, and I obeyed her without questioning. Sometimes I wondered if G was really a grown man or just a big boy because Myrtle relegated him to the same child status that I held in our house. Myrtle called both of us "triflin' backward niggas." I believed there was no person or force bigger, stronger, or meaner than Myrtle Jenkins. She was the ultimate authority on everything. But she too had a higher power that she obeyed.

Myrtle and G went to church four times a week; read their King James Version Bibles; and listened to gospel music to the exclusion of all others. They didn't drink, smoke, dance, curse, or play the lottery. They believed that if they committed these sins, God was going to cast them into the fiery pit of brimstones for eternity. And they told me that children could go to hell too.

"God don't have no mercy on little people's souls," Myrtle said, scaring the wits out of me.

Myrtle was a small woman, slight in stature. The color of uncooked brown rice, her skin was stretched taught over her cheekbones with no smile or laugh lines visible. She had no special features to speak of other than a receding hairline you might find on an old Jewish rabbi. Sometimes I wondered how her hair would hang when it seemed like the next strong wind would blow it away. When she was feeling lovely, she'd do the black woman's version of the comb-over by wrapping her hair into a swirl around her head, securing it with bobby pins and giving the illusion of an old school beehive.

G and I were not the same color as Myrtle. I noticed this one day and said, "Mommy, me and Daddy are the same, and you're different from us."

"How's that?" she asked, turning her nose up at the both of us.

"Me and Daddy are black, and you are white," I explained looking at my caramel-colored hands and G's dark cocoa complexion.

Myrtle's face wrinkled up like a paper lunch bag. "I'm white? Girl, how you figure dat?"

G giggled.

"'Cause me and Daddy are chocolate covered, and you are vanilla colored."

"Chile, please," she sneered. "I'm just as black as you and your daddy. Just 'cause I ain't dark-skinned don't mean I ain't black. It certainly don't make me white!"

"See, baby," G paused, and gently laid his hand on top of mine, highlighting the difference in our dark complexion as Myrtle kept hers to herself. "You got all kinds of blackness. You got some folk that's so black they almost look blue. You can cut the lights off and see only their eyeballs or their teeth if they smile. And then you got some black folks that are so light-skinned that they can pass for white folks. We got people like that on my side of the family."

"Any white person can look at me, and tell you that I ain't no white woman," Myrtle added.

Myrtle had thinner lips than G and me. She was always biting them. When she wasn't, she kept a toothpick clinched between her teeth. She rolled it back and forth, slowly bounced it up and down, sucked hard on it, and clamped down on it even during whippings at church. She took it out only to spit rage at me, bark orders, verbally assault G, and shout "Amen" and "Hallelujah" with the other so-called saved, sanctified, and filled-with-the-Holy-Ghost church folks.

Myrtle was a product of the era in which a woman's worth was measured by marrying, serving her husband, keeping her house clean, worshipping God, and having children. She dropped out of junior high school, unlike G who completed the twelfth grade. They both prided themselves on the fact that they had "common sense" and scoffed at people who were what they considered "high-minded" or "high-se ditty." All they both needed to know and learn about life could be found through reading the Bible and faithfully attending church.

Prior to life at 123 Hilltop Drive, God did not exist for me and I had never stepped foot inside a church. Now I was expected to sing Negro spirituals, believe and pretend to be moved by the Holy Ghost, know the "Good Book" and pray. I did not believe there was a big almighty God in the sky, because life here on earth hadn't seemed fair to me since that day my foster mother told me the truth about myself.

I thought the songs they sang in church were frivolous repetition. I didn't believe people should trust that God would get them through terminal illness, cheating spouses, and eviction notices. I never felt the Holy Ghost take up residence in my little body and possess me to run through the sanctuary head first and at full speed like a steam engine until either the ushers caught up with me or I ran out of speed and passed out as a sign of my soul being saved at last. I wasn't moved to testify about the goodness and mercy of God, considering one of his soldiers was slowly but surely beating the life out of me.

Even on holy ground, I found no sanctuary from Myrtle. Small infractions like chewing gum, not sitting up straight, fidgeting, or laughing at a woman with her wig askew from catching the Holy Ghost would cause her to strike me with a lightning-fast flick of her wrist without missing a beat to the song or word of the preacher's sermon.

Myrtle would always tell me God saw everything I did. "God ain't no toy," she'd mutter. "Church ain't no playhouse. You need to get right with the Lord, little demon."

If God saw everything I did, it was probably because Myrtle was his spy. She always insisted that she had eyes in the back of her head. Bored out of my mind, one evening I tiptoed up to Myrtle to part her thin coif in search of her other eyeballs as she lay sleeping on the living room sofa. I discovered only scalp, and my disappointment was compounded by the backhand I received for my mischievousness.

G didn't invoke the fear of God's wrath in me like Myrtle did, but he too took God seriously. He always had some gospel tune on his tongue, was poised to quote scriptures no matter the subject of the conversation, and often sat for long periods on the toilet reading his Bible. The fear of God had made his wife a strict and rigid disciplinarian. But that same fear of the Almighty One made him a humble man who always extended kindness to anyone who needed it.

Although I loved his friendliness and laid-back demeanor, I found my adoptive father to be quite embarrassing and awkward. G was forty when I moved into his home. He was medium height with a neatly trimmed mustache and a stiff walk. His ears were small and pinned close to his

head, with tiny hairs sprouting from the tips of his lobes and from inside
the canals. He had meaty hands with cracked skin and splintered purple
nails from hammer misses. His round, hairy navel poked out of his dusty
brown shearling when he walked in from doing odd jobs around the
house on weekends. One of his favorite summer pastimes was sitting in
his lawn chair on the front porch dressed in khaki pants and a Fruit of the
Loom undershirt with yellow-stained armpits and an economy-size bag
of barbecue pork rinds resting over his stomach. He'd smack loudly, lick
his fingertips, and sing his favorite spiritual, "Precious Lord." Crunch.
"Lead me on." Crunch. Crunch. "Let me stand."

Through the week, I could smell G reeking of sweat, oil, and grease like
those grungy men who worked at those hole-in-the-wall auto body shops
on the outskirts of East Trenton. Normally I could close my eyes in a
room of a hundred people and tell you whether G was present based on
his scent—unless it was Saturday or Sunday when he took his weekly bath
to prepare for entering the house of the Lord, where he was known as
Reverend Jenkins even though he had never gone to seminary school or
been ordained. We went to the kind of Pentecostal church where men
were "called" directly by God to preach the Gospel.

When G emerged from the bathroom, he always looked like a new
man, or as if he lost some weight from all the dirt he washed off. All the
other days of the week, he simply washed his face, neck, and arms in the
sink after working eight hours in a mechanical parts factory. Myrtle was
forever calling him a "funky backward southern nigga from the sticks"
due to his bathing rituals. Bathing only once a week was a nasty habit he
never left behind from his Mississippi upbringing. On weekends, he
dressed up in suits he bought from the Red White and Blue Thrift Store
and proclaimed that he was a minister called by God. He looked more
useful with his work tools, big black boots, and stinky, green jump suit
with "JENKINS" stitched on a white patch underneath his collar. He looked
strong and full of purpose until he took it all off and tried to be a preacher
or, worse, my father.

G once told the congregation at the Trenton Pentecostal Church of
God that he used to do "worldly" things like smoking, drinking, playing
cards, dancing, cussing, and running after women. "But one day," he bel-
lowed in his southern cadence as he stabbed at the ceiling with his finger,
"God changed all that. God," he paused, "picked me up!" He pretended to
pick up an invisible heavy body standing next to him on the pulpit.

"Turned me around." He spun himself around once. "And he placed my feet on solid ground." He hopped forward and landed firmly and upright again.

"*Well-well*," somebody said in a singsong voice.

Every second and fourth Sunday when it was his turn to preach, I made myself as little as possible. I fixed my eyes on my lap and hoped none of the other kids were looking at me. I tried to lose myself in the aroma of the red- and white-striped peppermint candy I sucked on. When I toyed with the candy wrapper, Myrtle either snatched it out of my hand or pinched me on the fatty part of my upper arm. I usually sat there mesmerized by the plastic white Jesus hanging on a cross over the pulpit with blood dribbling out of its plastic side. Sometimes I flipped through the pages of the Bible looking at all the artwork. I never saw black people. I asked Myrtle about this once.

"Mommy?"

"What?" She sounded annoyed as she always did when I asked her questions.

"How come there aren't black people in the Bible? And was Jesus white?"

"No, Jesus wasn't no cracker," she responded. "White folks want you to think that Jesus and God was white. They make and draw everything to look like them."

Myrtle took the Bible from my hands and turned to some book in the New Testament. She read a description that said Jesus had hair like wool and skin like bronze. "See that," she tilted the book and pointed at the verse. "Now do that sound like a white man with blond hair and blue eyes to you?"

"No," I nodded.

"Well, how come there aren't any black people in any of the pictures?"

"That's how white folks are. Band-Aids are made for white folks. Hallmark Cards are made for white folks. And Jesus is made for white folks. That's how they tell lies when they got pen and ink in their hands. They do it with the Bible. They do it with history. They do it on the news. They do it on commercials. You would think the whole world was white and wasn't nobody else around that did anything and contributed anything. That's what they want you to think. They don't include nobody else in the story. It's all about celebrating them. Celebrating whiteness. But we ain't stupid," she said.

I laid my eyes back on the white Jesus hanging over the pulpit. Myrtle said that *we* weren't stupid. She was talking about black church folks. But I was confused. If they had already read the verse and they knew Jesus was a black man, then why did they have a statue of a white man hanging above the all-black congregation? Why did they cry under this image? Why did they stretch their arms out wide and lift their heads up to this blond-haired, blue-eyed plastic man? Why did they shout and speak in tongues under him?

Something didn't seem right about black people and Christianity. And because I couldn't figure it out as a little girl, I just sat back in my seat thinking that I'd rather be somewhere more interesting. Sometimes I entertained thoughts of hell and convinced myself that it was going to be my final resting place because I never took sermons seriously.

All G preached about was how the world was damned, everything was a sin, and how the Book of Revelations said God was going to destroy the earth by the year 2000. According to him, life was supposed to consist of praying, going to church four times a week, forgiving others no matter how bad they've been toward you, reading your Bible, speaking in tongues every now and then, and, when something goes wrong, simply believing that it was God's will.

Once in a while G surprised me. Sometimes he actually stirred up the congregation. And for those short moments, he made me believe he was a powerful man and that there just might be a God.

Looking back on my church life as a child, I liken Sunday morning services to spiritual orgies. Sexual undertones were apparent, though I didn't fully recognize them as a young child. Church seemed like some kind of twisted release from the strict lives that its mostly female congregation lived when they left that holy place. Many of those women were single mothers, lonely, unattractive, overweight, financially struggling, battling health problems, and always having bad luck despite being down for Jesus. And yet they were the backbone of the church. For those Pentecostal women, church was an intimate space that fulfilled their human need for comfort, touch, and love without violating the tenets of their faith.

The start of worship services began with the choir members dressed in long, white flowing robes marching fast down the nave, and then breaking off into two separate branches behind the pulpit, sort of like fallopian tubes. They sang soft mellow songs at first, setting the mood for what was about to come. And then things heated up. Everybody waited anxiously for "the man of God." The tension between the preacher and the congregation began.

"Church!" G tugged at his belt buckle and jerked his pants up higher on his waistline, as if he had big balls and was about to test out his manhood on the congregation.

"Speak brotha," hollered Sista Charleston, a fat woman with breasts so big they could rest on her thighs as she sat in the pew. Once in a while she would sit her open Bible on top of them. She never clapped her hands. Her breasts were too big to get her arms around.

"The Lord set me free!" G pretended to break chains over his head.

A chain reaction of events began. The children got quiet, like mice. We could hear the roar of the traffic from the streets and the winos breaking bottles and cursing as they passed the liquor store that sat on the same corner as the church. Somebody started to beat a tambourine. I heard people crying out long, wordless cries. A woman in the front pew stretched her arms out like wings as if God was going to lift her up through the roof and take her to glory right in front of us.

"He ... bap-tized me!"

"Preach on!" Brotha Williams danced his feet up and down the pedals on the old pipe organ next to the choir stand.

"He ... chas-tized me!"

"C'mon somebody!" One of Myrtle's sisters jumped to her feet, flinging the hell out of a worn paper fan.

"He ... a-nointed me!"

"Yeah," three or four people hollered out at the same time.

"He ... a-pointed me!"

Somebody else caught the spirit. I knew because I heard feet pounding somewhere in the back of the sanctuary. Everybody turned all at once to see whom God had touched at the moment. G smiled. I could read his face. This made him more excited.

"He took me out of my old body and gave me a what ... ?"

"What?" the entire congregation yelled back at him.

"Aw, y'all don't wanna hear me preach today." He threw his handkerchief off the pulpit as if he was quitting. By teasing them, he knew he could get them to respond.

"Preach! Preach! Preach!" they begged.

"He gave me a new body!"

"Neeeeew body!" they yelled back at him.

"He gave me a new walk!"

"Neeeeew walk!" A deacon sitting in front of me jumped to his feet and pointed his long black finger at G while holding his Bible in the other hand.

"He gave me a new talk!"

"Neeeeew talk!"

By then everyone was on their feet. But not me. The church folks' sudden response to G overwhelmed me. I could hear women whispering, "He sho' is preachin' today," as they wiped and fanned their faces. The place was like the pit of a dormant volcano that suddenly swelled and erupted. It scared me. Maybe God was in the house. What else could make all those people act so crazy?

"And hallelujah church, the Lord gave me a message." He stepped down off the pulpit and took a new handkerchief from the usher standing like a guard next to the pulpit. He gently dabbed the corners of his mouth and slowly dragged the handkerchief across his sweaty forehead.

Just when I leaned forward in my seat to hear him say what God told him, he asked the entire congregation to bow their heads and pray with him. Then he made the altar call. All those who were sick, troubled, or wanted to pray for somebody else lined up and let G lay his hands on their heads with blessed olive oil. The women closed their eyes and rubbed their arms like they were itching or cold. Their bodies swayed and shook as they waited their turn to be touched. Sometimes all it took was one small tap on the head, and they fainted. The ushers would catch them, lay them down on the floor, cover their legs with white sheets, and fan them until they woke up.

Old women with canes and walkers came to G for some of his healing power that God had blessed him with. He'd massage their thighs, ankles, and knees, fondling and kneading their skin between his fingers. When he finished, he snatched the cane or walker away and the woman would walk slowly at first, then march, and ultimately do a Holy Ghost dance to the delight of the congregation, which would sometimes break into shouts leaving the ushers feeling overwhelmed.

Sometimes G would cast demons out of people. When somebody had demons, the congregation stretched their hands out toward the person and chanted, "Jesus, Jesus, Jesus, Jesus" while G and the other ministers yelled, "Come out, you foul devil! Loose her! I rebuke you!" The possessed person spat up white foam as her body contorted like a seizure patient.

And then the person jumped up and ran around the church screaming, "Thank you, Jesus! Thank you, Lord!"

When the church service was over, like after sex, some of the deacons would sneak around some corner or alley and smoke. The women rushed downstairs to the basement to prepare the food if it was the first Sunday of the month, when they were also expected to wear white.

Once in a while, when Myrtle felt like being around her nearly two dozen brothers and sisters, we went to her parents' house for Sunday dinner. The men packed the large television room at the back of the house to watch sports on the movie-sized television screen. One of my uncles spread money on the table and counted the offerings that were collected that morning and filled out deposit slips to be dropped off at the bank the next morning.

My adoptive grandfather, Pop, and his wife, Elberta, kicked up their feet on the back patio and watched more preachers on the satellite channels while waiting for dinner. Trenton Pentecostal Church of God was my grandfather's church. God too had called him thirty years before during a tent revival in some backwoods in Mississippi. He often relived that night when he had stumbled into a back pew, drunk and cursing, possessed by the devil. The short preacher woman laid her hands on him and cast that devil out of his body. He said God revealed heaven and hell to him and then ordered him to preach the word.

Grandpop revealed other events through his sermons, like the night the Ku Klux Klan dropped his father's dead body off in front of their house wrapped in white sheets after lynching him and cutting off his ears and penis. He told stories of robberies and other crimes he committed. And he told the church how he never spared the rod with his children.

"God chastises those he loves," he said, as his words were met with amens from the congregation. "The Bible says the blueness of a wound cleanses away evil. That's why I whupped my children's behinds. I locked their heads between my legs and lit their butts up with a strap or switch," he said, demonstrating for us.

The congregation, including Myrtle, thought it was funny. But the first time I heard him tell that story, I got angry with Grandpop. I blamed him for all my butt whuppings. Because he had whupped Myrtle, she turned those same tactics onto my body. Preachers like my grandfather were responsible for promoting violence against black children with their "spare the rod, spoil the child" sermons.

Myrtle and my aunts scurried about the kitchen stirring pots, cutting cheese, seasoning greens, and setting the tables in the dining room and kitchen. I took my usual spot on the front porch and watched my cousins play their games. One of their favorites was playing house. The oldest boy and girl were the father and mother. There were a whole bunch of middle cousins who were older children, and then the smallest kids were considered the babies of the house. The boys pretended to build things and drive cars—manly things. The "mother" gathered leaves and pretended to cook meals. The "father" never disciplined the children and didn't spend much time inside the pretend house. The "mother" always kept a switch in her hand and took much delight in wielding it at my smaller cousins, sometimes hitting them until they all broke off running. My aunts and uncles would shake their heads in laughter. I stayed far away from the pretend house because I got enough whuppings with switches at home.

When playing house got mundane, they played funerals and church, a game we were forbidden to play. They began with the "devotional" part of the service where one of the girls broke into song.

"What's the matter with Jesus?" she sang.

"He's all right!" The miniature congregation clapped their hands and responded in song.

"Oh, what's the matter with Jesus?"

"He's all right."

That song went on for about five minutes until someone changed it. The other song of choice was sung by all at the same time.

"I shall not. I shall not be moved. I shall not. I shall not be moved. Just like a tree that's planted by the wa-ter. I shall not be moved."

The next part of the service was the testimonial.

"Would anybody like to stand up and testify about the goodness and mercy of the Lawd?" the leader asked. "C'mon, somebody. Talk about the goodness of the Lawd," my cousin urged.

Slowly, one of the younger girls emerged from her seat as everyone clapped and got excited to hear what she had to share.

"Church, I give an honor to God and Reverend Shane," she said clasping her hands. Shane was the older boy cousin who always played the preacher.

"Hallelujah," another cousin yelled out while fanning herself with her hand.

"The Lord is good, church. Last week the doctor said I was gonna die.

I had a lump in my breases. I got in the prayer line last week, and Reverend Shane prayed for me. He laid his hands on me. I went back to the doctor, and he said he couldn't find no lump nowhere!"

Everyone stood and applauded her testimony and proclaimed that they had witnessed a miracle.

"We got time for one mo' testimony," said the devotional leader.

Another cousin stood to testify. "God blessed me too. I ain't know how I was gonna pay my rent. I had no money. I was feelin' real tired and real lo'. I said Lawd, I need a blessing. Lawd, give me a blessing. I went out to my mailbox the next day, and there was an envelope full of money. I don't know where it came from. But I knew it was Jesus."

Shane, still dressed in his church suit, took his position at the invisible pulpit and led the church in a long-winded prayer. He mimicked G, Grandpop, and the other deacons. He got their cadences right, their pauses, gestures, and he knew the Scriptures. The girls fanned themselves and cut their eyes at him.

"Preach!"

"Yes, Lawd!"

"Hallelujah!"

"Thank ya, Jesus!"

"Well, well, preacher!"

"Preach on!"

Each child went down the row saying their lines. And then (out of nowhere) one of the girls began to shout with her eyes closed, hands raised to the sky, and danced around like she was on fire. Two of the older girls made a circle around her like we saw the ushers do at church when somebody caught the Holy Ghost.

And then everybody, including Shane, broke into shouting spells. From afar, I could see what they couldn't—and it wasn't the coming of the Lord. Grandpop had been watching them through the small bathroom window overlooking their makeshift sanctuary. He kept quiet and snuck around the side of the house holding a long, freshly picked switch. He put on his running shoes and closed the gate next to the porch so no one could escape. I hid behind a tree—out of sight, out of mind.

The long switch turned the corner before Grandpop's legs did, and the smallest of my cousins caught sight of it and yelled, "Jesus!" and took off running. My other cousins just thought it was the Holy Ghost until they heard the crack of the switch landing on Reverend Shane's back. They opened their eyes, dropped their hands and the Lord's name out of their mouths, came to their earthly senses, and ran for safety.

"Heathens!" Grandpop ran after all of them, trying desperately to cut up anybody's legs he could land the switch on. "I'll learn you about playin' with the Lord! I'm gon' beat the devil out of you!"

If he caught any unlucky souls, he locked their heads between his legs and whipped them unmercifully while ordering the devil to come out. The rest of us looked on frightened. When he finished, he let the child go and looked out into the huge yard, tired, and knowing we were all hiding from him.

"And let that be a lesson to the rest of you," he said as he fixed his trousers and made his way back into the house to watch his preaching programs.

Our aunts and uncles always agreed with the whipping. It was okay for us to play house, to whip each other, and for Grandpop to whip any of us for any infraction. But we were never to play with the Lord or mock our parents' cultural religious practices because church was something that kept black families and communities together and restored their faith and hope in life. The church, the songs, the Bible talk, the crying, the shouting, and even the plastic white Jesus all had meaning. The black folks I went to church with came there to find stability, calm, and courage when they got disoriented by the world around them. Sometimes they couldn't see an end to their pain and stress. So when they came to the House of the Lord, as they called it, they unleashed their desire to talk about their anxieties, frustrations, fears, pain, and hopes. Church folks talked to the preachers, deacons, congregation members, and Jesus. Everybody had their own personal relationship with Jesus. Jesus knew their fears and gave them hope. Jesus was their everything, they said.

I didn't know the plastic white man like they did, though I wanted to. But even as a little girl, I felt there was something absurd about praying to objects, mumbling to the wind, and keeping faith the size of a mustard seed. I didn't understand how the black church could help a race of people who week after week kneeled on its floor and at its altar, cried, spoke in weird tongues, spit up demons, and did Holy Ghost dances while their problems remained. I did realize, however, that without family, community, hope, and faith, black folks had nothing. And though I was often confused by all those elements I realized their importance, even for myself and the treacherous road ahead of me.

SEVEN

Blacks who survived infancy and adolescence knew what slavery was all about. They were fully aware of the restrictions forced on them and the oppressive power that whites wielded over their bodies, minds, and spirits. Blacks witnessed beatings, tortures, and executions of their parents, and sometimes their peers. The contradictions of a slave society were brutally clear to them. Slave children watched their parents act like leaders, protectors, providers, and men and women back in their quarters and then become submissive and obedient in front of whites.

At whim, many slave owners changed the names of black children to show parents that they had no control over their offspring's destiny. Like some parents, enslaved children knew to demonstrate submission and obedience at the slave owner's pleasure. The slaves faked what the master demanded. It has been argued that masters treated slaves so brutally because they were considered property and because blacks were considered to have no souls and no humanity. But masters did recognize the humanity of slave women, men, and children. Because if they didn't, so many masters wouldn't have given so much attention to breaking, whipping, and subjugating the flesh, hearts, and spirits of their slaves. Denying that slaves had humanity was a means for white masters to disassociate themselves from their own barbaric treatment of black human beings. Pain is common to all humanity.

When slave children watched their parents being flogged, they felt their parents' pain. When slave parents stood helplessly watching their child being whipped, they felt the pain of their child. And when slave parents whipped their children, they often claimed that it hurt them more than it hurt the child and said the beating was for their own good. Beating children is not exclusive to that era, to slavery, or to race. Still, in many ways, black parents have always had to break, whip, and subjugate their children's flesh, hearts, and spirits not because they've considered children as property or subhuman in the same way white masters did. They've done so because they recognized their child's humanity and viewed whipping as a survival mechanism.

Children are naturally curious and defiant, and they test boundaries. To train their young not to step out of line in the slave community and to protect them, black parents believed they had to mete out the same kinds of violence that white masters did. Parents whipped children in the private sphere of the slave cabin, but especially in the presence of whites. In essence, they had to beat the spirit out of their children and any notion that they were free like whites.

Violence characterized the central nervous system of the institution of slavery. Whipping was a critical dynamic used to express power. For slavery to work, masters had to whip their slaves to make them obedient and subservient. In turn, slave parents whipped their children to help them recognize the absolute power of whites and to prepare them for their future in bondage.

History repeated itself in my home. Myrtle whipped me to make me fear her supreme rule. She whipped me to make me submissive. To break me. To kill any spirit that might well up in me and make me rebel or challenge her authority. She also said she whipped me to prepare me for the modern realities of being a little black girl growing up in America.

EIGHT

There was a little boy named Tye Johnson in my first-grade class at the Bethany Lutheran School. He looked like a frog with his wide, wet lips and big eyes that followed you even when he didn't turn his head. Unlike the other boys in our class, Tye was skinny, small, and short for his age, just like me. His ribs, like mine, pressed through his skin. We could easily have been used for a skeletal anatomy lesson.

Neither of us could sit still: I tapped my foot against the floor, and Tye rocked back and forth in his seat. Our veins stuck out of our foreheads and the brown side of our hands. We chewed our fingernails when we were anxious or scared. When black women came near us, we got quiet, stepped back from them, or ducked if they moved suddenly. He and I feared our mamas and other black women. We expected to be yelled at, hit, criticized, called names, and handled roughly when they fixed our clothes, hair, and faces. And I believed that all black women had the right to treat us this way because I often heard that expression "It takes a village to raise a child," from church folks and friends of Myrtle and G. Tye and I had crazy mamas. They never seemed embarrassed about raising their voices to cut us down in public or doing minstrel numbers for our white teachers by acting out the harsh and aggressive black mammy stereotype.

One afternoon Mrs. Shaw, our teacher, was threatening one of my classmates with loss of recess if he didn't correctly pronounce the word she had written on the board. The boy had a stuttering problem. His mama had found a way to stop the nervous tic when he was at home: whenever he got stuck on a word, she took a wet dish towel, grabbed it by both ends, twirled it tight like a thick whip, and then snapped it across the back of his neck.

"Get it out!" she'd yell, and the words would flow from his lips. There were no wet rags in our classroom, but his mother had given Mrs. Shaw permission to beat the devil off his tongue.

I knew how to say the word: B A P T I S M. It was one of those really important godly words. I was worried for the boy. I knew he was supposed to learn the word for his own sake. He had to first say it, then learn its meaning, and then have it done to him so he could go to heaven. But really, I was more worried that he'd lose his playtime if he didn't get it out right. I needed him to play on our side for kickball. No one else could kick farther than him.

All of a sudden a loud "Ooooooohhh!!! I'm tellin'" came from the back of the class. The voice was a girl named Kenyatta Thompson. We knew not to trust her to keep a secret, and we could always depend on her to tattle. Whenever Mrs. Shaw left the classroom Kenyatta was always left in charge.

Mrs. Shaw snatched her eyes off the stuck boy, and the rest of our eyes followed her to the back of the room.

"What is it now, Kenyatta?" She sounded annoyed.

"Tye called Sandy a white honky," she said with a disturbed look on her face as she stared at Sandy's bowed blonde head.

Sandy was one of two white kids in our class of eighteen. The others were black middle- and working-class kids whose parents refused to put their children in public school.

Silence arrested all of us. I heard only the deep swallowing in my throat. "Is this true, Sandy?" Mrs. Shaw asked as the chalk disappeared in the palm of her pale hand.

I certainly didn't want it to be so. A white honky! That wasn't like calling somebody fat, stupid, ugly, or an apple head. Tye was gonna get it. What did Sandy call him to provoke that response? It didn't seem to matter.

Sandy didn't lift her head. Judging by her demeanor, she looked as if she wished Kenyatta hadn't tattled. I guess it was hard enough being the only white girl, but to have a classmate call her a white honky!

Sandy mumbled a low, "Yes." My heart dropped to the pit of my stomach. Sandy lifted her head and looked into Mrs. Shaw's red face: "He called me a honky."

What was a honky anyway? I asked myself that question as I heard the chalk break in Mrs. Shaw's clenched fists. By now her knuckles had tensed up and turned white.

I had heard my adoptive parents and other relatives use names like *crackers, rednecks, whities, white folks,* and *devils* to describe white people. The names were justified with explanations. I was told that white people's skin looked like the color of saltines, and that's why they were called crackers. They were rednecks, especially southern whites, because the backs of their necks were red and sweaty. They were the worst kind of racist white people. *Whitey* was more of a sarcastic way of making fun of whiteness. And they were called *devils* because historically they were the one group of people in the world that had done the most destructive and devilish things wherever they had been across the globe. But no one could ever explain to me why white people were called honkys.

"Everyone!" Mrs. Shaw threw the chalk at the tray underneath the blackboard, missing it, and not caring that the two pieces hit the floor and broke into small pieces. "Put your heads down on your desks right now! I don't want to hear a peep out of anybody!"

She disappeared into the main office just outside our classroom. We all knew what was going to happen next. She would give an emotional report to our evil principal, a red-headed tyrant named Brenda Steinert. Tye's mama would be called to the school right away.

As my head lay on top of my arms, I knew Tye was beginning to get sick—so sick he didn't even bother to obey Mrs. Shaw's order to put his head down. Why bother? He was gonna get it anyway. I knew what was happening to his body. His hands were sweating. His tongue was dry. His heart was banging against his chest. And his bowels felt like they were going to drop. The only thought in his head was: *I'm gonna get a whuppin'.* Those were the same things that happened to me.

I always tried to prepare myself for a beating. Sometimes I stalled by saying I had to go to the bathroom. I'd pack toilet paper into the back of my pants. But when I eventually got caught, Myrtle started making me strip all my clothes off to whip me. Sometimes I'd speed-pray for G to magically appear so the whipping would be postponed. I even looked at the ceiling and asked God to change Myrtle's mind about beating me. Sometimes I convinced myself that she would have a heart attack or drop dead before the first hit.

"I won't do it again, Mommy," I pleaded with her.

"I *know* you won't do it again," she responded sarcastically while braiding the switches together or wrapping the belt or extension cord once around her hand.

Sometimes I closed my eyes and tried to make myself die so I wouldn't feel the pain. But there was never any escape for me, and there was no escape for Tye when his mama got to the school.

Mrs. Johnson was skinny and looked like a frog too. I had never seen a woman who was so dark. She was so black she almost looked blue. She was loud and cursed a lot even though we were in a Christian school where that kind of language was not allowed. Sometimes she brought a handful of switches to school when she came to get a report of Tye's behavior and grades. If she got good news, the switches were thrown in the trash can next to Mrs. Shaw's desk. Bad news, and the janitor would sweep up broken pieces of branches off the floor that evening.

I didn't see switches in her hand when Mrs. Johnson stormed into the classroom. "You little nigger!" she yelled at the frightened boy. Tye's face turned gray as her hand swooped down like an eagle onto its prey. In the other hand, I saw a thick rubber hose that had been cut from somewhere. All of us simultaneously raised our heads.

"Who you think you callin' a honky, huh?" she snarled as she yanked his jeans past his knees.

She smacked the back of his head hard. The echo made our heads snap backward as if she had hit us all. She clawed the back of his neck and must have pressed a nerve that made his back bend toward the bottom of her skirt. His head disappeared between her legs, smothering his face, and muffling his screams as she whipped his back, buttocks, and legs with the rubber hose. Though I had experienced time after time that same ritual, I was still shocked because Mrs. Johnson had done so in front of our class with Mrs. Shaw and our principal watching from the side of the room with their arms folded across their chests in approval.

Just like slave mothers who whipped their children in front of masters and overseers, Mrs. Johnson whipped Tye to show that she recognized that her son had crossed the line of acceptability. Instead of talking to him and telling him how horrible his words were, she beat him into submission. But what about his humanity?

Out of breath, sweating, and hair askew, Mrs. Johnson released Tye from her locked legs. "Fix your clothes!" she ordered him as she fixed her own. "And shut up that cryin'!"

Tye swallowed his breath even though the tears kept coming. "You still cryin'?" she yelled. "You want somethin' to cry about? I'll give you somethin' to cry about!" she threatened.

Mrs. Steinert stepped in slowly. She touched Mrs. Johnson's shoulder softly and said, "Thank you, Mrs. Johnson, for handling this situation. We apologize for having you come up here from your job."

"No, it ain't no problem. Any time you got a problem with him, you just call me," she assured Mrs. Steinert and began to make her way out of the classroom. "He won't be callin' nobody else no honky," she said as she disappeared through the doorway with Mrs. Steinert.

Mrs. Shaw returned to the blackboard and erased B A P T I S M. The boy who had been stuck on the word was still in so much shock that he didn't seem to notice that the word was gone with the wipe of the eraser. Mrs. Shaw wrote new words on the board:

I WILL NEVER CALL ANYONE A WHITE HONKY!

"Sandy and Liam," she said to the two white students. "Take out a book and read. The rest of you take out a pencil and piece of paper. There will be no recess today. You will all write this sentence 100 times. And if I hear a peep out of any of you, I will add another 100 to that!"

Occasionally I heard Tye sniffle. He seemed more relaxed now that the whipping was over. I wondered how long it would be before his next one. A week. Three days. One day. A few hours. It depended on his mother's mood.

Tye's whipping confirmed for me that this sort of behavior between black mamas and their children was normal. I had seen kids get beaten in parking lots, the side of the road, grocery stores, church, and now school. Time and time again, I heard that well-known expression, "Wherever you wanna act like a fool, I'm gonna act like a fool right along with you and give you a good whuppin'."

Black children I knew got whipped whenever, wherever, and with whatever. This was part of our identity as black children. I didn't think there was another way except for the way that white parents raised their kids. But, of course, that way was white. Looking back, I know that was a false idea, yet I had absorbed the notion that this kind of discipline did not exist in white homes and was specific to blacks. After all, Myrtle had explained to me that being white and being black in America was different and that black children couldn't be raised the same way as white children.

I really did believe that Myrtle beat me because she loved me. She had to yell at me. She had to call me names. She had to whip me. She had to

put scars on me to toughen my skin. It was all for my own good. She had to prepare me for a life and a world that cared nothing about me because I am black and female. She couldn't baby me because I had to be just as good as the white man—and better if I was going to be anything in life.

"If I don't beat you, then the *white man* is gonna beat you," she said. "It's better for me to do it than for him to do it! Do you understand?"

"Yes, Mommy."

"Do you think the *white man* loves you like I do?"

"No, Mommy."

"Do you think the *white man* cares anything about you?"

"No, Mommy."

"Do you think the *white man* is gonna give you anything?"

"No, Mommy."

"Do you think the *white man* wants you to be anything?"

"No, Mommy."

"Get ahead in life?"

"No, Mommy."

"Have a house?"

"No, Mommy."

"Live in a *good* neighborhood?"

"No, Mommy."

"Go to a *good* school?"

"No, Mommy."

"The *white man* don't want you to have nothin'! The *white man* hates you! The *white man* wants to kill you. The *white man* wants you to be just one . . . less . . . dead . . . nigga . . . layin' . . . in . . . some . . . ditch!"

Who was *the white man* Myrtle was talking about? What was *the white man*'s name? Was *the white man* tall? Short? Fat? Skinny? What did he look like? Was *the white man* President Ronald Reagan? Was it Peter Jennings from *World News Tonight*? Was it Bob Barker from *The Price Is Right*? Was it the police? Was it the mailman? Was it the meter reader? Was it the white man who owned the deli down the street from us? White men in business suits? Was it all white men? What about white women? White girls? White boys?

During my early childhood, Myrtle's lessons about white people didn't make sense to me. No white person had ever given me a reason to think they hated me, were out to beat me, or kill me. No white person had ever called me a nigga. No white person had ever laid a cruel finger on me. The

only person who had ever called me a nigga, and the only person I thought hated me and was going to kill me one day, was my mama, who said she beat me because she loved me and wanted to protect me from the white man.

I didn't know it then, but this behavior was all Myrtle knew. It was all Mrs. Johnson knew. It was what their parents knew and what their parents' parents knew. It was a behavior that had deep roots in the plantation legacy. No matter how much I tried to understand Myrtle's justifications for all my whippings, with each slap, punch, switching, belting, and extension cord flogging, there was no way that any of it would ever make sense to me. I didn't know then that this cultural sickness of violence against black children had stemmed from America's plantations. I simply thought it was a black thing, and that alone made me wish I had been born a little white girl.

NINE

The treatment of slaves varied from plantation to plantation. Some masters treated their workers in a relatively human fashion. But most whipped, branded, stabbed, tarred and feathered, burned, shackled, tortured, maimed, crippled, mutilated, and castrated their slaves. I once read a portrait describing plantation cruelty:

> A cacophony of horrendous sounds constantly reverberated throughout such plantations: nauseated Black men vomited while strung up over slowly burning tobacco leaves, vicious dogs tore black flesh. Black men moaned as they were hung up by the thumbs with the whip raising deep welts on their backs and as they were bent over barrels or tied down to stakes while paddles with holes in them broke blisters on their rumps. Frequently, Blacks called God's name in vain as they fainted from the master's hundredth stroke or as they had their brains blown out.

This kind of cruelty was meted out onto slaves for a number of offenses: running away, questioning the master, rolling their eyes or looking the master in the face, failure to complete tasks, visiting their mates, learning to read, stealing, breaking tools, arguing or fighting with whites, working too slowly, quarreling or fighting with other slaves, drunkenness, claiming they were free, and giving sexual favors to persons other than their masters.

No matter how much slave parents tried to shield their young from plantation terrorism, children not only witnessed these atrocities, but were not exempt from even the cruelest treatment. The first time a slave child experienced violence from white hands, the usual reaction was to either run away or seek revenge. But slave parents quickly taught their young that anger was not an option. They had to develop ways to protect the child's self-esteem and raise hopes. Parents taught their young about a master higher and mightier than their earthly ones. They also taught them how to pray and hope for freedom.

Sometimes faith and prayer helped slaves overcome their fear of masters. They were fully believing that masters could harm and even kill their bodies but couldn't touch their souls. Acting on their moral resistance, blacks could call on God for strength. Still, most slaves died with prayers in their hearts, keeping the faith, and never knowing freedom.

For a short time during my own bondage, I believed that prayer would change things for me. God would hear my cries. God would take away my pleas for help. God would take away my pain. God would change the heart of my enemy. God would have mercy on me. All I had to do was drop to my knees to pray and have faith the size of a mustard seed. But after many beatings and injuries and moments when Myrtle almost took my life, I came to believe that the acts of prayer and faith are mere psychological diversions for those who are powerless. More important, I learned that God does not exist in desperation.

TEN

G said that for me to know Jesus better and to establish my own personal relationship with him, I had to pray and read the Word of God. By the time I was in fifth grade, he gave me a New Revised Standard Version of the Bible. I had convinced myself that if I read and prayed myself into delirium, then maybe I'd see God.

The first story I learned about was the Creation. I imagined complete darkness and a big, strong, white man with long, yellow hair walking around talking about how lonely he was. In my mind, I could see all the planets, sun, moon, stars, oceans, and animals God brought into existence with his hands and words. And then I saw him gathering up dirt to make Adam and then robbing him of a rib to make Eve. Still, things didn't always make sense to me.

"Daddy?"

"Yes, baby," G answered breaking his nod into a deep sleep.

"What was before God?" I asked.

"Nothin'," he answered.

"So there wasn't nobody else here before him?"

"Nope."

"There wasn't nobody else here at the same time as him?"

"Nope. God is the beginning and the end," he explained. "He is the father and creator of all life."

"But look at this." I jumped to my feet holding the Bible in hand. As I pointed to a verse on the first page of Genesis, G pushed his glasses up on the bridge of his nose and leaned close to me. "Right here. Genesis 1 and 26. 'Then God said, "Let us make man in our image, in our likeness, and let them rule over the fish of the sea and the birds of the air, over all creatures that move along the ground."'"

"That's what it says," G nodded and looked me in the face as if the text was straightforward and unquestionable.

"Who is *us*, Daddy?"

"What?" He looked annoyed.

"It says, 'Let *us* make man in *our* image.' Who is *us*?"

"Lemme see dat," he said, gently tugging the Bible away from my hands."

"If nothin' was before God and God was the beginning, why does it say 'Let us make man in our image'?"

I could tell he was reading the verse over and over. And I knew he'd pull something out of his britches to explain the contradiction away.

"Us." He paused. "Us-us, us is the Father, the Son, and the Holy Ghost," he said.

"But Jesus wasn't even born until the New Testament," I said.

G looked at the book again, confused. And then he turned the book over to look at the cover. "See, that's the problem," he said tapping the cover with his finger. "You got one of them new versions. How did I miss that? I should have gotten you the King James Version." His voice got excited: "The King James Version, now that's the most accurate version. I don't know why yours is written like this." He shook his head.

"The Word is the Word," Myrtle's demonic voice came from nowhere, startling both of us. She was always lurking and appearing from nothing. "Don't question the Word of God," she warned.

As a little girl, I grew to believe that people like my adoptive parents didn't really understand the Bible. For me, it slowly became a long-winded novel or piece of sociological literature with stories about a society of a different time. What was written was a reflection of all that went on then, people's thoughts about it, and moral suggestions about how people should deal with problems and be kept in line. I believed that the Bible was a rule book that people used thousands of years later to apply to their present lives, perhaps out of fear.

While my adoptive parents and other holy rollers we knew simply said "amen," "hallelujah," and "preach on" when a verse was read from the Bible, I was made to feel that my confusion, curiosity, and questioning were sinful. So Myrtle found ways to try to brainwash me with The Word.

Every night just before going to bed, I sat on my bedroom floor waiting for Myrtle. I could hear her slowly making her way through the hall, creeping like a strain of darkness. Though I knew she was coming, her sharp yellow face with that tint of brown clear as day still scared me. Her hair was always in pink sponge rollers and held down by a black hairnet. Heaviness surrounded me as I tried to breathe through the oppressive stillness in the air. As she got closer to me, the thud she made by hitting her Bible against her right thigh got louder.

"Why you lookin' at me like you don't know the drill?" she snapped. "Get to it, stupid," she ordered.

I began the song, "Genesis, Exodus, Leviticus, Numbers, Deuteronomy . . ." From Genesis to Malachi, I sang all thirty-nine books of the Old Testament as Myrtle held her Bible in her hand and went down the index list waiting for me to mess up.

"Now the New Testament," she said.

"Matthew, Mark, Luke, John, Acts, Romans, Corinthians." I recited the newer books without missing a beat.

Then came the hard part.

"John 3:16," she pinned her eyes on my face.

"'For God so loved the world that he gave his only begotten son that whosoever believeth in him should not perish but have everlasting life.'"

She dabbed the tip of her finger on her tongue and flipped through more marked pages.

"Romans 3:23."

"'For the wages of sin is death but the gift of God is eternal life.'" My heart still beat hard against my chest.

When the drill was over, Myrtle never gave me an approving look or complimented me. She just sat there reeking of misery. I would watch her draw meat from her teeth with a toothpick. When she finished, she sucked her teeth and rolled the toothpick around in her mouth to intimidate me. It always worked.

She sat rigid as a catatonic, looking like the devil holding her Bible. Only her chest moved. I can't remember if she ever blinked. I never looked her in her eyes or face for long moments out of fear of getting slapped for doing so.

I moved quickly around the room, slipping out of my clothes, folding them neatly, and placing them on the brass nightstand at the foot of my bed.

"Humph, girl," she dragged the "l" and snickered. "You ain't got no kind of shape. You as flat as the kitchen table. Ain't got no titties."

It never failed. She always had something to say about how skinny and frail I was. But it was her fault that my growth was being stunted. How could I grow under her oppressive hands?

Myrtle let her leather-bound Bible rest on her lap and placed her hands on top as if she was waiting for some kind of magic to come out of it and electrify her body. I dropped to my knees and folded my hands across the bed. I closed my eyes. I felt nervous about shutting my eyes around her, especially when I was that close to her hands and feet. Just before I'd close my eyes, I'd always think of that one verse that Jesus told one of his disciples that he should watch while he prays.

She gave her cue: "Stacey, this is the prayer that Jesus taught us."

I parted my lips. "Our father, who art in heaven . . ." I enunciated every syllable slowly and clearly just like she wanted. "Give us this day our . . ." I heard the loud thud before the pain let me realize that she had whacked me across the back of my head with the Bible.

That was it! I knew God had to see that one. If He didn't see, I know He heard it. There was just no way she was going to heaven after using the holy Word of God to hit me over the head.

"Get the devil off your tongue and say it right," she scowled. I had missed a verse. So I started over, hands still folded tight, eyes still shut, heart still bumping up and down in my chest. I didn't expect her to be alive by the time I said amen.

When I got to that verse about forgiveness—"Forgive us our trespasses as we forgive those who trespass against us"—the words clung to the roof of my mouth. I had to forgive Myrtle because God forgave me. But forgiveness seemed like a catch-22. I knew it was hard to forgive somebody who did me wrong, but it seemed impossible to forgive somebody who kept doing me wrong. Why waste time forgiving somebody who would continue to do me wrong? I wanted to go to heaven, so I had no choice but to swallow my honest feelings and be obedient to God's words.

At the end of the prayer, we said "Amen" in unison. On a good night, when I hadn't gotten hit with the Bible or yelled at, I felt proud that I had recited perfectly. I lived for Myrtle's approval, for her to say, "Well done." The smile would always fade from my lips when she said, "You can do even better next time."

I just wanted her to like me.

Our eyes met. And then mine navigated her body to see where all the tension was. It wasn't in her face. It was in her hands that were still gripping the Bible so tight I saw her veins pulsating through her fingers. I was convinced that Myrtle had plastic skin, wooden bones, and a heart of stone. I didn't know any other person on earth who seemed as unreal and unfeeling as her.

"What you standin' there for?" She gave me a stupid look. "You think I'm sitting here to save my life? You know what I'm waitin' for, you little pee rat."

Every word that came out of her mouth shook me on the inside, but I couldn't let her see me shuddering. I didn't want to get slapped for acting like an imbecile, so I inched closer to her face. I searched for a pleasant aroma but smelled nothing but anger and bitterness mixed with Lifebuoy soap. I wished for warmth but instead felt cold and tension. I hoped for a positive vibe to settle my fear. Instead I grew more terrified as I heard her take a deep swallow.

She shifted the toothpick to the corner of her mouth without using her hand. Her eyes grew narrow. I puckered up. I held my breath and told my heart not to beat too loudly. My lips touched hers. Her lips didn't move. They felt cold and dry, like rubber.

I stepped back. There was less than a foot between us. I waited. Those sweet words I hoped for when I backed away from her never came. That smile I wanted from her was merely a false hope. And where was God? He hadn't punished her for hitting me with the Bible.

I studied her face. Her lips were the color of dark dried plums. Her hair held a dusky aurora. In the soft light of my room, her skin turned oak-leaf brown. We measured each other with our eyes. I began to feel as if I was in some swamp with heat hanging over it. My pulse hammered from my wrists down to my fingertips. I took my eyes away from her and looked down, like I was supposed to when I was in her presence. That way, she knew that I knew she was boss.

I had learned to live with a woman I didn't love or respect, and I felt she didn't love or respect me. Living like that was like learning how to die. I had become a shell. I denied what I felt. I hated without showing it. I knew how to weep without tears. Despite my shame that was my reality, I went on searching for some inkling of love to rise from her.

And then I told that lie: "Goodnight, Mommy. I love you, Mommy."

When she disappeared into her room I turned on my side and whispered my real prayer:

Dear God,

I hope you can hear me. I have to whisper 'cause she'll beat me if she hears me talkin', even to you. Can you please make her stop beatin' me? I'll do anything. Just make her stop.

And God . . .

Can you please help me find my real mama? Please. I know *she* wouldn't treat me like this. I know *she* loves me. I promise I will never tell her what Myrtle does to me. It won't matter 'cause when we find each other, everything is gonna be all right. We will be a family. Tell my real mama that I love her and I think about her every day and I can't wait to be with her.

And God . . .

Please forgive me for all my sins. I know you must get tired of me asking you that. But I promise to be a better little girl.

Amen.

Though I prayed hard every night, I really believed that God's ears were too small. God was not only invisible, so were his actions. As I got older, I came to believe that I couldn't do anything down on my knees with my eyes shut, head bowed, hands folded, mumbling to an invisible white man in outer space. I had to be the one to change my reality. I had to find a way to stop Myrtle from putting her hands on me and saying cruel things to me. I couldn't wait for God to stop her from controlling my destiny. I had to put my own stamp of approval on my head. I had to tap into some secret space inside me—a space that Myrtle's beatings and words hadn't touched. I was going to have to break out of the prison she created for me.

ELEVEN

Some blacks believed slavery would last for eternity. And others knew in their hearts that freedom would come, even if not in their lifetime. The more slaves knew about freedom, the more they desired it, and the more unsettled they became with their bondage. While some slaves continued to keep the faith, others knew well that freedom wouldn't come simply by exercising their imagination, so they turned their desire and faith into action. The physical and mental cruelty of slavery was likely to drain every ounce of womanhood and manhood from blacks, ridding them of self-respect. As a result, some slaves lost their will to resist. But not all slaves could be broken.

The scars, the rape, the whippings, the cries of their children, and the sale of family members spawned slave rebelliousness. Slaves resisted by breaking tools, working slowly, refusing to learn their trades, killing livestock, stealing, running away, suing for their freedom, attacking whites, burning their masters' properties, poisoning and murdering whites. For many whites, these were the worst kinds of slaves, whom they described as dangerous, insubordinate, bold, evil, restless, turbulent, vengeful, barbarous, and malicious.

For the early part of my childhood I was taught to resist only the devil and the temptation to sin, not my oppressor. But the devil was not some invisible spirit. It had flesh and blood. The devil had a color. A smell. A voice. A face. A name. Myrtle Jenkins was the devil.

Although some slaves searched deep within to find the will to resist, they rarely got their due. Those who were caught resisting faced castration, hanging, burning, or mutilation. Punishments and executions were often done in front of other slaves to discourage any further will to resist.

Freedom is a primal necessity of every man, woman, boy, and girl. It is only natural to rebel against oppression of any kind. Those who enslave, rule, or oppress teach against rebelliousness because they fear the power and potential of their slaves and their children.

TWELVE

Resisting Myrtle was not something that crossed my mind. I believed that her treatment of me was normal. In my environment, there was no one who said that beating children was wrong. Everyone called it love and God's will. Pain and whippings were for my own good and would make me stronger. I didn't have a childhood friend or classmate who said whippings were wrong. Instead, we made fun of each other when it happened to one of us.

"Dang, yo' mama fucked you up!"

"That's why yo' mama whupped yo' ass last night," we teased.

We studied each other's scars and bruises like our school lessons. We were fascinated by the details of the whuppings. We always had the same concerns and asked the same questions.

"What'd you do, man?" Something we had done or didn't do provoked our parents' wrath, thereby justifying our punishments.

"What'd she beat you with?" Oh, the instruments of pain!

"Aw, man, a switch?" We all smelled the sweet branches. Felt the thorns pricking and stabbing and welting our skin. Those of us who lived in the boondocks knew them better than the city kids, who didn't live around bushes and trees.

"She hit you with the buckle?" Cold. Hard. Square. Circular.

"Did it hurt?"

"Does it still hurt?"

"Can I touch it?"

"Do I look real bad?"

"It's still swollen a little right here."

"It looks like you got a extra lip."

"Is it broken?"

"It looks better than it did yesterday."

"She still mad at you?"

"You got beat again last night?"

We all had stories. Some were funnier than others. There were stories about shoes turning the corner to hit a child in the back of the head as he ran. There were the stories about being whipped out of sleep for forgetting to do something. Stories about being whipped in the vegetable aisle of the grocery store with thick and long carrot sticks or celery stalks. There were ones about our mama's pulling the car over on the side of the road to slap everybody in the back seat with one swift backhand. There were the ones about stalling tactics, like putting toilet paper in our underpants to cushion the blows or playing dead during the ritual of violence. The child, whoever it was—swollen, cut, blackened, marked up with welts—represented survival and strength. The laughter made the pain smaller and the whipping somewhat rationalized. Laughter gave us power over the scars, the pain, and our parents. Pain is what bound us together as black children. None of us died from a whipping. But none of us really knew then that every time we got whipped, our parents were slowly murdering our souls.

I never met a child who resisted the lash of their mother. We all knew that grabbing the belt, switch, cord, hanger, high-heeled shoe, or blocking our abuser's hand was even more dangerous than the actual whipping. We knew not to run, hide, or talk back. But the day came when I found my courage and will to resist despite the consequences I would face.

I was ten when it happened.

A blinding snowstorm hit the tristate area the day after New Year's. The snow was so deep the woman who lived next door to us couldn't walk her dog. I could hear Mrs. Paulette's scratchy voice outside my bedroom window.

"Pee! Pee! Pee!" she begged the curly black poodle as she held it in the air above the thigh-high snow. The dog wiggled its legs and head in a desperate attempt to free itself from her grip. "C'mon, Precious. It's cold out here," Mrs. Paulette whined.

Was the dog going to slip out of her hands and disappear under the snow? Or was he going to pee? The spectacle between Mrs. Paulette and Precious arrested my attention as I pretended to dust the window ledge.

The phone rang. I knew it was G by the way Myrtle's voice turned from a warm and polite, "Hello," to a cold, "What's up?" G wasn't coming home. My heart got scared and dropped to the pit of my stomach. The roads from Bordentown into Trenton were too chancy to drive through. He decided to stay at work and do a double. Myrtle agreed that the overtime hours were good.

"I'll see you tomorrow then," Myrtle sighed. "Be careful. I love you," she said just before I heard the phone hit the receiver.

"Tomorrow," I mumbled. Tomorrow was an eternity. Wrightstown was too far away for G to hear me begging for his return. Too far away for him to see the fright in my eyes. Way too far away for him to get a glimpse of me tracing Myrtle's raised handprint she had slapped onto the right side of my face earlier that morning.

"That was the Mississippi Mass Choir," the radio announcer's voice blared out from the stereo in the living room. "And this is W ... I ... M ... G, giving you the best in old and contemporary gospel music."

"Pee!" Mrs. Paulette's voice snatched my ear back outside. But suddenly I wasn't so interested. I didn't care if the dog pissed on her or if she dropped it and couldn't find it until all the snow melted away. I left the dust rag on the windowsill and made my way to the bathroom.

All my senses were under attack. My bowels got watery. My stomach filled up with air. My hands began to sweat. To make things worse, the tips of my earlobes were still sizzling, and that small section above the nape of my neck that black people called "the kitchen" felt as if it had been completely burned off. After breakfast, Myrtle had taken the metal hot comb to my head and slapped me every time I moved away from the heat. Along with belts, switches, and extension cords, hot combs were the other items I wanted banned from civilization.

"Hold your nappy head still!" Myrtle hollered as I heard that nasty bubbling noise the comb made when it connected with my grease-sodden hairline. I made the promise never to put my own children through such torture to reverse natural kink.

Along with the smell of burned hair, the stench of reheated chitterlings, turnip greens, black-eyed peas, hog maw, cornbread, and slimy okra stomped out the kitchen, turned down the hallways, and declared war on my nostrils. One of those dishes alone was always enough to make me dread the walk to the dinner table. But all of them together took on a whole new dimension. The leftovers were remnants of our New Year's celebration. Myrtle said that it was a tradition for black people to eat those dishes to ring in the New Year.

"This food will give us good luck," she explained. Ironic. So many old black folks I knew had diabetes, kidney failure, heart problems, and strokes. And people like Myrtle always said it all came from eating too much soul food. Where was the luck? Some black man told me later on in life that those kinds of dishes were scraps from the white master's table.

"Black people made magic out of those odds and ends," he said. He said it wasn't the best food, but black folks had to make do with what they had to survive. Year after year, I reluctantly followed that tradition. And I always felt like the most unlucky child, like the slaves who consumed food scraps while surviving under their master's reign of terror.

"This is Donny Hathaway with 'I Love the Lord, He Heard My Cry,'" said the radio announcer.

"Phht," I sucked my teeth and dipped my washcloth underneath the running faucet. A cool towel would help the throbbing and keep Myrtle's hand from getting bigger on my face. But at the rate I was going, I was bound to have another handprint over that one or one slapped onto the other side of my face before the night was over. It was one of those days when I couldn't seem to get anything right. Days filled with whippings and other minor abuses represented the very problem with the bondage of my childhood.

"He heard my cry," I mocked the radio announcer in a grumbling voice. "He don't hear my cry. Fuckin' ears too small," I said and quickly checked my surroundings to make sure Myrtle wasn't in earshot distance of hearing me.

I pressed the cool washcloth against my face, relieving it from the electric pain running through it. "He don't hear nothin'," I said as I took the warmed cloth away and returned it to the running water.

Something made me stop wringing the water out of the cloth to open the medicine cabinet. I don't know what it was that made me open it. Certainly there was no magic welt reliever or scar remover on the shelves behind the mirror. But something got inside me—fatigue, fear, anger, rebellion—made me reach past the witch hazel and Pepto-Bismol. My fingertips must have had magnetic fields in them because when they stopped moving, they rested on a pack of double-edged shaving razors.

"J E . . . S U S," a more tranquil song began to play. The melodious voices ended in a soft hush and then picked up again. *You are my joy within. You are my shelter from the wind. You're the forgiver of my sins.*

I almost started to sing along, not for the words or the meaning; I just liked the tune. It sounded good. But the small cardboard box of blades under my fingertips reminded me that neither Jesus nor gospel music was my savior. Slowly and carefully, I took one thin, cold blade out of the box. I knew very well that the only purpose a blade had was for cutting.

What was I going to cut? Cut off me? Cut out of me? Cut around me? I didn't know right then. And I most certainly wasn't concerned about the prospects of mending whatever I sliced up. I just let the spirit move me.

"Get in here and eat now!" Myrtle snarled.

Right then, I knew what I was going to cut. I would slice Myrtle's tongue out of her mouth so I'd never again have to hear her demonic voice. I'd flush the hurtful thing down the toilet so nobody could find it and stitch it back into her mouth. She could never call me ugly, stupid, skinny, bug eyes, or trifling or say my real mama didn't want me.

"You are my healer," the voices proclaimed in unison. "Thank you, Jesus," the voices got louder as I made my way from the bathroom to the kitchen.

I felt bold. Defiant. Fed up. Tired of the unrelenting fear and pain. I couldn't take any more of my body parts healing one day, only to be scarred the next. I refused to let down my guard, only to erect the barbed wire and gated fence around my senses of trust, safety, and the little semblance of love that was familiar to me. I couldn't go on with life as I knew it at age ten.

The wooden chair scratched the floor as I dragged it a small distance from the table. My eyes met two hotdogs and potato chips instead of the visual insides of hogs and pigs and other so-called lucky soul food. Despite my relief, I wasn't hungry. But I couldn't tell Myrtle. I never had the choice to eat or not. I ate when I wasn't hungry. I ate when she was hungry. And I most certainly never dared tell Myrtle when I was hungry because she made me feel guilty about that most primal feeling.

"I'm hungry too," she'd say sarcastically and then continue on doing her own thing. "You don't really know what it is to be hungry," she added. "You're blessed 'cause you don't know hunger. You're blessed and you don't even know it."

Myrtle was right. I didn't know hunger that well. I didn't miss meals in

their house. I didn't know what it was to fall asleep with an empty stomach or to have hunger pains.

Myrtle used my need for food as a way to remind me that she and G
were primarily responsible for my nourishment. When hunger pains did
come, they came out of my own refusal to acknowledge it. I didn't want
Myrtle to symbolically dangle food in front of me as a reminder that as a
child, an adopted child especially, I had nothing and came from nothing.
Myrtle and G had plucked me, this ward of the state, from obscurity to
feed and give me a home. These were two vital things that my biological
family had failed to do.

Though hunger pains in my stomach were rare, my mind and the middle part of my body where all my feelings came from experienced relent-
less cravings. My yearning for love, affection, attention, trust, and safety
wouldn't let me breathe right or sleep peacefully. The kind of hunger I
had made me so wary at the dinner table that I couldn't digest my food
right. Everything I ate went right through me. Fear kept me on the toilet.
Fear kept me skinny. Fear kept me hungry.

"You ain't got to wait for me," Myrtle said.

The blade was still in the palm of my right hand. So I kept it closed and
placed my left hand against my right as I rested my elbows on top of the
table to say grace. "God is great. God is good. Let us thank him for our
food. Amen."

I watched steam gently rise up from Myrtle's cup of coffee. Her red
mug sat on her plastic placemat adjacent to mine. The steam reminded
me of a wiggling woman's waistline. Myrtle would either sip her up, or the
frigid kitchen air would soon cool her dance.

A bad idea jumped into my head. I knew it was sinful. Wicked. Just
downright wrong! I was probably writing my ticket to hell just for thinking
about it. But something in me didn't care anymore about fire, brimstone,
and a red devil with horns and smoke brewing from his nose. I simply
wanted my pain to end, and there was only one way to make it end.

I heard the swirling sound of the large metal spoon against the bottom
of the cast-iron pot of chitterlings. Myrtle stirred and occasionally drew
the spoon to her mouth to test the pork juice. Her back was completely
turned to me. I looked closely at the stove to make sure there was no way
she could see my reflection. I no longer believed her lie about having eyes
in the back of her head. I had figured out her trick of being able to see me

with her back turned by looking for my reflection in mirrors, glass windows, or shiny surfaces.

Slowly and carefully, I opened my hand, still keeping my eyes on the back of her head. I quickly dropped the blade into her coffee mug without ever taking a second glance at the blade. I heard a tiny little bloop as the blade dropped into the hot black liquid. My heart beat faster than it had ever done in my ten years on earth. I was so nervous I nearly consumed half my hotdog with the first bite.

Almost thirty seconds after I dropped the blade into Myrtle's coffee, I wanted to undo what I had done. I felt guilty. Scared. Ashamed. I knew God didn't like ugly. And I didn't want to go to hell. I didn't really want Myrtle to die. I simply wanted her to stop hurting me.

I was about to stick my hand into the hot mug to get the blade, even if it meant burning or cutting myself to save Myrtle's life. But just as my arm began to shift from my plate to her mug, Myrtle turned around.

My heart almost busted through my chest.

The hotdog got stuck in my throat.

My eyes got bigger.

My bowels got weak.

I'm a dead little girl, I thought to myself.

Breathe, Stacey.

Breathe.

Swallow the hotdog.

Don't choke.

Look away from the coffee mug.

Pretend like you didn't do anything wrong.

It seemed as if Myrtle moved in slow motion as she took her seat. She tightened her Aunt Jemima scarf around her head and cracked her knuckles. She didn't even look at me. I was like some pet that was just there in the corner of her eye.

Myrtle opened her paper napkin and laid it in her lap. As she slid the coffee mug and saucer close to her, a voice in my head uttered, "Too late!" I watched closely as she added three tablespoons of sugar and another tablespoon of Carnation milk. She stirred. Blew. Sipped. Stirred. Blew. Sipped.

The blade must have sunk to the bottom of the mug. Why hasn't her spoon hit it? Maybe it melted.

Stirred. Blew. Sipped.

Maybe the lights will go out.

Stirred. Blew. Sipped.

Maybe the pot of chitterlings will explode.

Stirred . . .

Maybe the snow will get too heavy for the roof and collapse right down on her head.

Blew . . .

Maybe she won't see the blade.

Sipped.

I wasn't that lucky.

Myrtle's eyeballs turned gray. Her nostrils pulsed. I knew I was in trouble. I tried to focus on the ridges on my potato chips. Looking at her would have been a dead giveaway that I had something to do with the blade in her mug. She gently sat the mug down on its saucer and pulled the blade out with two fingers. She wiped the coffee off the blade with the napkin she snatched off her lap. At first, she curiously stared at it while holding it between two fingers.

I swallowed hard.

Our eyes met.

"You must think I'm stupid, don't you?" she growled and held the blade inches from my face. "You must think I was born yesterday! You g'on tell me that this razor blade got into my coffee all by itself?"

I couldn't talk.

"Do you hear me? You little piss rat!" she hollered stabbing the air with the blade. "Do you hear me talkin' to you?"

"Yes," I muttered softly. The hotdog and chips left a foul taste in my mouth.

"So?" she barked.

"No, Mommy. It didn't get there by itself," I murmured. I just knew I was gonna get the whupping of the century. I deserved it too.

Myrtle put the razor blade on the table next to the saucer and pushed back in her chair to stand up. "Get up," she ordered.

When I stood up, I watched her walk over to the cabinet underneath the sink. She flung it open and snatched out a green garbage bag. "Take it," she said flinging it at me.

I was confused. Why isn't she beating me? What does she want me to do with this trash bag? Is she gonna cut me up with the blade and put me in the bag?

"Go upstairs," she paused. "Go upstairs, and put your things in the bag," she said, pointing in the direction of the staircase.

As I turned to walk away, Myrtle followed close behind me. I climbed the steps, still feeling confused. She didn't follow me up the steps. Instead, she just stood at the bottom of the staircase and said, "You obviously don't know which side your bread is buttered."

While I walked up the steps, I kept envisioning bread with butter on both sides, thinking it would be quite messy to hold. Halfway up the steps she said, "And don't put nothin' in that bag that me and your father got you."

I froze. It was a trick. I didn't have anything that they didn't buy me. Suddenly the bread and butter metaphor made sense. Myrtle and G gave me the bread, the butter, and the knife to spread it.

"I have nothing, Mommy," I said, turning to face her. I clutched the garbage bag so hard that the plastic began to stick to my sweaty palm.

"That's right!" she nodded and folded her arms across her chest. "Now get your butt down here. You're so stupid! You wanna cut the hand that feeds you!"

I figured at that point she was ready to beat me, so I braced myself. When I came within inches of her, she just looked down at me watching as I trembled before her.

"Take off that shirt, those pants, and them shoes," she said.

The entire time I kept my eyes glued to her as I stripped. Stripping for a whupping was nothing new to me. She never liked whipping me with clothes on. Clothes were too expensive to ruin, and she wanted me to feel the full intensity of her blows.

As I stood before her in my white undershirt, panties, and socks, I expected her to attack me. But she didn't.

Myrtle dropped her arms. "Pick up that trash bag," she said as she began to walk toward the front door.

She unlocked the door and opened it. The cold blast of air hit me and sent a shocking and painful chill through my frail body. She pushed the screen door open. It was a struggle because there was so much snow piled up on the porch.

"Get out of my house, you little heathen!" she yelled.

Something inside my chest tied itself up into a big knot. Maybe it was the hotdog. I couldn't believe she was making me go outside into a blizzard almost naked, and I couldn't believe she was kicking me out of her house.

I began to beg. "Please, Mommy, don't make me go," I cried.

"Get out!"

"Please, Mommy, don't." I was terrified of Myrtle, but I was more terrified of being alone in the big, cold world with nothing and no one.

"Get out!"

"I'm sorry. I'll never do it again. I promise," I pleaded.

Like thunder, she boomed, "I SAID GET OUT OF MY HOUSE!"

Myrtle raised her hand as if she was going to slap me. I quickly made my way past her and stepped out onto the porch. The icy snow hurt my feet, and my tears felt as if they were gonna freeze up on my cheeks.

"You stand there and wait for DYFS to come pick you up," she hollered and slammed the door in my face.

The cold air hurt almost as much as the extension cord or any of the other weapons Myrtle beat me with. I could see every breath I took. The snow came up to my knees and was still falling hard and fast around me. I blew into my hands to warm them, but that didn't work. My socks got wet quickly. I rang the doorbell once, twice, three times. She didn't answer. She didn't even look through the curtains to see if I was okay.

I never cried harder in my life. I was so sorry for my sin. I knew I needed to be punished, but not that way. I wanted somebody to save me. But I didn't want it to be a social worker from DYFS. I was afraid they would take me away to some faraway place for bad little girls.

After standing in the blizzard for a few minutes I stopped rubbing my hands together, stopped trembling, and stopped crying. I couldn't feel the cold anymore. All my feelings froze over. I was numb inside and out. I didn't care if I lived or died.

The door opened, slowly. "Get in here," she said. "Now, you better not never forget what side your bread is buttered," she said as she snatched the trash bag from my hand.

From that day forward, Myrtle grew apprehensive and paranoid about my presence in her home. She started hiding knives, scissors, and other sharp objects. She put them in high places I couldn't reach. She locked up bleach and other toxic items. She randomly searched my pockets, under my mattress, and my toy box. And she never slept with her bedroom door unlocked when G was at work. Myrtle even threatened to send me away to a mental hospital or worse, a home for bad girls.

I had resisted, and I paid the consequences. I was scared for a while. But the incident showed me that I had courage. Myrtle still beat me day in and day out, but I'm sure she knew, as I did, that every word and strike fed my hatred of her. She knew that one day I'd look her in the face and talk back, hit back, or even kill her. That's what happens when a human being resists slavery.

THIRTEEN

One of the cruelest aspects of slavery was the breakup of families. Two of the many ways that families were torn apart was when a member was "sold down the river" or when a member ran away. To stand by and see a mother, father, wife, husband, or child sold away or run away was easily one of the most traumatic events in the life of a slave.

Mothers screamed and clung grimly to their children, only to be kicked away by a trader. Some lost their heads and ran off with the children or fought traders, masters, and overseers, to no avail. Many slaves who experienced such trauma never recovered. They became morose, indifferent, despondent. Some hallucinated and talked to themselves. Others committed suicide.

The breakup of families vividly exhibited the powerlessness slave adults often felt under that peculiar institution. Slave children felt the pangs even harder. Whether parents were sold or ran away, slave children who were left behind experienced a deep sense of abandonment and vulnerability. They were not only more vulnerable to the hands of whites, but also other blacks within the plantation community. Essentially they were not only slaves but also nobody's child within the system.

Other members of the plantation community were often forced to step in as fictive kin to sustain children in their grief. Some slave children loved and respected their new kin and found them to be as tender and nurturing as their biological parents. Others sometimes experienced abuse, neglect, and indifference. Fictive kin helped to teach a young slave about slavery and how to survive. But how did black children feel about their abandonment within their enslavement? What were their feelings about their extended family in the slave context?

I often heard the saying, "It takes a village to raise a child." I saw this concept played out in the ways in which black adults I knew took in children of relatives who had died, were on drugs, or had run off. Children were bound to those adults and thus incorporated into larger ideas about black community, family, and love.

Growing up, I never knew another black child who was adopted. As I approached the later stages of my adolescent bondage, I grappled with my own sense of abandonment and feelings about my own fictive kin as well as America's institution of adoption.

FOURTEEN

More than Myrtle's beatings, piercing words, and humiliating rituals, I hated being adopted. My blood, pain, scars, and her wretched voice temporarily reminded me that I had a purpose: to survive. For what? I didn't know then. But my daily struggles defined my strength, my tenacity, and my black girlhood. My physical scars could be touched. I could read their details. But the hole inside me was intangible.

I often touched my scars, even named them. I dabbed my blood with cotton balls, sucked it off my lips and cuts. I lifted my bandages and checked the scabbing process. Sometimes I tuned out some of Myrtle's lies about me being stupid and useless, and sometimes I believed her when she said I was unattractive and unwanted. I felt a deep, deep gash in my soul that I couldn't touch or adequately describe. Still, I knew it was there. That wound called abandonment would never close. And until this day, I'd never understand fully why it had to happen to me.

G often claimed that adopted kids were more special than biological children because they were chosen. But I couldn't trick myself into believing there was something so deeply special and wonderful about being adopted. I didn't feel like some unique gift to my adoptive parents. And I most certainly didn't feel blessed to have been placed in their home. The cold truth was that I had been unwanted and given up, for whatever reason. And perhaps I still would have felt this way even if I had been placed with better parents. Having no clue who I was or where I had come from made me feel that my life was meaningless. My early past was a mystery. So much of it made no sense. My childhood became this terrible never-ending existence of waiting and hoping for a miracle that would reveal my true identity and validate my existence.

As I was growing up, I wanted to become a teenager and then a woman with some sense of a foundation rooted in my own blood, genes, birth-place, and history. Adoption had stripped me of my birthright. I was an incomplete little black girl doomed for perpetual abandonment and emptiness.

At that time, the State of New Jersey gave biological family members a two-year period to change their minds about giving up their legal rights to a child, so by the time I reached seven, my time was up. Myrtle and G could finalize my adoption. The day that fat red-cheeked judge signed those white sheets of paper legalizing my adoption, I dragged my feet on the way in and out of the courtroom. I kept quiet as Myrtle and G relived every detail of the court proceeding. Their hands locked, and they swung each other's arms back and forth a few times.

"Thank you, Jesus!" G shouted at the sky. "Ain't God good?"

"Yes indeedy," Myrtle giggled.

G turned to me. "Ain't God good, funny lookin'?"

I didn't answer.

"Don't you hear your father talkin' to you, gal?" Myrtle scolded.

"Yes," I answered softly. "God is good," I said and rolled my eyes first at the back of their heads and then at the sky.

Myrtle, G, and the good Lord could have kissed my little black ass at that moment. All three of them and the State of New Jersey wanted to keep my soul frozen in time.

I kept kicking an acorn up the sidewalk as I occasionally crushed pinecones along the way. My heart was somewhere down in my stomach.

"You best realize this blessing, little girl," Myrtle reminded me. "You know how many little black kids there are in foster homes? They just waitin' and waitin' for somebody to come and get them. A lot of them ain't neva g'on find no home. Rejoice and be glad," she said.

"Our family is complete now," G said in a singsong voice.

"Now," Myrtle paused and looked back at me again. I put my fake, stiff, survivor smile on my face as I lost track of the acorn. "NO-BODY, I mean NOOOO-BODY can take you away from us."

That meant not even my real mother.

Before the legalization of my adoption, Myrtle and G's worse fear was the prospect of my being claimed by one of my biological relatives. If they had things their way, G would have rolled me up and stuffed me inside Myrtle's womb. He would have made me stay in there for nine months until she pushed me out again. He knew that having a baby would have made Myrtle feel like a complete woman. The fact that he would have pushed me inside her would have made him a man. But the cold truth was that I was somebody's else's child. Neither one of them, nor DYFS nor God could ever change that fact.

My biological mother could have flushed me down some fetid toilet. She could have thrown me in a Dumpster and covered me with garbage bags. She could have left me on some doorstep. But she handed me over to the New Jersey Department of Youth and Family Services. Back then I wondered if being swallowed down the throat of a toilet bowl was a better alternative to the pain and misery of life as the adopted child of Myrtle and George Jenkins.

Ironically, I never blamed my real mother for my adoption. I blamed adoption. Adoption was nameless, faceless, and voiceless. Adoption was like some kind of stork that picked up unwanted babies, dropped them off elsewhere, only to make mysteries out of them, and cut them off from their humanity.

During my childhood I had never met anybody who had been adopted. The only adopted kids I had heard of were the cute little black boy midgets Webster, from the show *Webster*, and Arnold along with his brother Willis from that show *Diff'rent Strokes*. Their lives were completely different from mine. All three boys were adopted by white people. Unlike Webster and Arnold, I wasn't a black midget boy who would never physically grow up into a black man. Webster and Arnold were stuck in the limbo of a continuous childhood, always cute and never a threat. Willis, on the other hand, always gave Mr. Drummond trouble. The stunted bodies of Webster and Arnold—comical little boys—stroked the ego of white paternalism, Hollywood style.

I was a little black girl—always a "gal" in Myrtle's world. In her house, she said, there would never be enough room for two women, so I'd physically grow but forever be childlike and deferential in her eyes. Myrtle had adopted me to stroke her own sense of paternalism. So I would conclude from this that the fiction of those television characters was not completely different from my own situation.

"You were adopted 'cause you were special," G once told me. "You were chosen. Ain't many kids can say their parents chose 'em."

Special, I thought. For me, *special* had some other connotation. *Special* was the same term used to describe mentally disabled kids who rode the short yellow bus, wearing helmets, rocking back and forth, and drooling.

There was nothing special about pretending things around me were real.

Jealousy swelled up in me when I saw other kids with their parents and could tell where they got their eyes, nose, hair texture, or height. Since that day my foster mother had told me she didn't know where my real mama was, I had walked down the streets of Trenton looking into the faces of random black folks, strangers, and wondering if it was possible that I got my eyes from the woman looking back at me. Did I get my complexion from the man standing at the bus stop with his hands shoved deep into his pockets? Would I be tall and grow big breasts like the woman eating crab legs and a potato seated at the table in front of us at the Red Lobster? Would I always have skinny ankles, like the man in green shorts running by the reservoir?

Holidays were the worst times to be an adopted child. Year after year, we made the same house stops. First, we went to Myrtle's mother's home in West Trenton. The house was always packed from wall to wall. My aunts piled food onto plates and chattered like busy chickens. My cousins played with each other, often excluding me because I wasn't really one of them. I usually took my place in the big television room at the other end of the house and watched whatever football or basketball game was playing. My uncles were so loud, always debating whether the Lakers would be a better dynasty than the Boston Celtics. People didn't seem to notice me until it was time to go.

"Myrtle, she's getting' so big," they'd say.

"Yeah, tell me about it," Myrtle said with dread in her voice.

"George you g'on have to get your guns ready for the little fellas," one of my uncles would always joke.

"Don't remind me," he said.

They always talked around me. Myrtle and G spoke for me. No one ever heard my voice. I always respected and never crossed my boundaries. I spoke when spoken to and came when called.

Our next stop was somewhere in Hamilton to visit Myrtle's goddaughter, Tera. Tera was the child Myrtle really wanted. She was a fat child and extremely attractive. She had long, silky, black hair, smooth caramel skin, and puppy eyes. I hated her. Tera never did any wrong to me, but she got every bit of affection and attention that I craved. I watched Myrtle as she kissed the little girl, stroked her hair, hugged her, and told her how beautiful she was while I sat on the couch, quiet and envious.

The final stop on our holiday circuit ended at my Aunt Crystal and

Uncle Shane's home in Cherry Hill, some forty-five minutes away. Uncle Shane, G's older brother, was the opposite of G. Uncle Shane never said much. He wore a serious, deep-in-thought expression as he sat in his chair with his ankles crossed tuning everyone out of his world. He greeted me with, "Hey, smarty-pants," and that was it until I said good-bye. Uncle Shane had given me that nickname because he thought I was a bright kid—sometimes too bright for the liking of most adults in my world.

I loved Aunt Crystal. She was warm and funny and asked me questions. She seemed curious about my perspective on the world. Of course, Myrtle was always nearby to enforce her rule: "What goes on in this house, stays in this house"—the rule that slave parents enforced with their children on the plantation. Slave parents feared that their children might share some information that would get them all in dire trouble. Myrtle didn't want people to know how I really got all my scars and injuries.

Aunt Crystal and Uncle Shane had two daughters, Niko and Conra. Niko was a year older than me, Conra five years. For Niko and me, Conra was a different species because she was a teenager. And for Conra, Niko and I were a pain in her behind. We spied on her and snuck into the private pink world of her room. As a teenager, Conra smelled differently to us. She put weird creams and makeup on her face. She didn't play. Niko and I didn't get her jokes. We didn't like her, and she didn't like us. Conra didn't get yelled at as much as we did.

The dining room table was always elaborately set. Aunt Crystal broke out her best crystal, chinaware, and cloth napkins. One year she taught me how to place silverware properly on the table. "Remember the word OWL," she said. "The O is for the spoon. The W is for the fork. And the L is for the knife. That's the order you place the silverware."

Aunt Crystal let me help her pour raisins and pineapples into her mixing bowl to make carrot salad. She even let me decide where certain dishes should go on the big table to make things look nice. I never got to sit next to her, though. When holiday dinners were at our house, Niko, Conra, and I sat at the kitchen table, while the adults sat at the big table. At Aunt Crystal's house Uncle Shane sat at one end, Aunt Crystal at the other. Niko, Conra, and I all sat next to each other squeezed on one side. G and Myrtle sat opposite us.

I sat at the big table looking at my relatives, knowing that they weren't my real people. How could I pretend? I looked nothing like them. Other than Aunt Crystal, I didn't understand their ways. I didn't have the same kinds of thoughts. I couldn't laugh at all their stories. I couldn't say, "Yeah, remember that time when . . ."

We had no common history. Adoption is the result of a loss or tragedy on both sides. My mother and I were separated. We lost each other for reasons unknown to me. Myrtle had loss too: all her babies ended up in the toilet.

They prayed before dinner and reminisced about dates, good times and bad times, and dead relatives. I had no choice but to find something interesting on the table, magnify it in my mind, and connect with it. The connection was that that object and I shared the same reality. That object and I were surrounded by characters, their voices, their pasts, but not connected to them except to be used for display in the life of the family. That object and I made the setting complete. I could have embraced their stories to connect with my adoptive family members, but I didn't want to connect with them because I often felt like I was different from and better than them.

Sometimes I wanted to shrink myself and become the turkey or the glazed ham with that big dried-looking pineapple on top. At least they'd pay me some attention. They'd pick at me, slice me, and choose my dark or light pieces. They'd say how good I looked and how they were going to have me for lunch for the next week and make a bisque and sandwiches out of me.

I wanted to be the smoked neck bone swimming around in the collard greens or the candied yams piled up in the glass bowl next to the macaroni and cheese Myrtle made at six o'clock that morning. I wouldn't have minded being the carrot cake sitting between the ambrosia and the sweet potato pie on the lazy susan sitting behind the big table.

But I was an adopted child sitting around folks who would always remind me that they were responsible for plucking me from obscurity and giving me a home, something they said no one else would do for me—something my biological family, for whatever reason, hadn't done.

"Stacey, it's your turn," Uncle Shane said year after year before we dove into the food. I was always the last to take my turn. "What are you grateful for?"

Myrtle gave me a cold stare. I tried to pretend she wasn't really there. G looked down at his chest, smiling, like he knew I was going to say something sentimental to make him proud of his little girl.

I could never give them an answer. Of course, I was grateful not to be homeless, hungry, blind, deaf, jacked up in some other way, or even dead. But I knew I didn't have to wait until Thanksgiving to give thanks for all that.

"A mother." Myrtle snapped. "A father." Her face grew dark. She was insulted because I hadn't parted my lips. "A home. Girl, you got a lot to be grateful for. You could be in that home in East Orange. Remember that while you eat your greens and turkey, little girl."

Aunt Crystal always had a way to change the subject or fix things. "Well, little Stacey has so much to be thankful for. Perhaps she's just a little overwhelmed trying to pick out the most important things. Give her some time. She'll think of it later," she'd say while scooping something onto my plate and winking at me.

When dinner was over, Aunt Crystal stopped drawing me into conversations. She and Myrtle cleared the table, washed the dishes, cut the turkey into pieces, stored the rest of the food inside the refrigerator, put the coffee pot on, and banned all children from the kitchen while they gossiped. Niko got into her moods sometimes and closed me off from her room. Conra always went to the movies with the other teenage aliens. Uncle Shane and G would take a ride somewhere. So there I was alone and constantly revisiting pictures and objects of Aunt Crystal's living room in my head. I amused myself until I eventually fell asleep. I felt that if I were a real niece or real cousin or real granddaughter, people would have paid more attention to me. But the cold truth was that I was different.

My classmates too had their way of reminding me that I was different. They saw me only in the context of the classroom and playground. Myrtle didn't allow me to play sports or do other extracurricular activities. She forbade me to talk on the phone or go to the movies, birthday parties, or slumber parties with kids other than her own nieces and nephews. She never explained then why she kept me away from other kids. But now I know why.

When you are a parent who abuses your child, you want to maintain absolute control and influence over that child. You can't allow her to spend time around other people outside the home. That child can't be allowed to see how other children live and are raised by their parents. That child can't be allowed to slip up and tell what goes on behind the closed doors of your home.

The other girls my age knew cuss words I was too afraid even to think of using. I knew nothing about boys except that they stood up to pee. I couldn't turn the jump rope right. I couldn't do any of the new dance moves like the cabbage patch, the electric slide, the whop, or the give it up. I wasn't allowed to dance or watch *The Soul Train* on weekends. I didn't know any of the lyrics to the hot artists like LL Cool J, Salt-N-Pepa, Big Daddy Kane, or Eric B. and Rakim. If I listened to that kind of "devil music," then I was going to go to hell, Myrtle said. So I spent most of the time standing against the fence wishing I wasn't so different. Being adopted intensified that feeling of isolation.

I had my moments when I made everyone laugh or think I was cool. I was the only girl brave enough to play the dozens with the boys.

"Stacey, you so skinny, you can turn sideways and disappear."

"You so short, you can sit on the curb and swing your legs," I would shoot back.

"Yo' mama so fat, she jumped in the air and got stuck."

"Yo' mama so stupid, she went to the post office for food stamps."

"Stacey, yo' mama so black, she went to night school and they marked her absent!"

"Boy, you was so ugly when you were a baby, yo' mama had to feed you with a slingshot!"

And then came the ooooh's from the other kids standing around us. I had silenced the competition. But then, it never failed: the low blow came in one form or another.

"At least I got a real mama and daddy."

"At least my mama wanted me."

"At least my mama didn't give me away."

"At least I ain't adopted."

When those words came, and they always came hard and clear, I felt as if someone had punched my chest open, reached inside, and squeezed every drop of blood out of me. The truth was that no one was that skinny, that short, that stupid, that black, that ugly. But there was no denying that I didn't have real parents.

So many times, I daydreamed. I conjured up what that magical day would be like when I met my real parents. It would be sunny and glorious. They'd welcome me with open arms. Maybe we would meet by accident in the street. Perhaps we'd meet on *Oprah*. It didn't matter one way or another how I'd meet my real family. I just wanted it to happen. Soon.

FIFTEEN

W hites on and off the plantation worked consistently to make black children submissive. No slave child came into the world naturally obedient or deferential. Black parents aided in this process—not in support of the institution of slavery but to safeguard their children's lives. Though physical violence was the linchpin of slavery, other abusive tactics were also incorporated to deter rebelliousness. The black child's spirit was always a threat to the vitality of slavery. Therefore, it was crucial to break the slave child's spirit in the first years of life.

Early on, slave children experienced the overwhelming power of whites. Masters forced slave children to bow in their presence and accept whippings from white children; they would be kicked for walking between whites on the street and punished for showing signs of anger or sadness. Such rituals forced slave children to be deferential and adhere to racial boundaries. These racially constructed conventions also allowed whites to create psychological distance from their barbaric treatment of slaves. White masters often forced young slaves to laugh, sing, put on plays, and fake contentment. But these were feelings masters wanted, not what slaves actually felt. Fear of the lash forced young slaves to respect their masters. While some psychologically accepted this way of life, others feigned deference to avoid punishment and masked their contempt for whites.

Like slave children, I feigned respect to avoid physical pain. I defined myself, my existence, my tomorrows, and my next breath through Myrtle. I even internalized her feelings. When she was sick, so was I. When she was sad, I felt sad. When she felt pain, I ached inside for her. I sought to envelop myself neatly and safely into her order. I wanted to understand and see the world through Myrtle's eyes. I sought to clean the way she cleaned. Hold my corncob and glass of tea the way she held hers. Walk like her. Speak like her. Laugh like her. Think like her. Be a miniature version of her. This was love.

I thought if only I could become one with Myrtle, maybe then she wouldn't apply the lash. And then just maybe, she would approve of me. Maybe my master would love me. I already loved her.

But how could the slave ever love the master? How could I have ever loved Myrtle? It seems like an impossible contradiction. Of course, I'd like to say I never respected or loved her. She chained my body, my spirit, and my mind to her supreme power. That's the very quintessence of slavery. If masters cannot chain the bodies, the spirit, or the minds of the weak, then slavery, oppression, and abuse cannot exist.

This psychological terror wreaked havoc on slave children well before puberty and adulthood. Were slave children fully able to maintain belief in themselves as worthy human beings? Did slave children who were forced to curtail their anger become too submissive? Did their concept of themselves reflect their master's treatment and perception of them? Or did black children express their aggression toward their masters and attempt to avoid total dependency? Did they turn on each other? Did their spirits survive?

SIXTEEN

Sometimes I wished for a brother or sister, someone with whom I could play bingo, Uno, or checkers. I wouldn't have to imagine another little person lying beside me at night to tell how *we* were going to grow up together and move away from Myrtle. Perhaps we would have had our secret language or ways of protecting each other. Being an only child was hard for me, because I was the sole witness to my pain.

I can still hear that russet grandfather clock ticking as it lay encased in a glass-like coffin in the living room. Tonight, like every other evening, I wondered if I was going to hold onto it or the antique marble coffee-table while she beat me for getting something wrong. Some bare twigs, twisted like nerves, scratched against the panoramic window as I watched Myrtle's blue Lincoln Town Car drag into the empty driveway.

"Shit," a little voice inside me said. "She's home."

I wanted to throw up.

I darted through the hallway and up the steps to my bedroom. If Myrtle caught me out of bed, a whipping was certain. Every day my adoptive parents left me home alone for about an hour until Myrtle got home from work. They didn't want to spend extra money on the after-school program. Since I was in the fifth grade, they felt I was old enough to be left alone in the house. So when G went to work the night shift at his machinist job, I had to stay confined to my bedroom. They hid the telephone cords, ordered me not to answer the door, and told me not to come downstairs for any reason unless there was a fire. Of course, I knew where they hid the telephone cords. I'd find them and call up as many schoolmates to chat as I could in less than a half-hour. I rummaged through photo albums, drawers full of papers, and blasted the radio. And I never got caught.

By the time I reached my bedroom window to peek one eye through the yellowed shade, Myrtle was just getting out of the car. She looked weary, almost dazed. Maybe something did happen to her, I thought to myself. Maybe she's sick. Maybe I won't get beat tonight.

Myrtle hauled herself and her bags past the slim tree that lent a creeping strain of maple shade over the driveway. She didn't even look up to see if I was out of the bed peeking at her through the window. My eyes moved across her skinny shoulder, collarbone, and breast. A thin silver necklace resting on her throat accentuated the bare section just above her cleavage. She told me she'd give it to me when I got older and learned to appreciate valuable things. When Myrtle disappeared, I briefly stared at the sunlight sculpting its late geometries across the tops of distant houses and trees.

I pictured Myrtle sticking her key in the door just as I actually heard it. I took one big deep breath and braced my body for whatever was to come that evening. At that moment, I wanted to set myself free like a balloon in the sky. But I knew I couldn't, so I jumped onto my bed and held onto my pillow and pretended it was a woman's torso—warm, nurturing, safe.

The front door banged against the hinge, gently shaking the shade covering on my bedroom window. I heard Myrtle's keys drop onto the coffee table and one of her bags crinkle, just as usual. Her footsteps approached the stairway. I was expecting to hear her callous voice ordering me to get up, but I heard nothing from her. That evening she walked all the way to the kitchen. But my body was still braced and ready as I gazed abstractly at the ceiling and inhaled the oppressive still air brought into the house by her presence. One, two, three minutes passed as silence kept repeating itself.

Did she forget about me? Did she drop dead? Suddenly my heart bumped up and down. I began to wonder if I had knocked something over when I ran through the hallway. Perhaps Myrtle was investigating the scene and planning a whipping for me. Maybe she was tiptoeing up the steps with a handful of switches she snatched off the bushes just behind the tree as she made her way into the house. Fear. Anxiety. Oh, how I wished I could speed up my childhood.

Myrtle broke the silence as she turned on the stereo and sorted music from static. I finally realized something was deeply wrong when she stopped at a station playing Big Daddy Kane's rap song, "Ain't No Half Steppin.'"

"She's playin' the devil's music," I whispered and smiled as I lifted my head from my imaginary pillow woman.

I bobbed my head back and forth and mouthed the words. This was a rare un-Christian moment for me. And I enjoyed it. All we ever listened to in that house was preachers and gospel music. Myrtle even blasted gospel music during my whippings to drown out my cries. At that point, I got out of bed and cautiously walked over to the doorway next to the staircase. I heard Myrtle pick up the phone receiver and press the sticky buttons as she dialed some number.

Before her voice broke, she gave a soupy sniffle. "Hi, G," she said softly. "Just got back from the doctor," she continued as I pressed my ear more intensely against the open air hoping to catch every syllable from her mouth.

"I hafta get surgery," she whimpered.

My eyes widened.

"She *is* gonna die," I whispered to the wall.

"The doctor said it's the size of a cantaloupe," she said. "That's why my stomach is so big and I'm always runnin' to the bathroom."

I envisioned the khaki-colored skin and rough, warty surface of the melons Myrtle kept on the countertop by the kitchen sink during summers. I could see her splitting one open with one of her big knives before cutting slices into the shapes of half-moons. She always messed up the taste by adding salt. I could taste salt on my lips just as a sudden rush of energy overwhelmed my body. Myrtle's voice had a soft timbre I hadn't heard before. I let one eye peek around the corner of the staircase. I could see her face. Her eyes were ash-colored, and the tears dropping from them rolled down to her chin.

"This means I can't ever have a child of my own," she said.

My pulse hammered from my wrists to my fingertips. My face wrinkled up. I was confused. Where did that comment come from? What did children have to do with the cantaloupe in her stomach? Was she the kind of woman who gave birth to fruit instead of children? I didn't understand the connection.

"G, you know I always wanted a child of my own. I wanted to give you a little girl or boy," she said as her voice got weaker. I could tell she couldn't hold back her tears any longer. My heart sank with Myrtle's hopes of ever fulfilling her sense of complete womanhood.

Like her sisters, Myrtle had been reared up to put God first, marry, keep a house clean, cook, and give birth to children who'd be brought up with the same direction. Myrtle was indeed faithful to her God. She married when she was twenty-one. The floors in our house were so clean you could eat off them. I could never foresee her marriage to G ending before death.

"The doctor said it's benign," she said, as I tried to figure out the meaning of the word. "But he said it has to come out, or it will get worse later."

I moved away from the staircase and walked softly back to my room. I searched my bookshelf for my dictionary and found it resting between a copy of the Bible and my Baby Sitter's Club book collection.

"*Benign*," I recited over and over again as I quietly turned the pages. I read the definition aloud, "Gentle, kindly. Salutary. Mild. Not malignant."

I was still confused. So I looked up *malignant* and read its definition. "Of a disease. Very virulent or infectious. Of a tumor, cancerous." After closing the book, I understood what was wrong with Myrtle: she had a tumor, but it wasn't a bad one.

I put the dictionary back on the shelf and returned to my pillow woman. Lying there on her soft plushness, I gazed up at the ceiling and imagined Myrtle laying on the countertop waiting for some white man dressed in a white short coat to split her belly open with a knife. I could see him pulling the cantaloupe out of her with his bare hands.

"You go to the doctor for a simple checkup, and the next thing you know somethin' big is wrong with you," I heard Myrtle complain loudly. Her voice got even more exasperated. And then it got low again, realizing she couldn't change her situation. Not even prayer would make the cantaloupe tumor go away. Still, she said, "This is the Lord's will."

I never understood why people said things like that when bad things happened. Somebody got sick. Somebody had a heart attack. Got cancer. Had a car accident. Got raped. Dropped dead. Black people were enslaved. Hung from trees. Hitler killed 6 million Jews. The Native Americans are almost gone. And all I hear people around me say was that it was God's will. If this was true, then God is terrible and demented!

"I love you," Myrtle said to G in a weepy voice before hanging up the phone.

What was going through G's mind? Did he feel limp? Helpless? Hopeless about having a child of his own? Did he think Myrtle was incomplete? Was she less of a woman in his eyes? Did he too think this was God's will?

"Mama," Myrtle's voice broke again. Myrtle had turned down the radio by then. She was losing her fight against her tears. I hated it when she cried. I think those were the moments when I wanted to love her most.

"It's me, Myrtle," she said.

I never saw my grandmother cry unless she was in church praising God. Her face was like some chiseled Native American mask expressing no emotion during tragedy or sad moments. Unlike Grandpop, Grandmom was not affectionate. Myrtle would spend hours scratching her father's scalp with a comb, cleaning his ears, and rubbing his shoulders until he dozed off in his chair. It seemed almost erotic. The man had a huge bald spot and two small patches of gray hair on the sides. When Myrtle finished, he took his toothpick out of his mouth and kissed her on her mouth as he did with his other daughters, granddaughters, and women in his church where he was the head pastor. This was love.

But Grandmom didn't get close to people like that, and she certainly was not very close to Myrtle. Out of respect, Myrtle called her mother once a week. Their conversations were never long. I could sense, even when they were in each other's presence, that mother and daughter had an invisible and intense veil between them. They said they loved each other, but they did not like each other. Myrtle also felt that she had gotten whipped more than her siblings. And she had, as one of her sisters would tell me years later.

"Myrtle was always doing something wrong," one of her younger sisters told me. "Always in trouble. Lying. Stealing. Cheating on tests. Running away. Cutting school. She used to beat us and tease us when Mommy and Daddy weren't around. We all got our butts beat from time to time," she said. "But Myrtle got it more."

I think deep down inside, Grandmom knew there was something wrong with Myrtle and was always praying for her. Sometimes I would catch her quietly studying her daughter from a distance. I imagined she was asking herself how she could have created such a strange woman. Did she blame herself? Did she think Myrtle had the devil in her? Did she think it was God's will?

My fingers played with my chin as I absorbed Myrtle's sometimes muffled words to her mother. "I have to have a hysterectomy," she said.

"Hys-ter-ec-to-my," I sounded out the word. Like *benign* and *malignant*, it was another word that I'd have to look up.

"They have to remove my ovaries and uterus," she said. "They have to empty out my womb."

I knew that a womb was where babies came from. I tried to picture what ovaries and a uterus looked like, but I could not conjure up any images in my head. Maybe my encyclopedia would have pictures. Although I couldn't draw up any mental pictures of ovaries and a uterus, I figured they were vital organs that made a woman's body work the right way.

Suddenly I found myself ridden with anxiety and fear. How are my ovaries? How is my uterus? Is my womb healthy? Was I not going to be capable of giving birth to a child of my own? Would I be incomplete too?

I tightened my grip around my pillow woman and tried to ease my fears about my future womanhood. My body was so hot I felt like I was stuck in some swamp with heat hanging over it.

"Stacey, get down here!" Myrtle's voice whisked up the steps and hit me like a cold blast of air. Right then I was reminded that womanhood for me was a long way away. I had to get through the rest of girlhood.

As I got myself ready to face Myrtle, I feared that she was going to take her bad news out on me in the worst way. I was afraid that she was going to see my face, a face she didn't give birth to, and start slapping me around. Despite my fear, my feelings were hurt when I replayed Myrtle's phone conversation with G in my head.

"I will never be able to have a child of my own," she had told him. A child of her own. What was I? Hearing Myrtle say those words made me feel unreal. My foster mother had already made me feel like some play doll years before. And there I was again, reminded of my inauthenticity.

All those beatings. All the yelling. All those bad names. All of Myrtle's rough treatment was done out of her love for me? This is what she said. So if she loved me, that meant she saw me as her child despite our lack of a biological connection. She would have treated her own flesh and blood child the same as me, right?

When I reached the bottom of the staircase, I started to think that maybe love did not dictate the way she treated me. Maybe she beat me because I was not her real child. Maybe she beat me because her womb didn't work. Maybe she was beating my real mother out of me because I probably resembled her and not Myrtle. Yes, she and G had plucked me from obscurity and given me shelter, food, clothing, toys, and a private school education. All those years. All that money. They were still waiting for the real child to come. Time had not made my body and facial features resemble my adoptive parents. The biological connection could never be faked. Perhaps this is what made Myrtle resent me.

For all my early adolescence, I wanted to make myself perfect for Myrtle. I wanted to lighten my complexion to high yellow. I hated my brown skin because I believed she hated it. If I looked more like her, then she wouldn't beat me so much. I had the same wish as Nicodemus in the Bible: to be born again. Jesus told Nicodemus that he had to be born again to enter the kingdom of heaven. He asked Jesus how it would be possible for him to reenter his mother's womb and be born again. Jesus told him that being born again was a spiritual journey, a moral cleansing. If only I could roll myself as small as I could, push myself between Myrtle's legs, and snuggle back into pregnancy, that floating bubble under her belly button. Nine months inside her body would have made all the difference, I believed. Myrtle would have pushed me back into existence, completing her womanhood and making me a real child. Only then could we get that mother-daughter thing right. But like Nicodemus, I could never enter Myrtle's womb and be born again. And Myrtle, physically barren and devoid of the quintessential power to nurture and love, would never possess the power to give birth inside or outside her womb.

My knife-blade lean body stood before Myrtle as she shuffled through the day's mail. She looked up from the pile of paper and envelopes and then measured me with her eyes. Scanning the dusky aurora of my hair that was tightly braided like yarn into six diagonal cornrows, I could tell she was counting the barrettes snapped to the ends of each braid. One, two, three, four, five, six. I knew they were all there. I made sure before I got down the steps.

"Lift up your shirt," she demanded, still holding an unopened letter in her hand.

I quickly and carefully untucked my shirt from my pants without wrinkling it. I knew that would make her mad. Slowly, I revealed for her my flat stomach, boney rib cage, and flat chest. Myrtle's face wrinkled into dark, disgusted features.

"You ain't big as nothin," she said turning her head to another letter. "You ain't got no titties."

I felt my heartbeat echoing in my stomach, and I'm sure she could see my heart pounding against my ribs through my skin. I knew not to let my shirt back down until she ordered me to. My eyes fixed themselves on her C-cups. I wondered if my breasts would grow to the size of hers. I worried that they wouldn't. I just knew I was going to be flat-chested for the rest of my life.

"Drop your panties," she growled.

Every day we went through this same ritual. Myrtle checked my clothes to make sure they weren't torn or dirty. Sometimes she examined my backpack and school supplies to make sure they were neatly organized. She made me take down my underwear and spread my legs. She looked inside my panties and pressed one finger against a place on my vagina that I never touched. She snatched her finger away and brought it up to her nose and sniffed. Maybe that was her way of making sure I was clean. I simply thought she was looking for some reason to beat me. I thought nothing else about this ritual. And long after the white man cut the cantaloupe tumor out of her belly, Myrtle's examinations of my body got more frequent.

Looking back, I believe that my adoptive mother had some morbid fascination with my physical and sexual development because her womb did not work anymore and she would never again have use for her own breasts to nurture a baby. Perhaps she was envious of my own potential womanhood. Any growth was a sign to her that she could not keep me enslaved in the state of childhood, of powerlessness. This little girl would become a woman, a complete woman.

SEVENTEEN

Like free white girls, enslaved black girls passed through the same physical developmental stages of life. But sometimes young female slaves did not realize when their girlhood ended and the next stage had begun. Their mothers, who experienced the pangs of growing up black, female, and property of the white man, often feared the changes in their daughter's bodies. Coming of age as a female slave was an especially treacherous time.

Even under normal circumstances, mothers often dread their daughters' coming of age. Black mothers wanted their daughters to grow up and become women even though their possibilities would be sharply limited by slavery. But as they watched their daughters shed signs of girlhood, slave mothers expected trouble from both white and black men. Slave masters often dressed both sexes in long, thin shirts and often denied boys and girls underwear as a way to humiliate them. When black boys and girls bathed in rivers, whites often came along and took their clothes away or threw them up in trees so they could watch the naked blacks run and fetch them.

Slave boys and girls alike faced the awesome task of obeying their white master and mistress as well their mother and father. This created a constant psychological tug-of-war between black parents who expected obedience while trying to apply some emotional significance to their children's lives, and whites who attached only economic meanings to black boys and girls as property and future cheap labor. To raise a black child to become a white man's "property" was a daunting task. It was common for daughters to survive girlhood without experiencing some form of sexual abuse.

Black mothers often limited their daughters' contact with the opposite sex. Attractive girls were most vulnerable on the plantation, so mothers often encouraged homeliness or otherwise tried to draw attention away from their own beauty and to camouflage their daughters' sexuality.

Slave mothers often played down the curiosity of their boys and girls when they inquired about childbirth and sexual development. Most slave girls grew up ignorant about the mechanics of sex and the functions of their own bodies. This withholding of information, this silence, sometimes led to fear, anxiety, ignorance, and trauma when black girls crossed the threshold into womanhood either naturally or through sexual abuse. The silence and secrets kept on the plantation would have consequences for black girls like me born generations later.

EIGHTEEN

I had questions about my own physical development but could not ask Myrtle. She wasn't the type of mother I could talk openly with about sex—or any less complicated subject. Myrtle was always critical of girls who grew up too fast. She wasn't worried about me being fast because she had control over me. But she often used poor blacks as examples of bad behavior.

As I watched other girls my age grow up, I felt that I was going to remain small and meaningless and be left behind like some kind of runt in a litter of puppies. Myrtle said that black girls seemed to grow faster than white girls. She and other black adults around me said that black kids grew faster because white folks put chemicals in milk, chicken, and candy. She never purchased certain foods like Popeye's or Church's chicken, Coca-Cola, Bubble Yum bubble gum, Nerds candy, or Uncle Ben's rice. Their goal, Myrtle said, was to make black people sick and sterile so that we would die out. I believed her.

The food in our neighborhood was fresher than in the 'hood. The stores were cleaner and more organized, and I didn't have to swat flies or worry about my fingers falling off if I touched something. Grocery stores in the 'hood sold dime drinks and penny candies, pork rinds, fatback, and salt two-for-a-dollar—things we didn't see in our white grocery stores. Every block in the 'hood seemed to have a church, liquor store, check cashing place, chicken spot, and hair supply store owned by Koreans. One other thing that frightened me most about the 'hood were the projects.

The first time I set foot in the projects, we were delivering canned goods during a Thanksgiving drive sponsored by our church. Myrtle refused to go, so I tagged along with G and helped him carry smaller boxes to "those less fortunate than us." I saw firsthand that I didn't have to go to a Third World country to witness poverty. The projects, or the PJ's as some called them, were less than a fifteen-minute drive from my house into the heart of Trenton. As soon as I walked through the door, I saw gigantic roaches lying dead on their backs. I wondered if they had died from urine inhalation or from starvation. Roaches weren't the only things littering the floors. I saw needles, broken pipes, bullet casings, puddles of urine, and sometimes drunken men who had fallen asleep in corners. I couldn't imagine how people could just drop their pants and pee right in the hallway or elevator or fall asleep out in the open.

The black people in the projects looked different from the black folks I knew. The kids looked hungry, hard, sick, and worn out like old people. Some of the girls' hair didn't grow. The boys' skin looked ashen and bruised. Boys and girls cussed, sometimes around their parents, who didn't seem to care. The mothers constantly sent young kids to the store to buy flour, sugar, milk, juice, Pampers, and cigarettes. And if there was no money, the child was sent to a neighbor to borrow goods. The children didn't seem to have a bedtime or any restrictions on when and where they could go. Life for black children in the 'hood was different from the life my black middle-class peers and I experienced. I never once thought I was better than the kids who grew up in the 'hood. My living conditions were better than theirs, and I knew I didn't want to live like them. But I did not think that those children or their parents chose to live in such conditions.

G said to me, "We all must be grateful for what we have. And remember, this could be any of us that live like this. Don't ever look down on folks and tell 'em they got to lift themselves up by the bootstraps. Some of 'em don't even have bootstraps. And just when you think you got it bad, somebody else is livin' worse than you. There is always some reason behind people's situation even if you can't see it. I ought to know, 'cause I grew up in the South. In the Jim Crow South. You don't know nothin' about Jim Crow. You too young. But thank the good Lord that ya'll youngins today ain't got to know nothin' about that kind of livin' 'cause it ain't no way for nobody to live."

Myrtle explained poor black people's situation differently. For her, history and racism had nothing to do with their lives. "See," she'd sneer at the poor blacks as we rode through the 'hood every blue moon. She would drive down Stuyvesant Avenue, one of the worst streets in Trenton. This was her way of teaching me a lesson about appreciation. She said I was spoiled and took everything for granted. Sometimes she threatened to leave me there. She'd quickly lock the car doors as some black man with a swagger crossed the street in front of our car. He didn't look like he was going to rob or do us harm. He was minding his own business. But nevertheless Myrtle feared his presence.

"This is what happens to you if you don't go to school. This is what happens when you don't have God in your life. Look around you!" her voice got louder. "See this?"

"Yes, Mommy," I answered as I pressed my face against the back window.

"Triflin' niggas! All of 'em! They live in dirty piss-infested houses. Roaches crawlin' everywhere. The kids are stupid and nappy-headed. All the women do is shack up with the men and make babies. Look at them little girls." She slowed the car down. "Look at that one." She stomped on the brakes as a teenage girl rubbed her plump belly. "Umph, babies havin' babies."

Myrtle sounded like the white people on television who were always talking about urban poverty, crime, teenage pregnancy, and black pathology. Their stories were always cloaked in numbers, charts, test scores and studies, and sketches of wanted black men. All that academic and professional language seemed like covert ways of calling black people niggers. But I never knew which Myrtle hated more: white people or poor black people.

"Don't ever be a nigga," she warned me on one of our drives.

I was confused. I thought all black people—rich, poor, educated, stupid, beautiful, ugly, Christian, devilish, upstanding, criminal—were niggas. For so many years, Myrtle taught me that white people thought all blacks were niggers. In white America I would never escape race no matter how hard I worked. And then she told me not to be a nigga.

"Mommy, what's a nigga?" I broke the question to her as our car crept past two groups of a dozen chocolate- and pecan-colored little girls with beads and cornrows in their heads. One group of girls played double-dutch while the other group surrounded a large boom box and danced to rap music.

"Them," she yelled. "See them? They are niggas! Niggas are ignorant low-life black folks. All them little hoochies over there know how to do is shake their little butts. Look at how these children grow up! It's an abomination in the eyes of the Lord!"

I didn't see what Myrtle saw. I wanted to get out of the car and play with the little girls. Yes, their neighborhood was different. Many lived with only one parent, and some didn't know who their fathers were. I lived with adoptive parents and didn't know who my real mother or father was. We went to different schools. Maybe they didn't go to church. I hated going to church. But they were black like me, and they were little girls. That was enough for me to feel connected to their lives. I wanted them to teach me how to dance and play double-dutch. I wanted to learn their hand and step games and speak their language. I wanted to sit between their legs and let them braid my hair like theirs. I felt I was missing that part of my black girlhood because Myrtle was so persistent about making me look and act like a white girl. I had to dress like them, walk like them, sit like them, talk like them, and be like them. Why? Because Myrtle said I had to grow up to be "a credit to my race."

"There is a war," she explained. "There is a war between niggas and black people. *We* are black people. *They* are niggas! Black people work hard and make a decent livin'. We go to church. We keep our homes nice and clean. We don't destroy everything we get our hands on. We don't steal. We don't go out drinkin' and druggin' and wastin' our lives away. We don't shake our butts all day. We raise our children to be obedient and to live right. Niggas make things harder for all of us black folks to try to get somewhere in this white man's land. Black folks don't live like this. Black children don't grow up like this."

As if she was honking at some stubborn mule in the middle of the street, Myrtle got angrier at the sight of all those little black girls growing up "fast." She banged the center of her steering wheel hard, frightening the girls with her horn.

"You all need Christ!" she yelled at the closed windows. "Heathens!" One little girl looked strangely at Myrtle. "Yeah, you! Heathen! Go to church!"

The girl could not hear or make out Myrtle's words, but she could tell by the tone of her horn and the sour expression on her face that she was being unkind. First, the little girl stuck her tongue out, and then she gave her the middle finger. "Fuck you, bitch," the girl screamed at our car. I wanted to laugh but knew that I'd surely get a swift backhand and a whupping from Myrtle when we got home.

"See," Myrtle darted her finger at the girl. "That's what I'm talkin' about. They ain't got no respect. Look at how they grow up. Flip and fast."

So black kids grew up faster than white kids, and poor black kids grew up even faster in other ways than black kids like me and my peers. Money, education, geography, and parents determined our growth. I lived in the suburbs. Never missed a meal. Wore nice clothes. Went to private school. Lived in a house with rules. Still, I felt my growth was stunted, not by race or class, but stress reeked onto me by my adoptive mother.

Every September I could see the transformations my classmates underwent during our summer vacations. The other girls came back to school taller, thicker, rounder in some places, and sprouted out in other places. As always, Tye Johnson and I were the smallest kids in the class. But he did not get teased as much as I did for lack of form. While the other girls got invited to play "house" or "doctor," I always remained a curious onlooker. Even Tye got to play the daddy or the doctor.

"I'll show you mine if you show me yours," the boys whispered to the girls or scribbled on notebook paper.

"You go first," the girl would smile.

"No, *you* go first," the boy insisted.

"Nope," she'd say back.

"You scared?" the boy challenged.

"I ain't scared. But how will I know you'll show me yours when I show you mine?" she'd ask. Boy and girl went back and forth, each one a little excited and growing more curious—and both a bit scared of what the other would think of their most private parts. We called this game "show-and-tell."

I was quite curious about what lay behind boy's zippers. I knew they wore different underwear and stood up to pee. And I actually believed that it was their penises that made them stronger and run faster. But as I stood by watching show-and-tell, I wasn't that fascinated. Their penises looked like little brown worms curled up on a wrinkly sack.

"That's it?" I whispered the first time I saw what hung between boys' legs. But girls had more. They had "titties" and a "pussy," which to me represented some secret world in their pants. Looking at the changes and diverse forms on girls' bodies gave me some insight on what to expect when my own body finally woke up and changed.

I had a deep and intense fascination with breasts. The bigger they were, the more I stared. A woman at church named Sista Charleston had the biggest titties on earth. To this day, I have yet to see breasts as big as hers. Hers were so big that when she sat down on the church pew, they could rest on her thighs and kneecaps. She couldn't reach her hands around them.

And sometimes she would lay her Bible and eyeglasses right on top of them and didn't have to worry about either slipping off. I loved getting hugs from big-breasted churchwomen. I felt safe and warm in their boob worlds. To me, breasts were a sign of nurturing and complete womanhood.

I also had a deep affinity for dark-skinned, heavyset black women. I feared fair-skinned, thin black women. I thought they were arrogant, mean, and hot tempered, so I kept my distance from them. I also believed that they had some deep disdain for dark-skinned blacks. This, of course, is not true. I believe I harbored such feelings because Myrtle was fair-skinned, arrogant, mean, and hot-tempered. She was also thin and had small breasts. So when I tried to imagine everything warm, nurturing, and safe I imagined the opposite of her. I imagined my real mother was dark-skinned, thick, and had big nurturing breasts.

When I was twelve, Myrtle bought me a pink cotton training bra. Sometimes I stuffed it or one of Myrtle's cross-your-heart-bras with toilet tissue and put a bulky maxipad in my panties. I would wear the bra and maxipad for ten minutes, get on my knees, and pray real hard. When I stood up, I noticed that my breasts didn't fill up the bra. The pad was still white and dry when I unzipped my pants.

"Still a little girl," I shook my head. I was going to be left standing alone with toys, cartoons, and an evil mother that controlled every aspect of my life while all the other girls became women.

Eventually I stopped wishing for breasts and bloodstains. I had to focus on staying alive and not doing anything to provoke Myrtle's anger. It became clear that any sign of my becoming a woman was a threat to Myrtle's position as woman of the house.

"There ain't enough room in this house for two women," she often said. With those words, I knew she was acknowledging my coming of age. She also said things like, "Keep your legs closed and your dress down. I don't wanna hear you mention nothin' about no boys. You bring any babies in my house, and I won't be takin' care of no little crumb snatchers. You make your bed hard, you lay in it. You make that red wagon, you pull it," she warned.

I think more than anything else, Myrtle despised the fact that one day I would shed girlhood and have the potential to become a mother, unlike her. For me, leaving girlhood was a sign of hope. Growing meant that I would get smarter and stronger and then unhinge myself from Myrtle's chains over my life.

That morning came, unplanned and unexpected. I turned over and stepped out of my bed to prepare for another day of school. Then suddenly I felt that slow warm rolling down my leg.

My heart jumped out of my mouth, and my eyes got bigger in my head. "Oh no," I whispered, covering my gaping mouth with both hands. "Not now." I lifted my nightgown to discover my white panties drenched in blood.

The right thing for me to do was to walk up to Myrtle as she sat next to G at the coffee table and show her the blood. But I couldn't. I just couldn't. I couldn't let her or G know my secret, and I certainly didn't want her probing between my legs. So I ran my hand up my leg to stop the blood. Carefully I stepped out of the panties and balled them up in my hand. After cleaning myself up and stuffing my panties with one of the bulky pads, I wrapped the soaked panties in toilet tissue and dropped them deep into the garbage where Myrtle would never find them. Before leaving the bathroom, I reached into the economy-size box of tampons and grabbed a handful. I stuffed them inside my backpack just before leaving the house for school.

Neither Myrtle nor G noticed anything different about me that morning. Couldn't they see that I was no longer a little girl? Hadn't they noticed the transition? Though they didn't, I worried about them finding out. I knew I couldn't keep up my act for long. Eventually the tampons and maxipads would run out—and what if I had an accident one day?

"Have a good day," G said as he dropped me off in front of school. I hated the fact that G drove me to school in his long cream-colored 1973 Cadillac. He called that car his "Ladyfriend." My classmates called it "The Batmobile."

"Good morning, Miss Stacey," Father O'Connor greeted me with his same corny smile he greeted every student with every morning rain or shine. He stroked the big cross on his neck and asked me, "How do you feel today?"

That morning I felt like a grungy old sick cat that wanted to crawl up into some dark hole and sleep my life away. But I simply answered him, "Fine, Father O'Connor."

There was something creepy about the priests and nuns at Incarnation Catholic School, where I transferred into in the seventh grade. They weren't normal people. They weren't supposed to make mistakes. They had to be holy all the damn time. That's not human. Fact is, I found all women and men of any kind of holy cloth to be strange.

"The Lord be with you, Miss Stacey." Father O'Connor's voice followed me down the hall.

"And also with you," I muttered.

I had nearly ten minutes before my religion class began. It was enough time to take care of that sogginess I was beginning to feel between my legs, so I made a stop at the girl's bathroom. I had five dimes in my pocket—five dimes for five tampons I could buy from the white metal machine next to the paper towel dispenser and save the ones I stocked up in my backpack. No one else was in the bathroom with me. That meant that no one else would know my secret.

I packed myself into the last stall at the far end of the bathroom and covered the toilet seat with pieces of toilet paper just as Myrtle had taught me to do. Squat to pee. Cover every inch of the seat for number two. And to flush, hold the handle down with the bottom of your foot. But don't ever sit on the seat of a public toilet. Other people are nasty, she told me. The first few days of trying to use a tampon were pure hell.

I had ten minutes to get that tampon inside me, and I knew I was going to need just about every second to make it happen and still make it to my seat before the bell rang. There was no way I wanted to explain to Sister Helena Peters that I was late because I had my hands between my legs.

TEAR OFF PAPER
GENTLY INSERT INTO VAGINA
PLEASE DO NOT FLUSH APPLICATOR

The first time I had read those directions, I cringed. "What?" I frowned and looked, appalled, at that little cardboard stick with the string hanging from one end. "I gotta put this thing inside me? What if it gets lost?"

My heart began to do that flipping it did when I was anxious or scared. The stall disappeared as I closed my eyes and sucked in my breath. My trembling hand pushed the tampon against my vagina.

"Please go in. Go easy." I winced as soon as the pressure turned to pain.

I felt weird and nasty touching myself. Myrtle had told me that touching my "kitty-cat" was a sin and could get me a one-way ticket to hell.

Time was running out before the bell would ring, so I pushed harder, tensing up even more—without any luck.

The tears came down hot, fast, and furious. I cried because I was going to be late for class. I cried because I couldn't make myself relax. Cried because it hurt. Cried because I didn't like touching that part of my body. Cried because I had just turned into a young woman and didn't want to be. But I cried mainly because forcing that tampon inside me reminded me of one of Myrtle's dirty rituals.

As I sat there on that toilet seat struggling with that tampon, I could see myself standing in the middle of the bathtub naked. It was hard for me to breathe, just as it was hard for me to breathe as I waited for Myrtle to wash me. I could see her in my head wearing that red bandanna she always wore to clean the house and my body. I could feel her coming close to me as she slid back her sleeves and knelt down next to the tub. I could still smell the glue that held the tiles together. I could even see that block of Lifebuoy soap and hear the rich lather building up in the washcloth.

She snarled, "Open your legs." I opened my legs wider as I sat on that toilet.

Unlike me, Myrtle knew exactly where to find that spot to shove her fingers inside my twelve-year-old vagina. She grabbed, yanked, dug, and rubbed parts of me I didn't even know the names of.

"You think you grown 'cause you got a little bit of hair down there? Huh?"

"No, Mommy. I ain't grown," I whimpered.

"Who's grown?" she tugged at my pubic hair.

"You, Mommy!"

"That's right! I got the biggest titties in this house. And don't you ever forget it."

The tampon finally slid inside me, relieving my pain. Myrtle, her hands, the smell of Lifebuoy soap and tile glue disappeared. The steam, the tub, and the washcloth were gone. But the trauma of Myrtle's daily ritual was not.

It would take me years to admit that Myrtle had sexually abused me. Many times I tried to convince myself that what she did was not sexual abuse. I had thought of sexual abuse as something that nasty men did to little boys and girls. I pictured some man in a long coat hanging around playgrounds with puppies and bags of candy. But Myrtle was my mother. She didn't fondle my private parts at will nor did she go around humping my leg or make me touch her genitals. So how was her behavior the same as the nasty men in raincoats?

A bad touch is a bad touch no matter who does it. Sexual abuse in any form is always about power and control. When I look back on what happened, I realize that there was another dimension to Myrtle's sexual violations. I don't think her intent was to become sexually aroused or get off on touching me. Though she had never been diagnosed, Myrtle displayed all the classic symptoms of obsessive-compulsive disorder.

Cleaning was the only way Myrtle could give her life any meaning. In church, the preacher used to talk about getting your house in order. She took that message literally to mean our house on Hilltop Drive. She slept with a rag next to her bed and always walked around the house with one in her hand. If everyone else was enjoying dessert, she was wiping up their crumbs and scrubbing the dinner dishes. Myrtle couldn't enjoy the view of a beautiful spring day because she'd see that tiny spot on the glass and reach for the glass cleaner. She scrubbed and wiped everything in her world constantly. To her, everything was a germ. My body, like kitchen utensils, a dusty knickknack, the window ledges, table crevices, toilet seat, was an extension of her need to clean everything. I too was a germ. My body became an extension of her sickness.

I knew it wasn't normal for a mother to bathe her child after a certain age, but I couldn't make sense of the kind of sexual abuse I endured. I was confused. Embarrassed. It became a secret that I would deny for years because I truly believed that others would look at me and say what Myrtle said to me: "You're a dirty little girl."

So I kept the secret to myself, just like I kept getting my first period a secret. I had become a little woman, and nobody else on earth knew but me. There wasn't a soul at school I could share my secrets with. I was afraid that if I trusted someone, she'd tell another student or one of my teachers, who would then turn and tell Myrtle. But later that day, I shared the news with one other person—the least of all people, and I knew that if he told another soul his God would punish him.

"Stacey!" a voice rang out from across the classroom. It was Gina Robinson, a white girl with big poofy brunette bangs and a long, crooked nose. She had a habit of toying with the tiny rubber bands attached to her braces. Sometimes they popped out of her mouth when she laughed. "How come you didn't come to the school dance on Friday?" she asked in a singsong voice.

Everyone turned to me and waited for my answer. I wanted to disappear. Instead, I turned my head toward the wall next to my desk. Many days I had turned my head to the wall and stared at the statue hanging there to keep my classmates from getting clear looks at new bruises and scars on my face. I studied the statue of the Virgin Mary holding her son's dead, gray-colored, bloody body on her lap. That day I thought to myself that the Blessed Virgin must have had some strong legs and arms.

"Everybody was there but you," Rose added. Rose shot hoops with me on the playground every day.

"What happened?" some voice asked.

Sister Helena, a drill sergeant of a nun dressed in her penguin suit, clapped her hands and demanded silence. She paid no attention to my classmates' inquiries. She motioned her hands like a chorus director and everyone shot straight out of their seats. I was saved for a moment. But I knew that later I'd have to face my classmates' questions and comments.

Somebody would say, "Your mama is mean."

I'd snap at them, "She ain't my real mama."

"She doesn't let you do anything."

"Were you home getting another beating?"

"I feel sorry for you."

Everybody knew that Myrtle was a mix of Joan Crawford and Sybil's mother.

We saluted the flag, said Hail Marys, crossed our chests, and listened to Sister Helena's religious lecture. That day she talked about purgatory, as she always did. Sister Helena said that purgatory was a place of temporary suffering where people get the chance to spiritually cleanse themselves before entering heaven. Some people don't cleanse their souls, she said. "And they are lost forever." She gave us a serious look as if to say she didn't want that to happen to any of us.

"Who do you think determines our eternal resting place, whether it be heaven or hell?" Sister Helena posed the question to the class.

"St. Peter," said Germaine, a tall black kid with a box fade haircut and large, bulging eyes.

"The Blessed Virgin," said Wesley. Wesley reminded me of one of those creatures from that show *Fraggle Rock*.

"Jesus," some boy said in an old man voice.

"God," somebody squeaked.

After working her way around the classroom for answers, Sister Helena's ash-colored eyes finally searched out mine. I snatched mine away from hers. "Stacey?" My body stiffened. "What do you think? Who determines whether we go to heaven or hell?"

I paced the floor in my mind as I listened to heads turning, coughing, somebody tapping a pencil on the desktop. All eyes were on me again. They didn't care about my answer. They were still curious about my scars. Sister Helena had just given them a good excuse to turn around and stare at me.

She asked me again. "Who determines our fate, Miss Patton?"

"We do," I mumbled. "We decide whether we are gonna go to heaven or hell."

They all frowned at me. Some twisted in their seats, looking odd and uncomfortable. I heard garbled whispers.

"Can you explain what you mean, Miss Patton?" She folded her hands and leaned forward on the podium. For a split second, I wondered if Sister Helena took baths or if she had more than one of those penguin suits. What did she look like underneath all that?

Sister Helena didn't like me and had made that clear to me and to others. She had a way of making me feel stupid in front of my classmates. She once told me that I was going to skip purgatory and go straight to hell and burn on a special brimstone with "STACEY PATTON" branded on top of it.

"Every day you go on living, the flames get hotter and hotter," she said to me once.

"You must know the devil real well," I murmured.

"And what makes you say that?" she shot back at me.

"How else would you know that hell flames keep getting hotter and hotter for me? The devil must have told you, right?"

I could never weigh my words carefully with Sister Helena. I always said the wrong thing. Sometimes I said the right thing but at the wrong time. Other times I got in trouble for keeping my mouth shut. I had a habit of letting my mind leave the classroom and go off floating like a balloon set free into the sky.

"Sister Helena, I think heaven and hell are in your mind," I said.

"Heaven is a state of mind? Hell is a state of mind?" She looked confused. It was a familiar look she always gave me. I was convinced she thought I had mental problems. Most people in my world thought I was one can short of a six-pack. Let me say that when you get beaten almost every day of your life, it affects your mind.

"Yes, Sister. Some people die a good death. Some people die a bad death. Some people die with heaven on their mind. Some people die with hell on their mind."

"But isn't death always bad?" Gina Robinson asked me, flipping her poofs out of the way.

"How can somebody die a good death?" a voice buried somewhere in the front of the class asks.

"A good death," I looked down at my lap to make myself feel comfortable. "A good death happens when a good person dies. People say good things about them. How they made people smile. How they would give you the shirt off their back. How they weren't mean. How they lived right. Other people hold on to the memory of that person until they die."

"And a bad death?" She leaned forward and smirked at the same time. She seemed to doubt I could come up with a way to explain that concept.

"A bad death happens when somebody is lying dead in their coffin, cold and full of hate, anger, meanness, and bitterness. They died unhappy. They didn't forgive people. Other people couldn't forgive them."

The array of eyes studied me. Were they really listening to me? Or were they tracing my scars or wondering why I didn't come to the big school dance?

"That's a bad death." I continued my thought. "That's dying with hell on your mind. If you die with hell on your mind, then that's how you're gonna spend your eternity—in a hell you created while you were living."

I couldn't explain it then, but I felt that all the good things we thought about heaven and all the bad images about hell simply sprang from our imagination. But I didn't think people had to die to go to hell. Besides, I wasn't dead, and I had been living in hell with the devil, my adoptive mother.

Sister Helena moved her lecture to a different topic, and I took my mind back to the seat of my pants. Maybe the blood would stop if I wished it away. Maybe I could postpone my period for a few years. Maybe I should just tell Myrtle the truth.

"And this gorgeous hunk came to the rectory yesterday," Sister Helena said, interrupting my thoughts. She was always talking about men. This confused me. Nuns were not supposed to talk like that. I raised my hand with a fury.

"Miss Patton," she smirked.

"Sister," I paused, "Are you havin' sex?"

The entire room broke into a mix of laughter and gasps. Minutes later, I found myself in the hands of our principal, Sister Margaret, a stocky red-faced nun who walked hard down the hallway. We could hear her coming from meters away. The click-clacking of her shoes made us hope to God she wasn't coming for one of us.

"You asked Sister Helena what?" she barked at me. She went for her favorite part on my body, my eyebrow, pulling it toward my hairline.

All I could do was say, "Ouch, Sister." I tried to keep up with her quick pace. For sure, I thought she was going to pull my eyebrow off my face.

"What gives you the audacity to think you can ask a holy sister if she's having sex, Miss Patton?"

"'Cause she's always talking about big hunks who come to fix things in the rectory," I explained.

"What do you know about hunks, Miss Patton?" She pulled my eyebrow harder.

"Nothing, Sister. I don't know nothin' about hunks. Sister Helena called him a hunk, not me."

My classmates were peering out of the window, like they always did when I said something crazy and had to pay for it. Sister Margaret always walked me out of the school building and yelled at me. She put one hand on her hip and sliced the air in front of my face with her other hand. She didn't scare me, though. I knew she wasn't going to hit me. That was Myrtle's job. She did humble me, though, because I was afraid that she might report my behavior to Myrtle. But she never did.

Sister Margaret still held strong to my eyebrow as we entered the church. When she let go, she dipped those same fingers in the holy water by the door and crossed herself in the name of the Father, Son, and Holy Spirit. Suddenly I felt guilty about all the times I sank my whole hand in the water and splashed the person in front of me.

"In there," she whispered and pointed toward the confessional like a crossing guard. "Confess now! Save your soul."

I closed myself into the small, dark space and sat on the square slab of a bench. I had never confessed my sins to another person. I had always heard about what it was like, how beneficial it was, and how ridiculous it was. I knew the priest couldn't see me. He couldn't tell anybody what I said. So I took in a deep breath and let it out along with all my sins that Myrtle hadn't made me pay for already.

"Father, forgive me for I have sinned."

"I asked Sister Helena if she was doing the wild thing with the maintenance man that comes to the rectory.

"Two weeks ago, I lied about not having homework.

"I stole that Snickers bar from the refrigerator.

"I threw beets and liver in the garbage when Myrtle wasn't looking.

"I stuck my middle finger up hundreds of times.

"I said *fuck* while I was playing basketball during recess.

"I say *shit* every day when nobody is around.

"I laughed at a dog that had three legs. I called him Tripod.

"When Myrtle goes to the store, I turn the radio on to Power 99 FM and dance to devil music. I'm not allowed to listen to worldly music or dance.

"I prayed that God would make Myrtle die.

"Last Sunday I played with my new breasts before I went to sleep.

"And I got my first period and didn't tell anybody."

I tried to think if there was anything else more to tell the priest. I'm sure there was. That was my one chance to confess the main stuff. My hope was that I could be redeemed. Then I'd get a clean slate, only to mark it up again. But I didn't know when I'd get the chance to go into a dark booth with an anonymous man who'd help me clean it again. I couldn't think of anything else, so I stood up to leave. Just as I reached for the latch, the little window opened. It was the priest.

"Wait a minute," I said. "You weren't listening to me that whole time?"

"No, my child," he said sounding all godly.

There was a fiber-optic silence and cold darkness between us, except for the slight strand of pee-stained light coming from the small window. I couldn't do it. I couldn't sit back down there and revisit all that I had just admitted to the walls. I didn't have the energy. Yes, I had done all those things. And so what? If God was going to send me to hell over dancing, playing with breasts He put on me, a stolen candy bar, laughing at a dog, white lies, and speaking what came to the mind He gave me, then He didn't have more important things to do. Besides, God was all-knowing. He knew I was going to do all those things before I did them. So what was the use of confessing to some man who had probably done worse things than me?

"Never mind, Father," I said and walked out.

I had not only secrets but growing pains of all kinds that I felt like I had to endure all alone. I wanted so badly to become a little woman. But when it finally happened, I didn't see the purpose in growing up. Height, hips, breasts, and bloodstains would not separate me from childhood or my bondage. I still didn't know who I was and where I came from. I believed that discovering my true identity was the only way I would free myself.

NINETEEN

When slaves decided to flee from the tyranny of their masters, it took all their moral courage and bravery. They hoped to free themselves from their legal status as property and unhinge themselves from the institution's yoke. Day and night, slaves talked about running away. Thoughts of freedom kept them awake and haunted their dreams when they slept. They consulted each other in confidence about their plans. Though their desire for freedom was irrepressible, there were immense dangers and powers stronger than them that lay ahead. What slaves faced in their quest to be free was daunting.

Numerous things prompted blacks to run away. Some ran to escape being sold to a crueler master and harsher conditions. Others left because they were treated badly or to see a spouse or other family members on a different plantation. Whatever reason a slave had for running away, the desire to fulfill the most basic and primal instinct of all humanity is clear: to be free. To control one's own life. To have a voice in one's own destiny. Most of the enslaved gave no credence to the paternalistic myth that blacks were happy and content in their bondage.

The reality for those who contemplated running away was that successful escapes were rare. Slaves had no money. No maps. They faced the psychological burden and self-denying act of leaving behind family and friends. Hunger often forced them to beg, steal, or eat garbage. Some bolder slaves took guns, money, clothing, musical instruments, and some even rode to freedom on their master's horse. Guided by the North Star, they headed for the northern states. They hid in swamps by day and traveled by night, sleeping high up in trees. They faced hills, meadows, mountains, rivers, bloodhounds, and, of course, white folks.

Whites used numerous tactics to hunt down runaways, including dogs. Slave hunters were given financial rewards for turning in fugitives. Slave codes also made it legal to kill a slave found away from the house or plantation. In some states, a male slave returned dead was more valuable than a child or woman brought back alive. When runaways were caught, they faced severe punishments: branding, cutting with knives, flogging, castration, death.

Sometimes slave children ran away when they experienced their first whipping by a master or overseer. Their parents would find them, and often comfort and educate them about the cold and harsh realities of slavery before bringing them back to the plantation.

Mothers who embarked on their quest for freedom sometimes brought their children with them. Most of the children were too young to understand why they were running. But their mothers stressed the importance of walking fast, staying quiet, and suppressing hunger pains and tears.

One hundred and twenty-five years after the demise of American slavery, I was twelve years old. I was chained to the tyranny of an abusive adoptive mother who had been sanctioned by the State of New Jersey to take care of me.

For years, I had contemplated running away. I thought about it day and night. I never told anyone of my plan. I had no money. No place to run to. No right to run away because I was a child. And I faced the prospect of being tracked down, not by thirsty bloodhounds or slave hunters but by some adult who would capture and return me to my bondage. Still, my desire boiled in me. I just needed the right time and the right incident to motivate me to flee.

TWENTY

I spent the first twelve years of my life anxiously waiting. Waiting for change. Waiting for life to show me that my suffering had not been in vain. Waiting for a sign to let me know I had some purpose in the world. Waiting to end up somewhere. I thought I was going to die before finally taking that step toward the other side of waiting. But even if I survived and moved beyond my bondage, what was to become of me? I still didn't know who I was or anything about my past. I had no connection with my roots. How could I know where I was going if I didn't know where I had come from? My life was in some way connected to those who had come before me. I just didn't know how.

I felt small and stuck for most of my early years. I felt as if I had been dropped onto the wrong theatrical stage with strange characters whose lines were written in a foreign script I'd never learn. Destiny had reduced me to a prop on stage with no role other than to be occasionally noticed and moved from time to time at the main character's discretion. Most people call this "being dealt a bad hand." Still, somehow I had to do something to make the most of my unlucky cards. It was up to me to take control over my life even though I was a preteen.

I hated being scared and walking on eggshells around Myrtle all the time. Listening to the night air to see if her waking breath turned into sleepy snores so I could finally shut my eyes in peace. I was tired of tasting my own blood. Picking scabs off my skin. Plucking switches off bushes. Taking trips to get the belt. Hearing that I was ugly, stupid, and wasn't gonna be nothing. I could no longer stand Myrtle's fingers up my ass or vagina during bath times, especially since I had gotten my first period. I was tired of waiting for some responsible adult to take pity on me and finally help me. I got tired of waiting for God to intervene. God never existed during my whippings. God never existed during my moments of desperation. The whole concept of salvation and the Lord's saving grace seemed like a tease.

I knew I had to stop praying, get off my knees, stand up, and run, but I didn't know how. All I kept hearing was Myrtle's voice rattling in my head: "The world is a big and mean and cruel place. Nobody is gonna give you anything out there. People will step on you! They will crush you! Won't nobody care. You will be layin' on the ground flat and dead, and the rest of the world will keep goin' about its business."

In my twelve years, I had seen dead roaches, flattened ants, crushed flies, and even some roadkill. But I had never seen a flattened human being lying out in public as people walked on by. Still, I believed Myrtle. I believed that kind of reality existed in some place darker than the world I lived in at 123 Hilltop Drive. Her words were not just a metaphor to me. They frightened me. Could people get crueler than Myrtle? Meaner than her? Colder than her? Did other people in the world have hard and quick hands like her? Did they beat each other with switches, belts, hangers, shoes, and extension cords?

Myrtle always reminded me not to forget where I had come from. "You didn't have nothin'," she told me. "You wasn't nothin'. Nobody wanted you. But it was out of the goodness of our hearts that your father and I gave you somethin' and made you somethin'. And you ain't g'on be nothin' without us. You remember that, little girl." Myrtle's point was that she and G had plucked me from the obscurity of the State of New Jersey's foster care system where children had been known to linger into adulthood. Some had been known to fall between the cracks before they turned twelve, unwanted and nobody's child. I should be grateful. I should count my blessings.

"Nobody will love you like your father and me," she reassured me day in and day out. "And if you think anybody out there in the world will, then, *honey-child*, you got another think comin'."

Every now and then I looked up the word *love* in the dictionary. I read the definition over and over: "A deep tender feeling of affection toward a person. A sense of underlying oneness. An intense emotional attachment as for a pet, a child, or treasured object." The definition did not fit my relationship with my adoptive parents, especially Myrtle, because she always handled me roughly and treated me as if she hated me. G was somewhat of a different story.

Yes, my adoptive father was weak. I was embarrassed of him. But the truth is, he was at the time the closest thing I had that resembled a paternal figure. He was not physically impressive. He wasn't smart. He was a buffoon who joked all the time and made only himself laugh. He was that kind of man whom white sociologists like the late Daniel Patrick Moynihan wrote about in his case studies of black family dysfunction. He was ruled by his domineering black wife and had virtually no voice in family or household matters. Because G never protected me from his wife's tyranny, I did not respect him. And to this day, I hold him just as accountable as Myrtle for my years of abuse. He stood by, a helpless and emasculated black man, and watched my pain and torture, like many slave men were forced to do on the plantation.

Another part of me can honestly say that I loved G even though I did not spring from his loins or respect him as a man. But today I am a woman with decades of therapy under my belt and distance from the vulnerable, brainwashed little girl I was. I have no love or respect for the man I called Daddy for almost a decade. Perhaps that's my anger speaking. I can, however, look back and find sweet moments with G that I cherish. He was playful and affectionate when Myrtle wasn't watching.

For me to understand why my adoptive father was so weak, I had to look at his roots. His history was also part of what made him a friendly, warm jokester. Each summer G rumbled through our musty basement to dig out his wooden ice cream maker. He lugged it up the steep steps and out through the back porch. He hosed and scrubbed it down before filling it with ice. He mixed the powdery packets of strawberry and vanilla with sugar and milk into the ice. He and I sat next to each other on the concrete steps as he turned the metal handle for nearly an hour until all the ice melted.

From time to time, he stopped, took his glasses off, and wiped the sweat from his eyes. And then he eyeballed me, "This is gonna be better than Breyers," he promised with a grin.

"Better than Häagen-Dazs?" I asked.

"Yep."

"Better than Ben and Jerry's?"

"Yep."

"Better than . . ."

"Better than all of 'em," his voice filled with excitement.

"Does it take Häagen-Dazs, and Ben and Jerry's, and all of them other ones this long to make the ice cream?" I asked.

"Probably not," he answered.

"Then how come it's taking you so long to make this ice cream for us?" I asked.

"'Cause they got machines that make the ice cream for them," he explained.

And then he stopped and pulled his shirt sleeve past his shoulder. He raised his hairy arm like a superhero and then flexed his muscle. "I got these," he said. "I make ice cream for us with my strength and my love," he said. "Them other ice cream makers don't use this kind of strength. And they don't use love to make their ice cream either. You just watch. You will taste the love in yo' daddy's ice cream."

He made me smile. It was the smartest and warmest and most meaningful thing I ever heard G say to me. I could feel his words inside me. From that moment forward, I sat there silently and patiently smiling as I watched my daddy make me some ice cream. He looked strong then. Full of purpose. Determined. He was making his love visible for me. It was moments like that when I felt I mattered, like I was somebody's little girl. When G finished all that spinning and grinding, he got two spoons from the kitchen, and he and I ate the ice cream right out of the wooden container until Myrtle yelled at us.

"Triflin' Negroes," she yelled through the screen door startling the both of us. "Look at ya'll. Just like white folks. Eatin' out of the pot and dipping your spoon back in. Get some bowls." G and I secretly exchanged smiles behind her back. Myrtle never spoiled those moments for us.

G learned how to make ice cream as a boy growing up "Down South" or "Down Home" in Mississippi. He was from a town called Tchula (pronounced Chu-la). The population is less than 2,000 people, more than half being female. Nearly 70 percent of the population is black, and the rest is white. It is a place where nothing much happens, and things seem to always stay the same. Most people born in Tchula die there. If they do leave, they go to Jackson, the capital. Or they go to Memphis or Atlanta, where there are more opportunities and a more exciting city life. Very few, like G and his older brother, make it up North to places like Detroit, Chicago, or even Trenton.

The summer before I got my first period, we had gone Down South for vacation, as we did every summer before. I hated taking that trip. We packed the car with large suitcases, a cooler full of Pepsi and ginger ale, fried chicken wrapped in aluminum foil, salad, white bread, fruit, chips, and sandwiches. The drive from Trenton to Tchula took us two days. We always spent the first night in a Howard Johnson's or Days Inn hotel somewhere in Memphis, Tennessee.

Once we crossed the state line and G saw that sign, "Welcome to Mississippi, the Magnolia State," he grew excited and stepped on the gas. "All right!" he got loud. "I'm comin', Mama," he yelled at the windshield.

There was always a stretch of the ride when G suddenly turned off the radio, got real quiet, and drove as fast as he could. His body got stiff. He never looked out the side windows, only straight, as if he had one focus and that was to get past that half-hour stretch. I never understood why he got that way until I got older and learned about Mississippi's tragic relationship with black people through stories I heard from G and other people who left the South during the Great Black Migration. Black folks told stories of having to step off the sidewalk to let white folks pass. They had to eat at separate lunch counters. Ride in the back of the bus. Sit in the balcony at theaters where they'd throw popcorn down at the white people. They had to call whites "sir" and "ma'am." They weren't allowed to try clothes on in the stores. The Ku Klux Klan burned crosses on their lawns and stormed their homes. White men raped black women. Black men got lynched for looking at white women or for allegedly raping white women.

On both sides of the road, there were green swamps that covered nearly half of the trunk of the trees. It seemed like some massive flood had come through the area a long time ago and nobody ever bothered to pump the water out. Sometimes we passed what seemed like never-ending fields of cotton, where the sun beat down all day.

"We used to have to pick this cotton for the white man," G said with disdain in his voice. "They called it sharecropping. Just another form of slavery. Some say it was worse than slavery."

"Umph." Myrtle frowned at the fields that G refused to look directly at during our drive. "I couldn't have done it," she shook her head.

"You would have done it," he assured her. "If you wanted to stay alive, you would have done it. Ask your daddy," he told her. "He grew up in Mississippi just like me. He picked this stuff for the white man too."

"I still say I couldn't have done it," Myrtle said.

"It's a different kind of white man down here, Myrtle. They used to rope black people up and hang 'em from trees. If you stepped out of your place, that's what happened to you. If you lived too high up on the hog, that's what they did to you. They'd bring their kids and family. Lay out blankets. Bring food. Play music. Dance. All this to watch them lynch some poor black man who just tryin' to own a piece of land. Feed his family. Save a bit of money. They acted like lynching somebody was some kind of party. Some festival. They would cut off the man's ears. Cut off his privates. Cut off a woman's titties. If she was pregnant, they'd cut the baby out her stomach."

"*All right. All right*," Myrtle complained. "I don't want to hear no more. You know I can't take hearin' them stories. I can't stand white folks as it is."

I wanted to hear more. I found the stories scary but intriguing.

"All I'm sayin' is that things are different than they used to be. But the South is a different kind of place. Much different than the North. Time don't move the same way. People don't walk the same way. They don't talk the same way. Don't think the same way. Different kind of white folks down here."

"Well, at least down here if the white folks don't like you, they call you a nigga to your face," said Myrtle. "You know where you stand with crackers in the South. But up North, the whities smile in your face and call you a nigga behind your back. You never know with them. That's why you can't trust white folks no further than you can see 'em."

"Black folks always got a place in the white man's world." G stopped for a short moment. He continued, "North. South. East. West. It don't matter where you at in their world. You always got a place, and it ain't never on equal terms with them. In all four directions, they got different ways of lettin' you know that you ain't nothin' but a nigga."

"That's right," Myrtle agreed.

"It ain't never gonna change." G sounded hopeless. "Not in my lifetime. And probably not in her lifetime," he said glancing through his rearview window at me.

"Not 'til Jesus come," Myrtle said as she continued to stare at the cotton fields.

"Jesus g'on set everything straight when he comes," G promised. "The first will be last, and the last shall be first."

I was scared of Mississippi and its white folks. Each year, I felt that we were traveling backward to some primitive place that refused to evolve. I hated that place. It was too hot, even in the shade. I hated the roosters that crowed next to the window at the break of dawn each morning. The mosquitoes, dragonflies, and fire ants. Downtown Tchula was a circle with only four or five major stores like Piggly Wiggly. Winos and other older men sat around drinking and playing cards all day. I found it boring sitting on the porch swing all day waving at everybody who drove by and honked their horn. It was hard for me to understand the way the people spoke. And I couldn't get used to the country-style soul food. The disparity between the haves and have-nots was blatantly clear. The white people had better homes and more money. And the blacks had virtually nothing but badly put together houses that sat off in the woods.

G's mother, Carol, was in her seventies when I first met her as a little girl. She's dead now, and so is his father, George Senior. His father was also in his seventies. He was over six feet tall and had a strong body that had been broken down by a stroke after years of drinking and tobacco chewing. George senior walked only three places in the house: to the bathroom, the kitchen table, and back out to the front porch, where he sat chewing dried tobacco and inhaling snuff. I often watched his ritual in disgust.

George Senior would reach into his shirt pocket with his working hand. (Myrtle said his other hand and the entire left side of his body was dead from the stroke.) He would pull out a brown, sweet-smelling block of chewing tobacco or a tiny container of white snuff. The white snuff was a mix of menthol and cocaine that he deeply inhaled into his nostrils, exhaled with gusto, and sneezed sometimes. He would then break off a piece of the block of chewing tobacco and pinch it between his thumb and forefinger before placing it between his lip and gums. From time to time, he would lean his body forward and squirt brown juice from his mouth into his tin spit can. The sound and the sight of the juice hitting the can made my stomach turn.

"You know you goin' to hell for doin' that to yourself," G lectured his father every summer. "Your body is a temple. It ain't yours. You are God's property."

"Shut up, boy!" his father yelled back. "I brought you in this world, and I can still take you out," he raised his eyebrows and turned his head toward G.

"Yeah?" G chuckled. "And how you g'on do that, old man?"

His father picked up his wooden cane and pointed it at him. "With this. I will break this cane off on your hide. Don't think 'cause you a city boy with a big Cadillac and a pretty woman from up Nawth that you can't be broke by your daddy. Mind y'own business and let me be with my snuff. Ain't botherin' nobody. Boy!"

Carol never said much to me. She reminded me of an old stubborn bulldog, both physically and in her shady disposition. Only one of her eyes worked. Her left eye had slowly begun to deteriorate, until she went blind in it. All day she sat in her rocking chair in front of the television sewing or shelling some kind of beans or peas for that day's dinner. She wore flowery cheap housedresses and thick glasses. She and George Senior didn't sleep in the same bedroom, and they didn't say much to each other.

When guests came by to visit because they knew that "Junior" was in town from up North, she introduced me as "Junior's adopted daughter." If someone asked if G had any kids, she replied, "Yeah, but *it's* adopted." Old bag. I never liked her because I knew she despised me for not being her *real* grandchild. Since G was her younger son, perhaps there was supposed to be something special about him having a son or daughter to show off to his mama. So Carol ignored me, and I ignored Carol.

G's youngest sister, Vera, and her two daughters and son also lived in the house. Ella was a year younger than I was. Jerome was two years older. We spent most of the time chasing and teasing the roosters, sometimes throwing rocks at them until they turned on us and started chasing us, wildly flapping their wings. Every summer there was a new litter of puppies or kittens that we looked after. We played hide and go seek and built things out of random items we discovered in the tool shed out back.

I got the sense that Carol didn't like Ella much either. She constantly scolded and talked roughly to her. Ella often stormed out the house rolling her eyes and mumbling under her breath, "I can't stand her" or "I hate that witch." Carol kept a long switch in back of the television set. Switches in Mississippi didn't look like switches that grew in Trenton. I was happy that I didn't live among the switches that grew Down South. Those things were extra long and thick, and they didn't break.

When Ella did something wrong Carol ordered her to get the switch from behind the television. Carol never left her rocking chair to whip Ella. Ella would stand almost out of the doorway of the living room and Carol could still reach her with the switch. She hit her maybe four or five times, and then it was over, unlike Myrtle's long plantation-style floggings. That same switch remained behind the television set year after year. I saw it each summer and had great respect for and fear of it. Once, Myrtle threatened to go into the field and find one just like it to bring back home because of its durability.

One evening on the last summer that I visited Mississippi with my adoptive parents, we all sat around the television watching a tape of comedian Richard Pryor. In one skit, Pryor talked about his relationship with his grandmother and the switch.

"My grandma raised me," he said to the audience as he paced back and forth across the stage in his bright red shirt and black pants. "She would whup me with anything. She'd grab the cord out of a douche bag and whup me with it." The audience and everyone in the room broke into laughter. "And she'd make me go into the woods and get my own switch to whup me with it. That was a long walk."

"Yep," said G.

"That's right," Myrtle agreed.

"And I couldn't come back with no little switch," Pryor continued. "If I came back with a little switch, then she'd go and uproot the whole tree and beat me with it."

We all laughed again.

"That's some fucked-up psychological shit," Pryor said. "To make you go and pick out a switch to get your own ass beaten with. That's fucked up."

Pryor went through the stages of the whipping. The walk. Hoping it would snow. Wishing his grandmother would die before the whipping. Listening to the switch cut in the wind as he flicked it back and forth. Crying as he got closer to the house. Watching his grandmother snatch the switch from him and start the whipping. He danced around the stage like he was on fire, yelling and screaming. The audience roared with laughter. So did we. This scene was all too familiar. We laughed because it looked funny. We laughed at this experience that bound us together. I wondered if they had the capacity to reflect on the pain and terror when the laughter stopped. Pain is what seemed to connect black people and make blackness authentic, I thought.

But as everyone in the audience and in the room caught their breath, Pryor changed his tone and did something powerful and brilliant: he told the other side of the story. He pretended to be his grandmother. His microphone became a bottle of peroxide. In his other hand, he held an imaginary cotton ball. He showed his grandmother trying to fix the wounds she had inflicted on his body.

There was silence in the audience and silence in the room. A cold, uncomfortable silence. I couldn't look at Myrtle. But at that moment I remembered all those times she had beaten me and then broke out the ice cubes, cotton balls, peroxide, and cocoa butter to fix my wounds. And then she told me, like Pryor's grandmother told him, that she didn't like whipping me but I made her do it.

"You bring this on yourself," she always said. "A hard head makes a soft behind." When she finished trying to fix my wounds, she told me, as Pryor's grandmother told him, "I don't like doing this. But if you do it again, I'm g'on whup you again." The audience and everyone in the room, except for me, abandoned their silence and laughed again.

Absurd. Absolutely absurd, I thought. I didn't laugh. Because that threat of getting whupped again frightened me. There was nothing funny in the kind of terrorism I experienced. But there was always something funny in the way that black people sat around sharing their stories of getting beat by their parents. They added colorful details and emphasis. Maybe they laughed because they survived to tell about it. But nobody ever, ever said they hated getting whippings.

I heard black people say, "I'm grateful for all my ass whuppings. I'm the man I am today because my mama whipped me." "I'm the woman I am today because my mama didn't spare the rod." "Whippings kept me out of jail." "I'm alive today because my mama beat me."

Some black folks who grew up Down South during Jim Crow claimed that whippings saved their lives from white folks. If the big dominant world beat them, then they could rationalize the beatings they got from their parents. Whippings did not save fourteen-year-old Emmett Till from being beaten and killed by white men on his summer visit to Mississippi. Whippings didn't save those four little girls who died in the church bombings in Birmingham, Alabama. Whippings didn't save the thousands of black folks who were lynched or died by other forms of racial violence. Could whippings have saved them?

No one dared say that they were angry with their parents when they got whupped. Why? Do they believe they would have been disrespectful to their parents to say so? Is this what happens when you become an adult? Do you gain distance from the pain, the tears, the fear, and the truth? The truth is that the brutality of whipping did not save thousands of black children and adults from the end of a rope, church bombs, or other racial evils.

I wonder how Ella felt. We never talked about our whippings. We never expressed anger. As black children, we were not allowed to express anger or to "show out," as our parents called it. Nobody cared if we disliked something. We didn't have an opinion or "say" in things. We were not allowed to cry for too long under any circumstance. We had to smile. Be content. Never complain. Know our *place*. And the adults around us proclaimed that we ought to be grateful for our whippings.

"If we didn't love you, we wouldn't whip you," they claimed.

At church, the ministers justified beating black children using verses from the Bible. "God chastises those he loves." "Spare the rod, spoil the child." "The blueness of a wound cleanses away evil."

"If I don't whup you, then the white man is gonna do it," Myrtle said. "And there's a big difference between me doin' it and the white man doin' it. I do it out of love and protection. The *man* beats you 'cause he don't care about you. He beats you to kill you," she explained.

At the hair salon, beating kids seemed to always be one of the hot topics of discussion. It was cast as some debate between how white folks raised their kids and how black folks raised their kids.

"White folks let their kids run wild," someone would say.

"That's right!"

"White folks let their kids run all over them."

"Yep. They talk back."

"Cuss their parents out!"

"Umph."

"Not mine, girl."

"And then they talk about some damn time out."

"Time out my ass!"

A few women laughed.

"They talk about democracy in the home."

"Democracy, my ass!"

"Yeah right," somebody huffed. "I pay the bills. I pay the cost to be the boss."

"I'll be damned if I let some little muthafucka that I pushed out my pussy cuss me out," a loud-mouthed woman from the back yelled.

"I ain't g'on be beggin' no child do what I tell 'em to do," an older woman proclaimed.

"White folks beg their kids to do shit they're supposed to do."

"I'm g'on tell that child to do somethin' one time," said one of the stylists flinging a hot comb above her client's head. "And once I find out that child ain't retarded, I'm whuppin' his ass!"

Everyone laughed as I looked on, silent and helpless with a blank face.

"Now they wanna send you to jail for whuppin' your kids," the same stylist complained. "Can't raise your kids the way you want to. When I was growin' up, everybody had license to whup your ass if you acted out."

"That's right," somebody shouted out.

"Whoever saw you actin' out snatched yo' little ass up and gave you a good butt whuppin'. And when you got home, you had to tell your mama and she turned around and gave you another whuppin'. People don't do that no more."

I was glad they didn't do that anymore. Getting whipped by Myrtle was enough.

"People forgot that African proverb that it takes a village to raise a child."

"Umph, talk about it."

"White folks always tryin' tell black people how to raise our kids. You can't raise a black child the same way you raise a white child."

"Nope."

"Sure can't."

"Not in this society," the stylist said in a preachy voice. "We got to prepare them. If a black child steps out of line, the consequences are greater than for little white Johnny or little white Sally. Police ain't g'on shoot little white Johnny or little white Sally. But your child. My child. And that child sittin' over there," she pointed at me, "is a little worthless nigga to them. They don't care nothin' about our black boys and girls. We got to beat our kids to keep them from gettin' beat or killed by the white man."

"But don't you understand," a slow, intense, smart voice arose from the back as she dipped her head out from under the dryer, removed her glasses, and closed the book she was reading. "Don't you understand," she continued, "that what you are doing to black boys and girls is wreaking a double terrorism on them?"

A hush fell over the place. Everyone glued their eyes on the petite woman whom no one had ever seen in the shop before. They seemed surprised that she had spoken and even more shocked that she, a black woman, was disagreeing with them.

"Don't you see that when you beat your children down that you are doing just what the white man wants you to do to them? They want you to break them. They want you to make them passive, submissive, deferential, and never question or challenge anything. You are breaking their self-esteem. Killing their spirits. Murdering their souls. This is what the white man wants you to do. You are doing his work for him. Don't you see that this behavior stems directly from the plantation? From slavery? Slave mothers beat their children so the master wouldn't do it. And look at you all standing here today saying you beat your children so the white man won't do it. This is so plantation. This mentality is so plantation. This is why black people are dysfunctional. Their minds are still shackled to a slave mentality. And you are passing it on to your children. What they need is love and assurance, not violence and more degradation. We need to teach black boys and girls how to cope and compete in this racist society. Not break them and twist them to fit into some limited place in it."

"So you don't beat your kids?" the stylist asked the woman.

"I don't have any children," she replied.

"Oh."

"See there."

"Uh-huh."

"Well, wait 'til you have some children. You'll think differently about that. Right now you thinkin' like a white woman."

"I don't have to have children to know that you don't have to raise them with violence," she shot back at them. "I am twenty-nine years old. My parents never once beat me or my siblings. So it can be done. You have to learn patience and educate yourself on how to do things differently. You can't always blame everything on racism, on the *white man*. Most times when you all are beating on your kids, it has nothing to do with protecting them from racism or the police or any other white folks. You do it because you are angry. Because you aren't educated about how to do things differently. Because this is what your parents did and what their parents did. You don't know a better way. Everybody tells us it is okay to beat black children. Our ministers. Our comedians. Our predecessors."

"Wait 'til she has kids." The stylist dismissed the woman. Everyone else agreed. "If she wanna act white, let her."

Frustrated, the woman slipped her reading glasses back on her face and put her head back under the dryer. She knew, like I knew, that her words were futile. Though she didn't know it, her words had given me hope. Finally there was a black woman who saw the absurdity of this kind of violence toward children.

Whippings didn't make me obedient or more respectful. They made me fear Myrtle. Fear black adults, black women especially. They made me angry even though I had to suppress that anger like some slave child. Deep down inside, whippings made me hate Myrtle. Whippings made me docile to some degree. They made me stutter. I was not confident. I couldn't look people in the face. I didn't think I had the right to stand up for myself. I didn't like myself. Most of all, I felt inferior—not because white people claimed that I was, but because black adults made me feel small, insignificant, devalued, and powerless when they condoned the murder of black children's souls.

I had to unhinge myself from this mental and physical slavery. I was certain that nobody around me was going to help me escape, so I had to do it on my own. I had to wait for the right time, the right incident to motivate me. Many times I had promised myself that I would run the next time Myrtle beat me. Even though I was only twelve I was like a woman who suffered from battered wife syndrome. Myrtle would hit me and then apologize. She would buy me gifts and promise she'd change. Her promises seemed to convince me that things would be different. Her good nature would last a few days before a slap in the face or a whipping crashed my hopes.

"You know I love you, right?" she'd ask.

"Yes, Mommy. I know." I nodded my head. But deep down, I believed she hated me because I wasn't perfect. Hated me because I wasn't fair-skinned like her. Hated me because I was another woman's birth child. Hated me because I was becoming a woman who would have a child of my own someday, unlike her.

When we returned back to Trenton after that last trip to Mississippi, I knew the time had come for me to become a fugitive like those slaves from Mississippi had done. I couldn't remain stuck in some backward, primitive misery. I couldn't live a life defined by somebody's else's constraints.

I wasn't going to end up a tragic victim of child abuse. Every year the news reported stories of children killed by parents after years of abuse. What a dreadful end to a dreadful childhood. How could people bring children into the world only to beat them to death? Or adopt them to do the same? I hate the witnesses interviewed for those kinds of news stories.

They all say they knew something was wrong in that house or apartment. They always heard the cries. The child looked skinny. The child always had marks. There were all the signs. But nobody did anything, just like my teachers, neighbors, aunts, and uncles did nothing to save me from my torture. Everybody wanted to just mind their business. Their business was more important than saving a child's soul from murder.

I didn't know what I was going to find or where I was going to end up if I ran away. Most of all, I feared that if I ran away, no one would believe my reason for leaving. Who would believe a child over two adults? People would take one look at Myrtle and G and see that they were not crackheads. They looked like decent people who kept a nice home in a middle-class neighborhood, sent me to private school, and went to church. I had heard stories of children being put in the youth house for running away from home. But still, my desire was strong despite the odds against me. All I knew is that I had to take the step beyond the other side of waiting and see what I could find. Anything had to be better than my bondage.

That day finally came.

"Didn't I tell you to organize these shoes?" Myrtle yelled, breaking my attention from my prealgebra homework.

The vacuum cleaner came to a soft hush right in front of my sliding door closet. I set my pencil in the middle of my textbook and gently placed it on the floor next to my other books. We went through this ritual every evening. I tried desperately to focus on my schoolwork, but Myrtle's priority was keeping the house clean. School was the only thing that mattered to me. It was the way I could escape into stories, history, numbers, and art. School stimulated my mind and kept me sane. But all Myrtle worried about were the crooked shoes in my closet.

"How many times do I have to tell you? Church shoes go in the front. School shoes in the middle. Sneakers, sandals, and casual shoes in the back. What can't you understand about that? You retard!" she snapped.

"I'm not a retard," I said to her in a blank voice.

"What?" her body stiffened as a look of surprise jumped onto her face. I was never supposed to talk back to her even if she asked me a rhetorical question.

"I said I'm not a retard," I answered.

"You talkin' back? What, you think you grown or somethin'?"

"No. I'm just tellin' you that I'm not a retard, and I don't like it when you call me names."

By that time, my heart was pounding in my chest. I couldn't believe that I had been so bold—and so stupid. I knew there was no turning back. She was going to hit me. I was just waiting for the moment and how she was going to do it.

Myrtle paused for a moment, shocked, dismayed. She looked around her, as if to see what she could pick up and hit me with. Since I had grown so much, she didn't like using her hand because she had to hit me harder, and this hurt her hand. I froze and waited for my punishment.

Suddenly I heard a loud jerk from the opposite wall and quick whisk past my head. By the time I looked over to the wall, Myrtle already had the vacuum cleaner cord wrapped in her hand. When I turned back to her, the cord was flying toward my face. She hit me once, twice, a third, fourth, fifth, and sixth time before I lost count. When she drew back for another strike, I did what every black child knew never to do: I grabbed the cord.

She was going to kill me.

"Let it go," she demanded.

"Please, Mommy."

"I said, let it go," she ordered as she tried to catch her breath. I tried to catch mine too. My face was throbbing and burning. Blood was trickling down my cheek from my eye.

"Let it go!"

"No!" I yelled.

Myrtle tried to snatch it out of my hand but couldn't. I reached for strength that I didn't know I had. I was determined not to let go and not to be hit anymore that evening or ever again. Myrtle drew back with her other hand and slapped me hard in my mouth, almost knocking me to the floor. But I still held on. I regained my balance. My legs got strong again. She slapped me again. Then came the blood in my mouth. She reached back again, this time I blocked the oncoming hit.

"I'm not letting go!"

"Let it go!"

"No! I'm tired of you beatin' me! You ain't my mother!"

The air went out of her body. Her hand was still drawn back, ready to strike me, but it was halted like a jammed gun. You would have thought I had struck back with a cannon ball to the middle of her body.

"What did you say?" She lowered her voice in a way that suggested that she didn't hear me right.

I couldn't believe I said what I did. It must have been the devil that made those words slip out of my mouth. I said those words in my head plenty of times, but I never thought I'd ever express them aloud, especially not in earshot of Myrtle.

"I said, you ain't my mother," I had the audacity to repeat it again. And then I got bolder and said more. "And my real mother wouldn't treat me like this."

"Oh, yeah?" She got loud as she dropped her hand. "How do you know?"

"I don't know," I replied flippantly.

"Let me tell you somethin' about your *real mammy*," she said with a look of disgust growing more and more intense on her face. "Your *real mammy* was crazy, just like you. You *real mammy* didn't care nothin' about you. That's why she put you up for adoption. What mother does that to a child if she really loves her? Huh? You tell me. I'm the only thing you got that's close to a mother. Gal!"

"You ain't nobody's mother! You ain't mine. That's why you can't have kids! You wasn't supposed to be a mother! Look at the way you treat me! That's why all your kids ended up in the toilet bowl! That's why you always scrubbin' the toilet bowl so hard. You can't flush down that truth. Ever! You wasn't supposed to have any kids! You ain't even close to a mother! Not for me! Not for anybody!"

"You little piss rat!" she yelled and continued to try to loosen the cord from my hand.

"Listen! I'd rather run away from here than have you beat me again," I yelled.

"That's what you want?" she yelled. "That's what you *really* want?"

"Yes," I answered.

"Then go," she said, freeing her hand from the cord and backing away from me. "Go on! Get out of my house!" she pointed in the direction of the back door. "You'll see that the grass ain't greener on the other side. You'll come runnin' back."

I didn't pick up a jacket, money, or food. I just turned away from her and ran through the hallway until I got to the back door. I nervously and quickly unlatched the door and opened it.

"Don't let the doorknob hit you in the butt," she yelled as she watched me from the doorway. "You'll be back. No one will love you like me and your father."

As I burst through the door, the cool autumn night air hit me. I could hear leaves crunching under my feet like potato chips. I ran as fast as my scrawny twelve-year-old legs could go. My heart still pounded hard against my chest. My face throbbed and burned even more intensely. And slowly, I couldn't see out of my left eye. It was swelling up.

I had no idea where I was going to run to. There was no North Star in the sky to guide me to some place of freedom. All there was in front of me were long paths and left and right turns. I could choose any. I didn't hear any bloodhounds or Myrtle's car, but I feared she'd come after me. Turning back was not an option. I just had to keep moving fast. Though I kept moving forward and didn't think of stopping that night, little did I know that even though I had escaped and would eventually end up someplace, many places different, I would still have to look back to finally free myself from the bondage of my past.

PART II
FREEDOM

ONE

A h, freedom!
   While former slaves welcomed their new freedom with jubila-
tion, songs, prayers, and hope, some were forlorn and fraught with fear.
Blacks and whites faced uncertain and precarious prospects after the Civil
War. For centuries, slavery had been a stabilizing social and economic
institution in American life. The emancipation of 4 million blacks not
only upset the legal definitions of their status but also what it meant to be
white and free.

   Black freedom meant more competition for jobs, education, power,
and even sexual ownership over female bodies. Following the Civil War,
the South was surrounded by utter devastation and social upheaval coupled with the loss of billions of dollars in capital that had been sustained
by black bodies. As white folks of all classes enjoyed various degrees of lib-
erty and citizenship, black people could not by law be considered citizens;
rather, they were property with no real intrinsic value attached to their
humanity.

   The newly won freedom of black children was especially problematic
for white society. Emancipation destroyed the black childhood that
whites had known for centuries. No longer would the development of
black children lead to fixed identities as slaves with limited possibilities.
Amid all the social disorganization, fractured communities, and government intervention in the lives of the freed people, whites and blacks
would face the challenge of redefining black childhood. During the first
two decades of freedom, black parents battled former masters over ownership of their children. Some whites continued to kidnap black youngsters and exploit them through illegal indentures and apprenticeships.

   The transition from slavery to freedom was arduous for both blacks and whites because the nation made no plans for it. While struggling to house, feed, clothe, educate, and build communities, blacks would have to face new forms of dehumanization at the hands of whites who believed that equality between the races was impossible.

For me, freedom meant an end to my adoptive mother's terror. An end to being whipped. An end to sexual abuse. A chance to loose myself from her distorted view of me. The opportunity to think for myself. Assert my identity beyond the projected limitations of my race, gender, and youth. Search for safety, nurture, and love. Freedom from my bondage meant that I could reclaim my little body and inner being and look forward to an optimistic future. But I didn't know all this in 1990 when I was running down the middle of the street trying to keep from being recaptured.

TWO

The bottom of my shoes slapped the wet street as my arms and head pumped back and forth. Dirty drips of water sprinkled up to spit at my neck, chin, and drooped mouth. My breath got stalled in my throat like bread I didn't chew all the way through before trying to swallow. I looked up at the sky's infinite darkness and caught a slender thread of moonlight defining the shingles on the suburban rooftops. The jagged stars looked as if they were on the verge of falling on me. Far above my head, the telephone lines played double-dutch as tiny drops of rain hung onto them.

Cold air shot up my nostrils like icy torpedoes. I had felt that sensation deep in my nose before. That familiar pain triggered memories of wanting to expel a sneeze, but it was stuck. Of accidentally snorting pool water and blowing it out as the chlorine stung my nasal paths. Of all the times Myrtle stuck cotton swabs up my nose to clean out snot and boogers. Of all those split seconds just before the bloody dams burst and rushed over my lips and chin after being slapped for something that made her mad at me. Those memories along with the pain itself slowed me a bit. But I couldn't let them stop me.

"Oh, fuck, a car!" I darted behind one of the bulging yet stately looking oaks that lined the long and winding Hilltop Drive. The car breathed sort of like a steady and calm robotic machine. I whined to the sky, "Please, please don't let it be her. Pleeease don't let it be her."

The pain in my nostrils began to subside a bit, but then fear replaced the pain, taking over the rest of my body. My bowels felt as if they were going to explode at any second and run hot and fast down my legs. I couldn't see beyond the car's headlights. I blinked with the eye that wasn't swollen. I blinked again, harder the next time, with my good eye even though it hurt the swollen eye like hell. And then I squinted to minimize the lights. My worst fear was that it was Myrtle creeping down the road in search of me. I could just picture her face in the windshield. The way her nostrils flared up and a wash of red rose from her throat upward into her cheeks and forehead. The way thick green veins bulged from the sides of her neck. The way her eyes narrowed and her jaw quivered and little gobs of spit formed at the corners of her mouth. The way she bared her teeth and clenched her fists when she spat rage at me.

My imagination made me see Myrtle's evil face through the blazing headlights. It was a face that made my stomach turn. Made the tiny hairs on the back of my neck stand out. Brought goose bumps to my arms. Dried my tongue and made it useless. I could see her scaly red knuckles curled around the top of the steering wheel. The brown trench coat buttoned all the way to her throat. And those pink sponge rollers packed underneath her red headscarf.

Was it really her?

The car crept close and closer again. I flattened myself as best I could against the tree, trying to become part of its lumps, bark, sap, and color. The car moved past the tree, just as slowly as it had approached. I rolled my head toward the opposite side of the tree trying carefully not to expose a shoulder, hand, foot, or one of my wiry-looking braids.

It was blue like Myrtle's. Boxy like hers. But as its rear end became clear to me, I didn't see the "Jesus Loves You" sticker on the bumper. It wasn't Myrtle. Time stayed suspended for a few moments. I heard nothing. Felt nothing. And then my body began to warm again, like a dead person coming back to life. I glanced over at the streetlight towering a few feet from the great oak that sheltered me during my paranoia. I started to pant. Sagging over to clutch my knees, I tried to regain my composure. Suddenly my body felt as if it was about to break from the inside out and fall into the street like shattered bits of dead flesh. Once I caught my breath again, I let out a soundless sigh of relief. Although that particular car wasn't Myrtle's, the next one could be.

Something lifted me up by my armpits. Some invisible hand of inspiration pushed me forward. "Run, black girl! Run!"

I had to save my own life. Against all odds, seen and unforeseen, I had to run. I had nothing, just my feet, my little arms, and this fire in me. I had to make do with what I had. That was a phrase I had heard old black churchwomen say so many times before: "Chile, sometimes you gots to make do with what ya' got. Work with what the good Lawd done gave ya!"

Just before I lunged forward to hit the ground running again, the brittle wind brought me Myrtle's voice, and I stopped dead in my tracks. "You little hussy! You ain't g'on be worth two cents without me or your father!"

For a moment, I wondered if Myrtle was right about me. When I ran out of that house, I wasn't thinking about how much my life was going to be worth without my adoptive parents. I never really thought about how much my life was worth with them. For as long as I could remember, I felt like their property, an investment. I never really felt as if they attached any emotional meaning to my humanity. So two cents wasn't much, but I thought my life would be worth more alive than dead.

My mind flicked back and forth. I was ambivalent about taking the next step. It wasn't easy running away from what I had known. I asked myself how I was going to make it out there all alone in the streets—the "mean streets," Myrtle would say. Who was going to feed me? Who was going to clothe me? Who would give me money? Who would save a little black girl? Who would believe me? What if it started to rain? Where did children go when they ran away from home? How did they protect themselves? Did they stop growing up? Did they die?

Maybe, I thought, maybe I should turn around and go back.

I stroked my chapped bottom lip with my tongue and brought in the metallic-tasting blood from the split. I wanted to see what my mouth looked like. And my face? A few times I had to flip the small flap of skin dangling from my cheek back onto the space it belonged. Myrtle had hit me so hard with the extension cord that it tore my face. I wanted to survey the damage and wonder how it would heal.

Thinking about the prospects of more pain and soul murder made me run again. "Faster, Stacey Patton." My heart began to feel as if it was folded in the collar of my shirt and sewn shut. I could see blue, white, and gray television ghosts flicker beyond blinded, curtained, and shaded windowpanes. I thought about banging on somebody's window in hopes of getting some help. But with my luck, some black person would answer the door, beat me for running away, and then drive me back home like some fugitive slave. All too often I had heard that expression, "It takes a village to raise a child." And then came the stories about adults who had permission to beat other people's kids before returning them to their parents, who beat them again. So I didn't take a chance of seeking help. I felt safer with the trees, cold air, and darkness.

I reached the end of Hilltop Drive just behind the Trenton State College campus. I had to decide whether to go left or right. I turned around and faced my escape route. Though I was still scared, I grinned a bit. I couldn't believe that I had actually mustered up the gall to run! I remember all those times I promised myself that I was going to leave.

"One more time," I mumbled. "The next time . . . ," I swore to the ceiling. "If she hits me again . . . ," I declared as I stared at the front door. Every time she forced me to pluck switches off the bushes, I made that promise. Each time I gaped into the top drawer of the nut-brown dresser at the snake pit of black and brown leather belts, I tricked myself into believing that there had to be one belt that hurt less than all the others. When I returned after surviving my ass whupping, I made that promise again. I made that covenant to myself when I hovered over the toilet bowl choking and watching my blood drip into the clear water, turning pink at first, and then totally red. As I stood to my feet again and watched the bloody water get sucked down the toilet's throat, I vowed to leave. At night when the sheets stuck to my pus-filled wounds, I held my pillow woman tight and yearned to be draped in the gentle warmth of my real mother. I wanted her bones to slip inside mine and take me away from 123 Hilltop Drive. Her love and power would course through me and lead me to freedom. When my real mother never showed up to save me, just before I drifted off to the safety of sleep, I whispered, "Next time . . . Next time . . . Next time . . ."

As I came of age, I felt a distance between Myrtle and me. She and I were nothing alike. As a form of resistance, I began to define myself in total opposition to her and her life. She was light-skinned. I was darker. She had straight hair. I had curly roots. She was a Christian. I was a nonbeliever. She was against abortion. I was prochoice. I was good. She was evil. She was wrong. I was right. Still, despite the contrast between us, I couldn't seem to keep my promise to my twelve-year-old self.

I always felt guilty for wanting to leave her. Myrtle had a way of fixing what she had done to me. Ice cream. Toys. Cocoa butter. Peroxide. She knew how to relieve my pain. I was like an abused puppy that never learned from the smacks and kicks. I always inched back, trusting that she'd be soft with me, stroke me, hug me, and speak softly to me. I wanted to trust her. I wanted her to like me. More than anything, Myrtle's words made me feel guilty for wanting to be free.

"You know I can't stand doing this to you, right?"

"Yes, M-mommy," I stuttered.

"You know I love you, right?

"Y-yes."

She'd pause. Look hard at me. Read my soulful eyes. Wring the blood out of the washcloth. Reach for a fresh cotton ball. Dip the bottle of peroxide again. Throw out the melted chips of ice and replace them with brand-new whole square cubes and wrap them in a towel. Put a bandage on my cut.

"And *you* love me and your father?"

Yes was the right answer. *Yes* was the only answer.

"Look at all we do for you," her tone changed.

She had to justify for me why I should love them. It was as if she knew when I was contemplating taking flight, so she used the material world surrounding us to remind me that I had nothing and came from nothing and would have nothing if I ran away.

"Private schools," she began her list. "Nice clothes. Nice home. You never miss a meal. You got your own room. Who's gonna take care of you like we do?"

"Nobody," I answered.

I really did believe that nobody would take care of me. Besides, I had been adopted. I couldn't forget that fact. I had started life as an abandoned baby, and that sense of abandonment haunts me to this day. I wanted to grow up fast so I could take care of myself and never again have to worry about being abused or abandoned by anyone. I swore that I would never ask anybody for anything. I hated being reminded all the time that I was adopted. That I was unwanted. That I had nothing. That I came from nothing. That I had privileges. That I had been taken in out of the goodness of my adoptive parents' hearts. I didn't understand why my adoptive parents always reminded me of what *they* did for me. It was their duty to take care of me. I didn't ask to be born, and I certainly didn't ask them to adopt me.

And love? My warped sense of love kept me from leaving. Kept me enslaved to dysfunction. Made me a constant victim. The love between an abuser and victim, like the slave and master, is strange. They depend on and nurture each other. Myrtle needed control, domination, and my submissiveness. I validated her existence. She defined her strength and worth based on my weaknesses, physical and mental. And me? I defined the world and myself for so long through her eyes. My life, my sense of self, depended on her approval. I lived for those moments when she praised me for getting something right. For those rare times when she said I was a pretty little girl. For the times she held my hand, though it felt cold and awkward.

Like most other victims of abuse, I was always hypervigilant. I tried to tiptoe around her moods. To please her. To do things before she asked me to. To anticipate her needs. To please her so she wouldn't yell at me and call me names. I hated being called stupid, trifling, and good-for-nothing. I wanted her to think more of me. I believed that if I kept things in order, did what I was told to do, then I could be perfectly responsible for keeping her from beating me again or attacking my sense of worth.

"Naw," I moaned and shook my head at Hilltop Drive. "I can't go back there." I turned and began to sprint until I saw blue and white police cruisers lined in front of an old brick stationhouse. I ran so hard toward the building, thinking I was saved.

Once I reached the stationhouse grounds, I began to calm down a bit. Before me loomed the oaken front door, solid and heavy. First, I had to navigate what looked like ten thousand granite steps. Just as I grabbed the frosty doorknob, I turned once more. No sign of the Lincoln Town Car. No sign of Myrtle. Maybe she expected me to come back. Maybe she thought I'd be too scared to run down a dark street by myself. Maybe she didn't want me back. Perhaps she didn't care either way. When I entered the stationhouse, I heard static sounds of radio checks and a drowsy syncopated tune of jazz notes loping from a small boom box sitting on the desk closest to the entrance.

A white police officer with a blunt nose and a small mouth stopped writing in his rectangular notebook and lifted his eyes over his glasses. His eyes were shiny, like chips of onyx. His hair was brushed into the red pompadour of a rooster about to announce the dawn. The officer's high stiff collar pinched his throat so tight I wondered how he managed to swallow his dinner. His hands were swollen. They looked like padded white skin-colored gloves. If anybody could save me from Myrtle, this man could. He was the police, the neighborhood hero. So I thought.

He cleared his throat. "Yes. Can I help you, young lady?"

I fixed the flap of skin dangling from my face again. And then I licked the new pond of blood that had formed in the middle of my split lip. He seemed unbothered by my injuries. Were the bloodstains on my shirt, my closed eye, and swollen face not enough to tell that officer that I needed help?

"Mr. Policeman." I paused and took in a deep breath. "I just ran away from home."

"*Ran away from home?*" he shot back at me, frowned and twisted the volume knob on the radio. The soft melodic notes disappeared, with a buzzing from the long-exposed light bulbs attached to the ceiling replacing them.

"What'd you go and do that for?" He scratched his chin then folded his pudgy arms across his brawny chest.

I gave him a look. Did he think I was pulling some childish stunt? Wasn't it obvious why I had run? I thought he'd be jumping to his feet and yelling, "Who in the hell did this to you, angel face?" I expected him to tug at his gun ready to shoot something. Instead, I had to explain myself to him.

"I ran away because she beat me," I said as my eyebrows converged in the middle of my forehead.

He slid his gold-rimmed glasses off his face. The frames softly clicked against the metal desk as he lay them down next to his notepad. He put his hands over the pile of lined papers in front him as if he was trying to protect them.

"Who?" His lips looked like he was about to whistle. "Who beat you?" He scratched the red stubble underneath his chin again.

I didn't want to tell him at first. I looked around the empty lobby, as if I were searching for someone else to blame besides Myrtle. I felt as if I were about to commit the biggest act of betrayal. Why did he have to know who beat me? Why couldn't he just take my word? Take my injuries as evidence? Couldn't he just hide me? Take me away somewhere safe? Nobody had to get into trouble.

"Who beat you?" he insisted.

"She did," I mumbled, dropping my eyes to the floor. I was nervous. I wanted to bite my nails. Pace back and forth. Instead, I started to count the tiles on the floor.

"She? She who?" He sounded agitated.

"M-my," I stopped. "My adoptive mother." I suddenly felt guilty for telling on her.

"What'd she go and do that for?" He slinked toward me like a rattlesnake.

"'Cause she's crazy." I didn't want to tell on myself either. I couldn't tell him that I was absent-minded and failed often at being perfect. Myrtle would have told him that I was rebellious and disobedient.

A long silence settled between him and me. He looked up at the clock just above his desk. I looked too. It was a quarter to eleven. His eyes met mine again.

"What'd *you* do?" My heart dropped to my knees.

What did *I* do? What kind of question was that? Was it common practice for police officers to ask battered victims what they did? Did he really think there was something that I, a child, could have done to deserve the ass whupping I had gotten from someone who was bigger and more powerful than me?

"Nothin' to deserve this!" I got defensive with him.

I stepped back from his desk, suddenly realizing that I was never supposed to get sassy with a police officer. Myrtle's reminder came into my head as I glanced at his gun and shiny badge, "Five-O don't mind beatin' and killin' a little black girl like you. They are some trigger-happy devils. So don't get out of line with them," she warned me over and over again. "You say 'yes sir,' and 'no sir' when they ask you somethin'. Your mouth can be enough of a weapon to make them crackers shoot you."

"Well, I'm confused." He shook his head and leaned all the way back in his chair until it groaned. "What in the world would make her hit you like this?" he asked with a puzzled expression on his face.

"'Cause my penny loafers were crooked," I explained.

He dropped his head and bottom lip at the same time. He looked puzzled. "Crooked?" he slanted his head to one side.

"Yes sir. They weren't lined up straight like all the other shoes."

I was expecting him to ask me why the penny loafers were crooked. Instead, he looked closer at my face and shook his head. Then he dabbed one of his fingers against his thick tongue and then turned to a fresh page in his notebook. His pen made a scratching sound. It didn't work so he reached into a mug full of pens and plucked out another.

"The night streets aren't a safe place for a young girl. You should never run away like that," he lectured. And then he had the nerve to say, "You ought to ask an adult for help."

I wasn't articulate enough to tell him that everybody around me ignored all the signs. The neighbors heard me crying. My teachers and relatives saw the bruises and even witnessed Myrtle abusing me. My adoptive father was so stupid that he believed the lies she told him. So who was I going to ask for help?

"What's your name, hon?" The officer's voice softened a bit.

"Stacey," I answered blankly.

"Last name?"

"Patton."

He asked my age, phone number, and address.

"Hilltop Drive." He nodded his head up and down. "Not bad." He looked impressed. "Nice area. Beautiful homes. We never really get a lot of calls over there."

When he finished writing down basic information, the officer led me down a long hallway adjacent to the main lobby to a room with a long, scuffed wooden conference table and about ten empty folding chairs. He bought me a soda and chocolate bar from the vending machine sitting in the corner of the room. And then he left me there, waiting and waiting.

I sat, palms resting in my lap. I watched the soda can sweat and the candy bar rest in the same spot he placed it. The thought of eating a chocolate bar and drinking soda made my stomach feel even queasier. Sugar surely wasn't going to settle my stomach or my situation. The stationhouse felt cold and smelled like nothing. I counted the chairs and the naked light bulbs over and over again. A layer of beige-colored paint had begun to curl off the walls, revealing a soft green underneath. Six five-by-seven black-and-white photographs of uniformed officers lined the wall directly in front of me. Their frozen gazes held my attention. The men were all white and stiff-faced. The only thing that distinguished one from the other were the dates printed on the bottom of each photo indicating when each was killed in the line of duty. On the tops of the frames, a coat of dust had formed. Myrtle would have a fit if she saw all that dust.

There was a small mirror slightly hidden behind the door. I pushed back my chair and quickly headed toward it. Pulling the door toward me, I was anxious to see what I looked like. My lip didn't look as bad as it felt. I expected it to be more swollen and cut up because it felt as if it was hanging over my chin. A black half-moon had begun to form underneath my shut left eye. I bared my teeth and noticed that one was chipped. I felt unpretty. Devalued. Scarred and battered. I feared that I'd never grow up to become an attractive woman.

I returned to my seat to continue sitting idly by, waiting. I hated waiting. I hated having my destiny in the hands of others. What were the officers down the hall talking about? I could see them down the hall standing in a circle and hear their voices blend into a quiet, indecipherable stirring in the air. Were they going to call Myrtle? Were they going to lock me up in a cell? Send me away to a place for bad girls?

I was nervous, dreadfully nervous. I stared at the way the ceiling lights illuminated their badges, like holy objects. I was bothered by their dark, freshly pressed, starched uniforms, dangling night sticks, jingling keys, sleeping guns, and the way they flexed their muscles and poked out their chests. Suddenly I began to feel that they had no intention of helping me.

Anxious and uncertain, I began to fondle the necklace warming against my neck. I wound it gently like a thin strand around my finger. Hanging from the tiny white gold links was a flat, plain, and delicate crucifix. Myrtle told me that Jesus died on the cross to give me life, happiness, love, and a chance at eternal life. The day she gave me that necklace was the first time I had ever heard of Jesus, and it was the first gift that anybody had ever given me.

Myrtle had pulled out a small white gift box and said, "Stacey, I got a present for you."

My eyes lit up. A gift? For me? My entire insides were excited. In the world of my foster home, nothing belonged to me. I shared everything—toys, books, candy, socks, and even panties. I ripped the tape off the edges of the box, which revealed another small fuzzy gray box, that held my first necklace.

Myrtle reached into the box and lifted the little treasure into the air. I watched the cross spin and then dangle in front of me, as if it were hypnotizing me. My eyes met Myrtle's eyes, and then we shared a smile. She unlatched the clasp and looped it around my neck.

"Little girl, you are special," she talked at the back of my neck. "You are chosen. You deserve the best. And that's what your father and I will always give you . . . the best. And this little token will always keep you safe. Remember that."

Myrtle's voice and the memory dissipated from my head. "Liar," I grumbled at the crucifix and snatched the chain until it popped. Pain slashed across the back of my neck. I tried to ease the slight burn by massaging my neck with my hand. The cross looked dull and worn out. Myrtle never allowed me to take it off. I thought about her words.

Special?
Chosen?

The best?

Jesus?

Safe?

The crucifix disappeared into the ball of my fist. The edges began to poke my skin. For me, Jesus was just as dead as those policemen in the dusty pictures. I felt angry, hoodwinked. I took one look at the wall again and threw the chain against it. At that moment I didn't care about getting in trouble for taking it off. I didn't care if Myrtle got angry with me for intentionally losing it. And I certainly didn't wonder if God was going to get pissed at me for disrespecting such a sacred symbol.

From behind me came a thin strand of sound, low and broken. "Stacey. Stacey Patton."

Startled, I turned to face the voice. It was a different white officer.

He knelt down in front of me. "I just wanted to let you know that I called your mother."

I wanted to die when he said those words.

"I let her know that you are here and that you are safe," he continued. "She's not comin' to get you," he explained. He flattened a first-aid bag of ice in his hands.

Good, I thought to myself. Relief whisked across my body.

"I called your father at work. He'll be here in a few minutes to pick you up and take you back home." Relief left the room again, and darkness began to cloud my mind.

"Back home?" my face crawled with terror. "You're sending me back home?"

"Yes," he answered in a vacant tone.

"Why?"

"Because it's late and there's not much any of us can do for you tonight." He threw up his hands as if he was helpless.

"But look at what she did to me! What if she does it again?"

"She's not going to hurt you," he assured me.

"How do you know? You're sending me right back there! She's gonna be mad that I ran away. Mad that I came here! To the police! She's gonna be mad that I told on her! She'll whup me again!"

"Calm down, calm down." He massaged my shoulder. "We've explained to your father that he has to stay home and not leave you alone with her. Tomorrow he will call the Division of Youth and Family Services, and a social worker will come out to your house and investigate the situation."

"What if he doesn't call them?"

"He will." His voice got stern.

"How do you know?"

"He's given me his word."

"His word?" I frowned. "That ain't enough! She's promised not to hit me over and over again, and she still does it. Her word. His word. Their words don't mean nothin'."

"I tell you what," he paused, "If they don't call DYFS in the morning, then you call 9-1-1 or get out of the house and come back here to get some help. Deal?"

"Why can't you just put me in a cell overnight?"

"A cell?" He looked shocked. "Why would you want to stay in jail overnight? Don't you think you'd be scared?"

"Not as scared as I will be if you send me home!" I hoped he'd see my desperation. Take my fear seriously, and help the other officers reconsider their decision to send me back home.

"I can't put you in jail overnight." He shook his head. "Besides, jail is for criminals. You haven't done anything wrong. So just make this deal with me, and everything will be all right. It's all going to work out fine."

He said all this like it was so easy. I was worried about facing G. Facing the devil again. A whupping. Death. I didn't want to have to run again. It had taken so much physical and mental energy for me to run away. I escaped once, and I expected to reach freedom, not to be returned back. I never wanted to see 123 Hilltop Drive ever again.

Why didn't they go to the house and arrest her? I would have felt safer going back home without Myrtle inside. I didn't understand how adults could be locked up for assaulting another adult. But I was a child who had been beaten by an adult, but nothing was done to her. This lack of application of the law was not fair! People get locked up for beating animals. What about children?

I slumped down in my seat, feeling defeated and hopeless again. The officer handed me the ice pack. "Here," he said. "Put this on your face to stop the swelling."

The coolness of the pack sent icy sparks across my head as I watched the officer stand to his feet again. He turned his wrist over to look at his watch. It got so silent in the room that I could hear him breathe through his hairy nostrils.

"It's the end of my shift," he said and fixed the big leather belt around his waist. "Good luck to you, kid."

"Yeah, whatever," I said sarcastically. "I thought the police was supposed to help people. Protect them! *Luck,*" I yelled at his back as he left the room. "Is *luck* gonna save me?"

He didn't have an answer for me. I surely didn't have one either. And besides, who in America answers to black children?

THREE

There is an index card taped to the closet door in my study on which I had scribbled a quote by Frederick Douglass on the unlined side. In 1876 Douglass had this to say about black freedom:

> You say you have emancipated us. You have; and I thank you for it. But was it your emancipation? When you turned us loose, you gave us no acres. You turned us loose to the sky, to the storm, to the whirlwind, and, worst of all, you turned us loose to the wrath of our infuriated masters.

Douglass's lament reflects the nation's struggle to deal with the question of full citizenship for its newly freed black population. After the Civil War, Congress implemented Reconstruction, which lasted from 1866 to 1877. The plan was aimed at reorganizing the southern states after the war, readmitting them to the Union, and defining the means by which blacks and whites could live together without slavery. The white South, however, saw Reconstruction as a humiliating and vengeful imposition. Although African Americans enjoyed a brief period of suffrage rights, political participation, land ownership, use of public accommodations, and other privileges of citizenship, opponents of black progress launched a counterrevolution against the former slaves' freedom.

For most whites, the best freedom for blacks resembled slavery. They wanted the former slaves to remain in their homes and under white surveillance and control. Graciously accept food and clothing rations as they did during slavery. Observe the same rules of racial etiquette and deference. Remain uneducated and economically dependent. Some whites even kidnapped black children or apprenticed them to uncompensated labor until they reached age twenty-one. Eventually the Supreme Court barred such illegal abductions of young blacks, and this move ultimately made black children even less valuable to white society because they could no longer be exploited for economic or psychological purposes.

Some people have argued that the conditions under which black adults and children lived after emancipation were actually worse than slavery. How did black children feel about their new freedom? Their present? Their future? I picture little black boys and girls loose under that sky, spinning in that whirlwind, and caught in the wrath of those infuriated masters that Frederick Douglass wrote about. The law had freed hundreds of thousands of black children, only to set them up into a different kind of slavery that had familiar remnants of the old system.

The night I had freed myself by running away, the Police Department helped put me back into bondage and in Myrtle's hands. Freedom, for a moment, had lost all meaning for me.

FOUR

The heavy stationhouse door banged like a shotgun. G had arrived and brought in a gust of cool air with him as he racketed through the doorway. He drew stares from three startled Puerto Rican men seated in a row of chairs adjacent to the front desk. They were waiting for their drunken buddy, who had been brought in earlier. He kept cussing and threatening the cops, so they handcuffed him to a radiator in the room next to me.

"Yo' man," he hollered. "Telephono! I want mi phone call. Uno phone call," he demanded. The cops kept ignoring him, and he didn't give up his demands.

"Yo' amigo!" one of the frustrated cops yelled down the hall. "Shut the fuck up! You'll get your phone call in a minute."

By the time G made it to the station, the man's hooting and hollering had turned into moaning. He kept complaining about his arm and wrist. But the cops ignored him.

G couldn't see me, but I could see him. He yanked off his black cap with its bright, almost neon yellow "Union Local 23" stitched across the forehead. A weak strand of light from the dim bulb above him muscled its way through the grainy air, just enough of a glimmer to warm his bald spot. Looking down at the burlap mat underneath him, he wiped his feet as we did so obediently at home.

"In the back," an officer from the new shift said blankly as he pointed G in my direction.

I listened to his big boots make a scritching sound on the floor. The scritch got louder and slower as he got closer. For just a second, I imagined that I was a trapped princess, like the ones in the cartoons and movies and fairlytales. My knight in shining armor had just come to save me. He was going to take me away to a life of happily ever after. But as usual, reality never lied to me.

Our eyes met in a blaze of reaction. Maybe G didn't know what to say to me because he just kept looking down at me with his lips tightly squeezed together. I didn't know what to say to him either, so I snatched my eyes away from him. I wanted to talk to him. To set the record straight. But I couldn't figure out where to begin. Should I have begun with that night? Or should I have started with the incidents that happened eight years before?

I felt his heat, sensed his anger and embarrassment. I could smell him reeking of sweat, oil, and grease. G was a peacekeeper. He wanted everything to look happy and perfect on the surface. I guess that's what made him feel like a man.

"I'm sorry for all the trouble, officer." G's voice cracked as he fondled the shredded brim of his trucker hat. "I assure you," he paused, "there ain't g'on be no more trouble."

The officer stood to his feet, looking strong and towering over G. They shook hands and exchanged nervous smiles.

"You know," G began to talk again, "the Bible says that trouble don't last always. Weeping may endure for the night but joy cometh in the morning."

I rolled my eyes. "Trouble," I mumbled under my breath and then sucked my teeth. Trouble was in every room at 123 Hilltop Drive. It was in the electrical sockets. In the baseboards. In the toilet. Under the kitchen and bathroom sink. In the drawers. Under the carpet. In the crawl space and basement. Caught in the wallpaper and dry wall. Lurking around every corner. Trouble lasted always in that house. I knew that better than G, better than Myrtle, and better than the imaginary white man in the sky. And weeping? Nobody wept more during the night than I did. And joy? It never came in the morning. And it certainly wasn't going to come that next morning.

"It's all right, Reverend Jenkins," said the officer as he patted G on the shoulder. "Just be sure to call the Division of Youth and Family Services first thing in the morning. They'll help you sort this whole thing out. And you," he turned to face me, "keep that ice pack on your face. And don't ever run away from home again."

I felt as if I was about to be sent to my death as I followed far and slow behind G. He was quiet and emotionless as we headed for the exit. No hug.

No kiss. No, "Baby, I'm glad you are okay." No lecture about the dangers of the mean streets. Nothing. He didn't even hold the door open for me.

The cold slapped me in the face, and I could hear the tongues of slight winds murmuring. G marched on toward his cream-colored Cadillac. I kept wondering just when he was going to verbally lash out at me. I expected him to at any second. Just before he opened his door, he patted his finger on his tongue and wiped a spot off the windshield. He had a habit of doing that—not just to his car but to my face. He would see something in the corner of my eyes or lips, and then came his spit-soaked finger on my face. I always frowned and bore it. When he wasn't looking, I'd take my sleeve or collar and wipe his juice off me.

He called that Cadillac "Ladyfriend." The car had a wide dashboard and steering wheel. It played only eight-track tapes. It stalled in winter and leaked smelly antifreeze in summer. When the temperature dropped too low, the horn would go off. G would jump out of bed, throw on his slippers and coat, and go unplug the thing so it wouldn't wake the neighbors.

"That's why yo' daddy drives a bootleg version of The Batmobile," my classmates teased.

"He ain't my daddy," I shot back at them before saying something derogatory about their mother or father.

Our doors slammed on cue. G violently jerked his seatbelt strap forward and then across his chest. I didn't bother to reach for mine. When he put his key in the ignition, the car coughed itself awake. We sat there for a few minutes in silence, listening to the rumble and absorbing the vibrations. A few times he pressed his foot down on the gas, held it, and then let it go to help warm up Ladyfriend.

He checked the rearview mirror, shifted to drive, straightened the wheel, pulled out of the parking lot slowly, and then began to head for Hilltop Drive. At the first stop sign, G stopped and looked both ways for traffic. As he drove through the intersection, he banged his hand on the top of the steering wheel and came to an abrupt stop in the middle of the street.

"Dagnammit!" he yelled at the windshield.

Dagnammit, I think, is the Christian version of *Goddammit.* Pentecostals don't believe in cursing. You curse, you go to hell. So they say *shoot* or *shucks* or *sugah* instead of *shit. Frick* instead of *fuck. Dag* or *darn* instead of *damn. What the heck?* instead of *What the hell?*

"You tell me what I'm 'posed to do," he hollered at the side of my face, sprinkling spittles on my nose. "I can't leave the house!"

I reached for my collar.

"Can't go to work in peace!"

My collar slipped from my fingers.

"Always somethin'!"

I reached for it again.

"Somethin' is always goin' on 'tween the two of you."

I wiped his spit off my nose.

"If it ain't one daggone thing, it's another." G got quiet and slowly pressed down on the gas again.

I slid the ice pack off the other side of my face. My mouth dried up again. I slinked down in my seat and looked at him with the eye that was still open. My hand had gone numb from holding the pack, so I slid it between my thighs and squeezed them together to warm my hand.

"Am I supposed to let her kill me?" I was calm when I asked him that.

Nothing from him. Not a word. Not the beginning of an answer. Not a look. I wanted to dissect the silence of his confusion so badly. He kept his eyes pinned on the black road in front of us.

Why did he yell at me? Blame me for running away? Why didn't he reach over and wrap his arms around me? Hold me for a minute? I wanted him to let me wet the front of his jacket with my salty tears. New tears. Saved-up tears. And tears I wanted to cry for no good reason at all.

I wanted to hear his plan. How was he going to protect me from Myrtle? Would he finally show me that he could be a real father? A man? A black man who could take back his dignity? Was he going to take me to a safe place? Would he have Myrtle locked up? Was he going to divorce her and take me away with him? The longer I sat there waiting for answers, it became more and more clear to me that I wasn't going to get any.

"I'm not gonna let her kill me," I promised him. "And I'm tired of waiting for you to help me. You don't do anything." My voice began to rise. "You just stand around and let things happen."

"What?" his head jerked back. "You blamin' me? Huh? What the heck do you mean, *I let things happen*?"

"Yes." I defended my statement. "You know she beats me all the time. You know how I keep getting scars and bruises. You know why I always have to go to the emergency room. You see my blood on the walls. You see me limpin' around. You hear how she talks to me. She talks to you the same way!"

"I *never* hit you," he defended himself. "I *never* once put my hands on you. I *never* treated you bad."

He was right. G never beat me. I looked over at his hands gripping the steering wheel. Those hands, rough and ugly, had always been kind to me. Every night he came home from work and tiptoed up the stairs to my room with his kind hands. He turned the hall light on so he wouldn't wake me. Sometimes he did, but I pretended to be asleep. I could feel his warm body hovering over me as he gently pulled back the blanket and top sheet. He lifted my nightgown and ran his fingertips up and down my back, legs, and arms tracing old scars and discovering fresh welts, bruises, and open wounds. My heart rate sped up when I felt his hands touch me so softly. That kind of touch was so rare for me that I felt a kind of excitement. When he finished, he always sat on the edge of the bed holding his head in his hands, sighing. Most times I fell back to sleep before he left my bedroom. Other times I felt him gently place the covers back over me and kiss me on my forehead. I listened for the click of the light switch and followed the sound of his footsteps in my head.

"You g'on kill that girl one day, Myrtle," I could hear him yell through the central air vent in the floor.

"What, nigga?" she complained.

"You heard me, woman! Don't 'What nigga?' me." He sounded like a man, and for a second I had hope.

"Don't start with me," she warned.

"I'm g'on start with you," he insisted. "One day you g'on hit that child the wrong way, and she's gonna die! Then what you g'on do?"

"What I'm g'on do," Myrtle got louder. I pictured her sitting up in the bed. "What I'm g'on do is whup her little butt as long as she's livin' under my roof with my rules. I ain't here to baby her like you do."

I heard G throw his shoes in the hallway. "If you beat a dog too much, it's g'on turn on you one day," he said crossly.

"I wish that little pee rat would try to turn on me," she grunted. I wondered if she was looking up at the ceiling. My bedroom was right above theirs. "I will take her out of this world."

"See! See how you sound! Stacey is a child. A doggone child. Why can't you get that through your thick skull?"

"When I was a child, I got my butt beat."

"So did I," he said. "But times are different. You can't go around doin' what your mother and father did."

"It was good for me," she said. "Didn't kill me. And it's good for her. And I ain't g'on kill her. I'm just tryin' to bring her close to being killed, so when she comes back to her senses, she'll live this life in a holy way."

"Ain't no sense in me talkin' to you." G sounded exasperated.

Then came the silence. The end of the discussion. G's defeat. The click of the light switch. The creak of the bed as he took his side. I lay there imagining him falling asleep with his hairy back to her, feeling helpless. The kind of helpless he probably felt as we rode back home.

I broke the silence again. "Just 'cause you never hit me doesn't make you any better than her. You are just as guilty of putting all these scars on me as she is."

"How you g'on blame me for all of that?"

"'Cause you didn't protect me! Why can't you be a man? You're a punk! You let her walk all over you," I yelled. One tear crawled down my face as my lips shook at him.

"You best watch how you talk to me, girl," he warned. "I'm your father."

"*Adoptive father*," I corrected him. "A real father protects his daughter."

G turned his head to look at me. I could see that my words hurt him, and then suddenly I felt guilty again. I should have tried to understand that he really tried to do the best he could. He had a good heart. He was a nice person. He often reminded me that I was his little girl and he wouldn't trade me for the world. I knew he loved me. But my anger told me that he had no excuse. My anger blamed him for all my pain.

"She is my wife!"

"*And?*"

His eyes glared at me in a way I had never seen before. "You are a child. I ain't g'on let no child come b'tween me and my wife. This is all just a trick of the devil."

We came to another stop sign and waited. I sat wondering whether if I was his own flesh-and-blood daughter, if he would have said all that to me.

"I tell you one thing," he continued. "If I had to do it all over again, I would never adopt a child. It ain't worth it. It's too much heartache and trouble. What they say is right: blood *is* thicker than water."

I felt as if he stabbed me in the middle of my chest with the handle of a broomstick. "What does water and blood got to do with how you love somebody?" I asked him.

"It makes all the difference in the world," he said.

His words crushed me. He was turning the broomstick clockwise and counterclockwise in a quick motion, the handle digging deeper and deeper into my chest. He was going to kill me with his words. But I wouldn't let him. I turned away from him and gazed out the window, speechless. I couldn't help but remember all those times he told me that I was chosen because I was special. I had really believed it didn't matter that we didn't have the same blood running though our veins.

I could hear the song he used to sing to me still resonating in my ears: "Thank heaven, for little girls. Thank heaven, for my little girl. Thank DYFS for little girls like you."

It was a lie.

I wanted to weep. Weep hard until my insides curled up into knots and I couldn't cry anymore. I wanted to scream. Curse. Punch him. But I knew better. That kind of anger was not tolerated. So I sent his words and my feelings into exile somewhere deep inside me. G hadn't rescued me from anything. He had only brought me deeper into the vortex of my hell, and it was abundantly clear to me that he couldn't, and wouldn't, help me out of it.

When we got to the house, he hunched over the doorknob and fiddled with what looked like hundreds of keys on a single lackluster chain. My body slowly tensed up. I was frustrated with myself for being back there again. I thought escape meant leaving for good and never looking back, let alone returning to the place I ran from.

As soon as we stepped inside the kitchen, I saw drops of my blood peppering and drying on the bright floor. I was surprised that Myrtle hadn't bothered to clean it up. She scrubbed everything, even her resentment at her own life.

The house had an eerie silence. There was always gloom peeking through the window blinds and keyholes. A smell of evil seeped out the air vents, and awfulness rounded the corners and hid under furniture. My fear and her rage made it hard to breathe in there.

There was no sign of Myrtle. I smiled when G called her name, and there was no answer. Where was she? Had she run away out of fear of losing me? Fear of being caught by the police? Did she die while I was away?

I wasn't that lucky. When I reached the end of the hall, I peeked my head into their dark bedroom and saw her lying there under the sheets. The air went out of me. She hadn't run away. She wasn't dead. I wasn't that lucky.

"Just go to bed, Stacey," I heard G's voice chase me.

I passed him in the kitchen again. He had snatched the mop down from between the wall and the refrigerator and was about to clean my blood off the floor. As usual, he tried to clean up the situation. Make it go away. Do nothing to change our problems. He probably figured that joy would come in the morning. We'd forget about all that happened that night. We'd wake up and go on with things as usual. He wasn't going to call DYFS in the morning. As I watched my blood disappear under the wet mop, I realized that I was going to have to free myself yet again.

FIVE

D id the black family collapse after emancipation, or did it continue to adapt to changing circumstances just as it had done during slavery? These questions have been at the center of debate among various scholars such as Stanley Elkins, E. Franklin Frazier, Herbert Gutman, and Daniel Patrick Moynihan for decades. Much of the work produced by sociologists, historians, and psychologists has been motivated more by policy debate than by genuine and unbiased scholarly investigation. Some have claimed that the black family became riddled with pathologies after slavery, just as doctors and politicians argued that freedom made blacks sick, insane, criminal, and sexually loose.

Blacks, according to popular belief, were an endangered species that would soon die off without the peculiar institution and white paternalism to keep them in line. Scholars also argued that the black family as an institution did not function according to white middle-class standards. They highlighted out-of-wedlock births, the absence of black fathers, the presence of weak black men, strong and domineering female-centered households, failures in education, crime and drug abuse, lack of sexual mores, the intergenerational transmission of so-called deviant cultural norms, violent child-rearing practices, and the overall instability of relationships. Black children, some argued, were born into a state of moral degeneracy. For white society, black youth became a source of contamination, criminality, vice, and social danger.

Slavery itself was a great compromiser for the black family. It had disrupted many African cultural traditions, family organization patterns, and sex roles and placed great stress on husbands and wives, parents and children. But the black family survived because of its ability to adapt to the constantly evolving demands of slavery. The same was true after emancipation. In freedom, black families faced poverty, illness, starvation, economic exploitation, disenfranchisement, segregation, and persistent racial terrorism. The specter of racism loomed over every aspect of their lives and ambitions despite class or region.

Racism continued to be a great compromiser for black families. Many scholars have failed, and continue to fail, to link the problems of black families to the history of slavery and Jim Crow. Instead, their work is aligned with myths that solidify stereotypes about black family disorganization and cultural as well as genetic inferiority. These untruths were used, and still are used, to justify various forms of discrimination. They also help white Americans deny their history of racism and their continuing covert and overt agendas against poor people and people of color.

The real truth is that after slavery, white society had a vested interested in keeping black families dependent, subordinate, and dysfunctional. The family in American culture has always acted as an institution. Within that institution, society expects certain functions to operate properly for the health of the nation and prospects for the future. The family, in essence, plays a vital role in the maintenance of certain cultural norms and social hierarchies. It is also a crucial aspect of democracy. But white society never intended for blacks to equally participate in the adult business of democracy. So the goal was to infantilize the race by trapping it in a continuous limbo of childhood, attacking the physical, intellectual, and moral development of black children and keeping the black family dysfunctional out of fear of the potential and possibilities of what the African American race could become—healthy, functional, competitive, independent, and equal. Besides, if the black family met all those ideals, then how would the white middle-class family and lower-class and immigrant white families define themselves, their sense of place, and solidify their identity? In truth, whiteness, white supremacy, and gradations of white identity have always been defined by what it is not rather than what it is. And what white is not is everything that it deems to be black.

I knew my adoptive family was dysfunctional, but I didn't realize this by comparing it to white families or by using eurocentric modes of analysis to come to my conclusion. I didn't live in poverty. Nobody used drugs or alcohol in our house. My family's sexual mores were not loose but rather overly conservative. Education, work ethic, and religion were constant themes. My adoptive parents taught me that I did not just represent myself and the family, but the entire black race.

My adoptive relatives as well as other black folks in our world didn't aspire to live or act like white folks. We didn't care what white people thought about us. We cared only about how they treated black folks and were more concerned about how black people treated each other. We rarely interacted with white people outside schools and public spaces. We drew on the functional aspects of family and community ethos for survival and a sense of black identity. But it didn't always work.

Many families, regardless of class or ethnicity, are dysfunctional. But in the popular American imagination, the black family has more often than others been branded with labels of pathology. Yes, Myrtle was that stereotypical harsh and domineering black matriarch, and though G was a present and responsible breadwinner, he was still a weak black man in our household, conforming to the stereotype. But at times neither slavery nor racism had anything to do with our problems. However, I do acknowledge that race remained a compromiser in my own black family experience. At times, Myrtle failed G, G failed Myrtle, and they both failed me. We were all victims of a past with mangled roots. Somehow I had to be the one to make sense of this history. I had to break the cycle because our past was not dead. For me, the past wasn't even past.

SIX

I woke up and stretched under the sheets like a cat. All the drama that I had gone to bed with the night before was still with me. Church folks always say that you should never let the sun set and then rise again before resolving issues that happened during the day, but this was not possible in my case. The morning after I ran away, my problems had not passed away in my dreams during the night. I wasn't like G who would just move on. But part of me wanted to throw the pillow over my head, curl up like a fetus, and sleep through my never-ending struggle.

My bones popped like tree limbs as I got out of bed. Outside my bedroom window, the street looked like a wet snake sleeping. The rain fumed down from the sky. I pressed the palm of my hand against the flat, cool surface of the glass and felt the wind curl around the house searching for cracks to enter. I caught a glimpse of a tan-colored puppy nestled underneath the tire of the neighbor's gray Toyota. I wanted to bring it inside. Hold it close to me. Clean it up. Give it a better chance at life.

The tension in the house scared me. I felt as if I was about to face a playground fight with a pissed-off black girl. The feeling reminded me of being cussed out. Seeing the girl twisting her neck around in all directions. Snapping her fingers in my face while making promises of what she was going to do to me. Carefully removing her large, gold-plated hoop earrings. Putting her hair into a single ponytail. Rubbing Vaseline on her face so my fingernails would slide off if I got close enough to scratch her. The tension peeled off the walls. Blew its breath through the central air vent and underneath my shut door. I swore that at any minute it was going to surround me and peel back my skin.

Every morning I woke up with that kind of unease. Myrtle's body heat had always made me jump out of my sleep. She would stand over me with a belt or extension cord draped over her shoulders or dangling from her hand. I would try hard to stay calm, moving as little as possible. I knew that any wrong movement could be the difference between no pain and new welts. It always took me a few seconds to get over the initial shock of seeing her droopy, heavy breasts with their raisin-colored erect nipples pointing at me. I tried not to stare at that hairy black jungle between her legs that I could smell just inches from my face. Sometimes she beat me out of bed. Other times she simply walked out of the room without saying a word. Every morning that she displayed her naked self in front of me, I wished I had died in my sleep rather than face a new day with such a rude awakening.

"No child is gonna stay under my roof and disobey me," Myrtle's crackling voice drew my ear against my bedroom door.

The war was about to begin again.

G and Myrtle had gotten up at their usual time, seven o'clock. They never ate breakfast during the week, but they drank coffee together and watched the morning news and read the paper. That morning I didn't hear the television. That morning, they argued about me. Arguing about me had become a constant theme in that house.

"Did you have to bruise her face up like that?" G asked, trying to keep his voice low. "You went too far. You always go too far, Myrtle."

Silence. And then I heard somebody's spoon drop.

"And now the cops know about this," G complained. "Do you know how serious this is?"

"Long as she's livin' under *my* roof, I'm g'on whup her little behind!" she shot back at him.

I wondered if she knew my ear was pressed against the door. She had raised her voice and said what she had to say in a way that suggested that she knew or wanted to wake me up with that declaration.

"Why can't you just learn how to talk to her?" G pleaded.

"Talk?" Myrtle said it like it was some absurd suggestion.

"Yes, talk. What's so wrong about talkin'?"

"Time out for talkin'," she harrumphed. "I ain't waistin' my breath on a child."

"I talk to her," he said.

"You baby her."

"And do you think she respects you?" He pitched her the question.

"Dogonne right," she answered.

His voice got lower. "She fears you."

"And?" Myrtle said. I imagined she was frowning and shrugging her shoulders like she didn't care.

"There's a big difference b'tween fear and respect. And there ain't no love in the middle," G said.

"*Whatever*," Myrtle huffed.

"You know," G paused, "you got to get rid of your daddy's ways."

Oh no! He didn't just bring up her father! Talking about her mother or father always pissed Myrtle off. Nobody could say anything critical about her parents, even if they were speaking the truth.

"My daddy's ways," her voice cascaded off the walls. "Phht, nigga please."

"You do," G's voice got just as loud as hers. "Your daddy ain't right about everything. I don't care if he is a man of God. He didn't always do the right things. And he didn't always do right by you and your brothas and sistas when ya'all was kids."

"You need to leave my father out of this!" Myrtle warned. "He ain't got nothin' to do with this."

"He got everything to do with this," G insisted. "Every generation got a way of doin' things. But what worked for your generation might not work for this one. You got to put them old ways that don't work to rest. But, no, you want to hold onto them 'cause that's all you know. You think beatin' a child is the best way to do things 'cause your daddy did that to you."

"Don't tell me what I know," she hollered. "Nigga, you don't know what I know!"

"See! Look at you. Can't talk to you 'bout nothin'," G complained. "Can't reason with you. Can't get nothin' through your thick skull."

"Just shut up and drink your coffee. I don't feel like hearin' your mouth this morning."

Dead silence. I took my ear away from the door as the details of the night before began to haunt me again. The pain in my face sharpened. I tried to ignore it as I reached for my school uniform and decided that I had to do what I always did: adapt and face the world.

Myrtle and G looked up as if they were surprised by my presence in the kitchen. Did they expect me to die in my sleep? Be too scared to emerge from my bedroom? The smell of perked coffee bobbed around the room. The stench would linger in the air all day. It would eventually fade by dinnertime, when she would clean the pot and throw the grinds in the trash bag by the door.

My eyes shifted to my empty chair and the bowl of soggy cornflakes waiting for me on the table. Myrtle had always poured milk over them when she felt like it, not when I actually arrived at the table ready to eat. G picked up his copy of the *Trenton Times* and searched for the sports section. He would read the horoscopes and then the funnies.

Something inside me wouldn't let me part my lips to say my ritual, "Good morning, Mommy. Good morning, Daddy. Thank Jesus for letting us all see another day together." I couldn't pull out my chair, sit, fold my hands, and say grace over my soggy cornflakes. That morning I was not thankful for that bowl of cereal, for that house, that mother and that father. I wanted to run again.

"Did you call the Division of Youth and Family Services?" I asked boldly and looked down on him like I had some authority to question him.

Myrtle poured more Carnation Coffee-Mate into her cup. G rattled his newspaper after taking a glance at the Pick Six lottery results. At church he preached that playing numbers was a sin because it was considered gambling, but I always saw him and Myrtle sneaking tickets into the house.

He didn't answer me. They both acted as if I wasn't there. So I reached inside myself to pull up some more boldness. I raised my voice: "If you don't call them, I will!"

G slapped the newspaper shut and folded it in half. "Is that what you want?" he yelled at me. "Is that what you *really* want?"

"Yeah," I said in a flippant tone.

Myrtle's head jolted up. She was irked at my "yeah" response instead of "yes." I was never supposed to answer her or any other adults with "yeah." I could tell that she wanted to slap me in my mouth for stepping out of line.

"All right, Stacey," G pointed his thick sausage finger at me as he shifted in his chair. "You g'on get what you want, but you ain't g'on want what you g'on get. Maybe this is what you need. You need to get out there in the real world and see that the grass ain't greener on the other side."

"I don't care about grass," I said as my eyebrows converged in the middle of my forehead. "I care about living."

"Living—" Myrtle sneered.

"You don't appreciate nothin'," G cut her off. He jumped up from the table, his chair falling backward and crashing to the floor. He headed for the phone.

Myrtle twisted her lips and tapped her spoon against the table. She looked like a powder keg, and then her cheeks started to tremble. Her eyes got watery.

"I'm sorry," she mumbled.

Myrtle looked away from me and reached for a napkin to dab her eyes. I uncrossed my arms and took the attitude out of my stance. My heart balled up in the middle of my chest. Seeing her tears broke something inside me. As they came rolling down her face, fast and furious, I not only saw but I felt her pain. Forget about me. How could I be so selfish? I wanted to know where her pain was coming from. Who hurt her? What made her so stiff and mean? Nobody, not even Myrtle, came out of their mother that way. Life had to make her the way she was.

"Stacey," she cleared her throat. "I-I," she stumbled on her words, "I-I never meant to hurt you. I just wanted the best for you." She reached for her spoon and began dipping it into her coffee and pulling it out to let the brown fluid drip from it. G was frozen. He had the phone clutched in his hand, as if he was waiting for me to change my mind.

"All I've tried to do since you came to live here when you were five is teach you lessons about life. You need to be taught how to live right," she said, still dabbing at her stream of tears.

At that moment, I remembered the first lesson she ever taught me.

Myrtle had picked me up from my first day of kindergarten at the Alfred Reed School, which sat directly across the street from Frank Moody Memorial Park on Buttonwood Drive. She held my backpack as I walked a few feet in front of her.

"Your teacher says you're gonna have a test on your alphabet this Friday." I didn't respond. I was too busy paying attention to two squirrels chasing each other up a tree, their gray tails shaking wildly and their little claws scratching the bark.

"You know, there ain't no other little black kids in your class," she said. I hadn't noticed. "I bet them little white kids know their letters. You can't be a little black girl in America and not know your alphabet. If you don't know your alphabet, then you ain't never gonna be nothin'!" she insisted.

When we got home, I took my usual position on the living room floor to watch *Sesame Street*. I wasn't allowed to sit on the couches or other chairs. A child's place in our home was on the floor. Furniture, Myrtle said, was for grown folks to sit on. As the theme song to *Sesame Street* played, Myrtle walked into the room holding a plastic bag filled with wooden alphabet blocks. I watched as she piled them in front of my legs.

"Put them in order from A to Z, and call me when you finish," she ordered as she walked out of the room.

I already knew the alphabet, but I was too afraid to tell her. If I told her I already knew my letters, then she would have thought I was trying to get too big for my britches and trying to tell her that she was wrong. A child was never supposed to tell the parent that she was wrong. I glanced up at the glass clock hanging between two goldplated swans on the paneled wall above the television. *Daddy will be home soon,* I thought to myself.

I couldn't stay focused on the blocks. *Sesame Street* was far more interesting. I wanted to know what the number and color of the day was going to be. What Kermit the Frog's news flash was going to be about. Were they finally going to let us see what was inside Oscar the Grouch's garbage can? As I fiddled with the letter M, I didn't hear Myrtle coming into the room.

Something cut off my breath.

My heart nearly dropped to the pit of my stomach and my bladder opened up like a busted levee, wetting the seat of my pants. Every time I tried to breathe, the thing over my head got sucked into my mouth and nostrils. I could still see Big Bird's yellow body on the television screen, but it was fading fast. When I put my hands on my head to feel what was trying to kill me, I felt Myrtle's hard hands gripping a plastic bag over my head. I had two thoughts: AIR, and I'm not gonna ever breathe again.

I was about to give up and accept the fact that I was going to die. But just then she snatched the bag off my head, and I collapsed against the floor. The room kept spinning. For a few seconds, I couldn't hear anything. I made a choking sound as I took my first breath.

"When I tell you to do somethin', you do it! You don't be in here watchin' TV and lollygaggin' around," she hollered.

Spit danced from her mouthful of crooked teeth as she roared at me. The tendons in her neck and the vein in the middle of her forehead were ready to explode. I was mad at myself because I made her mad. If I had just lined up the blocks like I was supposed to, this would have never happened. I brought the punishment on myself. The next thing for me to do was to fix the situation and make her happy. So I began to search the pile of blocks again for the letter M.

Less than a minute later, G walked through the door. "How's my little girl?" he smiled and planted a wet kiss on my forehead.

"Fine," I lied to him. If only he had walked through the door just a tad bit earlier. If only he could have sensed the trouble in the air. If only he knew what kind of monster his wife was. But he was always too late and clueless.

Thinking about my alphabet sped my heart up again. I heard it ticking in my ears, like an egg timer. I shot both of them looks and then frowned at them. Myrtle taught me that I couldn't do anything good enough for her. She taught me that she didn't like me. Taught me that I'd never be anything. Taught me to think of myself as a heathen, a hussy, a little nigga, a bony and funny-looking tramp. She taught me that I wasn't her real child.

Sorry. Myrtle was always sorry when she hurt me. She uttered those same words, but they were empty because she always hurt me again. I didn't think she'd ever change. She would always beat me down. Make me cry. Scar me. Call me names. She would continue to make me hate myself for not being perfect enough for her.

Her apology ended. Myrtle had nothing else to say to me. G looked limp and weary as usual. Right then I realized that moment was about to become one of the most pivotal in my life. I knew that I had to stick to my gut feeling. I couldn't allow myself to be duped anymore.

"I don't want to grow up to be like you! I don't want to beat my kids. I don't want them to be scared of me like I'm scared of you. I don't want them to hate me like I hate you. So call the social worker," I insisted. "Tell them to come and get me, 'cause I don't wanna be here anymore."

Myrtle picked up her coffee cup and threw it against the wall. It crashed and broke into five sharp pieces, and some little ones. She leaped out of her chair and lunged toward me. G threw his body in front of her to stop her from getting to me.

"Who do you think you are? I ain't no child! I will break my foot off in your little butt, you little pee rat!"

"She ain't worth it, Myrtle," G pleaded, pulling her back away from me.

Struggling with her flailing arms, he said, "Don't do somethin' you gonna regret. Put it in the Lord's hands."

I stepped far enough away from her so she couldn't put her hands on me. Her tantrum showed me for sure that I had to keep myself out of her reach for good. She shot me a look that could decapitate roaches.

"Get them on the phone," she yelled at G and walked away from him at the same time. "Call them! Tell him that I want this demon out of my house."

I felt that I was almost free. I just had to make it through a day of G begging and pleading me to change my mind. He finally called DYFS. But the story he told them was drastically different from the truth.

"Yes, ma'am," he said into the phone, turning his back to me. "I have a twelve-year-old daughter. She ran away from home last night."

"Tell her why," I insisted.

"She's back," he explained. "But she don't want to be here anymore. She's rebellious. Flippant. And mad 'cause she's adopted."

"No!" I hollered. "I'm mad 'cause *you* adopted me!" I stormed out of the kitchen and headed for a dark corner in my bedroom. I couldn't believe he didn't tell that woman the truth. He didn't tell her that his wife messed up my face. That she had been beating me for years. That she was crazy.

I could still hear G talking with the social worker, blaming me for everything. I felt helpless, small. And then there was a sign of hope. When I heard him repeat back an address for the name of a shelter for children, I got excited.

"Seven o'clock," he said. "Yes ma'am, we'll be there."

He hung up the phone. I heard him pick his chair up off the floor again.

"Well," Myrtle muttered.

"Well," he sighed. "We got a meeting tonight at the Anchor House at seven. They want all three of us to be there."

I smiled at the ceiling and promised to tell all. I wasn't going to hold anything back. I knew I had to convince people that I wasn't a liar. My home wasn't a safe place. I knew, and I had to make them know, that eventually somebody was going to get hurt or be killed.

When we left the house that evening, I felt ambivalent. One part of me felt relieved. The other felt scared and an oncoming sense of abandonment for the third time in my life. My real mother had given me up for adoption. My foster mother turned me over to Myrtle and G when I was five. And there I was again, about to be turned over to a youth shelter for abused and runaway kids.

I felt like a grungy old cat that had been passed around but not really wanted by anybody. I suspected that Myrtle and G would drop me off at the shelter and then move on with their lives. Somehow I had to make myself belong somewhere and to somebody. I had to make my life and my little self matter in the world.

I should have been completely happy with what was about to happen to me. After all, I didn't want to live with my adoptive parents any longer. I dreaded the beatings, being talked down to, the suffocating atmosphere—all of it. But the fact remained that Myrtle and G were legally my parents. They were supposed to take care of me and want the best for my future. They were supposed to invest in me. Love me. Keep me safe. Why were they so willing to thrust me out into the world? The fact that they were turning me over to strangers made me feel that they were giving up on me and that I wasn't worth the struggle to try to make things work. I was not important enough for them to try to change their ways. Myrtle always refused to go to counseling. She didn't think she had a problem. *I* was the problem, she said.

I stared straight ahead, rigid, like somebody in a coma with her eyes still open. G and Myrtle were quiet. Anchor House was in South Trenton on Centre Street, just minutes away from our church. The silent ride there reminded me of all those long trips I took when I was five. I always sat quietly in the back seat with my eyes pinned to the road, wondering where the social worker was going to take me next. There was nothing like being a little kid going for a ride with no clues as to what lies ahead. I never asked, "Are we there yet?" I guess I was to afraid to want to know.

We parked directly in front of the shelter. It looked like a convent, with metal bars covering all the windows. A homeless guy with black fingernails rushed up to our car and tried to sell us a pack of batteries. G and Myrtle ignored him. As we entered the building, the sounds of Spanish music and traffic faded behind us.

"Hello Mr. and Mrs. Jenkins," a white woman with spotted, veiny hands smiled and offered a handshake. "C'mon in. I'm Susan."

Suddenly I felt hopeless.

The building smelled like cheap cleaning products. You could hear each footstep you took even though the floor was carpeted. We followed Susan down a dark and narrow hallway past walls adorned with Norman Rockwell prints. The one that caught my eyes was of a scrawny white boy holding a stick over his shoulder with his belongings tied up in a rag. The boy was clearly a runaway.

We stopped at the end of the hallway and entered a bright meeting room. Susan let G and Myrtle enter first, and then me. As soon as the light hit my face, Susan noticed my injuries. Myrtle and G sat on the couch opposite me. They held hands and didn't even look at me. They were in this thing together. I could just hear what was on their minds: Myrtle thought she was right and I was wrong; she beat me because I deserved it. Disobedient children ought to get their butts whupped. And G was thinking that no child was going to come between him and his wife.

Susan slowly closed the door behind her and she took a seat in a small plastic chair midway between the two couches. Finally, she saw me good in the light.

"Are you okay?" Her entire face had changed. She looked horrified, almost angry, yet still trying to maintain a sense of professionalism.

"Uh-huh," I whispered back.

"What happened to your face?"

"She beat me," I said coldly. I couldn't feel Myrtle staring at me.

"Mrs. Jenkins, you did this to her face?" Susan pointed at me.

"Yeah!" Myrtle snapped. "I whupped her behind, and I'll do it again!"

I felt a sudden hollow ache inside me.

"When I was a kid, you couldn't talk back to your parents. Roll your eyes. Question them. You did what you were told to do, whether you liked it or not. You didn't act all high and mighty. If you did, you got your butt whupped. I remember the time my daddy—"

"Mrs. Jenkins," Susan interrupted. "We are not talking about your childhood! Times are different. Times have changed. You can't go around beating children."

"Oh, we supposed to do what white folks do?" Myrtle sneered at Susan. "We supposed to give a child a time out? Y'all don't beat your kids. That's why they run all over you. Just 'cause y'all raise your kids different don't give you the right to tell black people how to raise our children. Raising a black child in America ain't the same as raising a white child."

"Mrs. Jenkins, with all due respect, this is not an issue about race,"

Susan said. "This is about the safety of a child. Most people who spank their kids use one hand on the backside. You've clearly used something else to beat Stacey." Susan ignored Myrtle for a moment to look at me. "What does she beat you with?"

"Belts. Switches. Hangers. Shoes. Extension cords. Sometimes whatever she can pick up," I answered.

She turned to face Myrtle again. "You know, the law prohibits parents from hitting a child in the head or the face? Did you know that you can't leave bruises or scars?"

G tried to defend his wife: "The Bible says the blueness of a wound cleans away evil."

"The law today says that this is child abuse, plain and simple," Susan barked back at him.

Myrtle and G couldn't even look at me. Instead, they stared down at their own laps. They seemed disappointed that Susan didn't agree with them. Myrtle and G were used to being around folks who agreed with them about beating the devil out of children. They would share stories and laugh about their parents beating them wherever and whenever they "showed out." They laughed about choosing the switch and sucking back their tears and moans after the beating.

"Stacey's bruised face tells me that this has been going on for a long time. How long, Stacey? How long has this abuse been going on?"

"Since I was five. Since before they adopted me."

"You're adopted?" Susan looked surprised.

"Yes," I answered, feeling unfortunate and abnormal.

"Tell me something," Susan, frowning, said to Myrtle and G. "Why would you adopt a child only to do this to her?"

"She doesn't even treat a dog like this," I added. "They treat their pit bull better than me."

"I don't want her in my house!" Myrtle stammered and lunged forward, startling me. I threw up my hands to cover my face like I always did when she got angry or made sudden movements.

Susan jolted up. "No one is going to hit you here, Stacey," she promised. And then she turned to face Myrtle and G: "Mr. and Mrs. Jenkins, I'm going to have to ask you to leave now. Please go home and pack a bag for Stacey and drop it off tomorrow. She will not be returning to your home. DYFS will contact you in the morning, and there will be an investigation."

I stayed glued to my seat as I watched the three of them walk out of the room. It was amazing to me how that fragile-looking woman had all that fire and courage under her skin and bones. I didn't expect Susan to defend me or stand up to the two people I always considered giants who could never be told they were wrong. For the first time, I realized that some adults, and even white people, saw things the way I did.

G and Myrtle didn't bother to give me a last look. No good-bye. No quarters or dimes for a phone call. Nothing. They just walked out the door and kept going. I felt saved and abandoned all at once.

SEVEN

Were African Americans mentally, physically, and spiritually damaged by slavery? In freedom, did they relive the experiences of their bondage through nightmares and flashbacks? Or did some former slaves choose to anesthetize themselves or just simply forget the past?

Black folks never got the chance to heal from their wounds that were inflicted during slavery because they continued to face mental, physical, and spiritual degradation during Jim Crow. Even those who hadn't lived through slavery and those who hadn't yet been born couldn't forget it. Some blacks felt disgraced by the past. Others mediated their recollections through writing, art, music, narratives, reflections, and race leadership and work. This past trauma and pain wrought out of enslavement grounded African Americans' individual and collective sense of identity. The memory of slavery would continue to play over and over again in black minds because racism continued, and still continues, to perpetuate the memories of exploitation.

When I freed myself from my own bondage, I expected to find peace and feel safe in the world and in my own skin. I didn't expect my mind and soul to remain shackled to my past. I knew that I had physical scars that would either fade or remain with me until death. But I didn't know that I had some deep internal wounds that would affect how I functioned in the world and how I saw myself and others for years to come. All those years I had survived in part because I learned to disassociate from all the pain. I protected myself by pretending to be a wallflower, a piece of the carpet, a window, anything. Sometimes I removed myself from my world altogether and imagined places I had never been. Memories became my worst fear and declared war on me even as I moved away from Myrtle and G physically and emotionally.

EIGHT

Throughout much of my childhood I sat silently in my place, absorbing the conversations of adults. They thought they were wise about everything and above the mind of a child. But the adults in my world had no real wisdom at all. They rationalized everything through biblical texts and clichéd statements: What doesn't kill you makes you stronger. Keep your head up. This too shall pass. Weeping endures for the night, but joy comes in the morning. Everything happens for a reason. There's no progress if there's no struggle. Look for the light at the end of the tunnel. Have faith the size of a mustard seed. Pray on it!

The morning after I woke up, I realized that I was in a situation where I had to make my own rules. I knew all those tokens of empty religious ideas were not going to get me through the day.

I expected to find peace when I awoke, but instead I found myself on a different battlefield with a new kind of enemy. There was supposed to be a truce, peace, a happily ever after. Life was supposed to show mercy. Trouble was supposed to move on to another place.

For the first week I spent as a resident in the Anchor House, it hurt to open my eyes in the morning. There was no movement around me. No voices. Almost no noise. The high ceiling and walls were fiercely white. I felt that I had awakened in the heart of winter, even though it was only late October. Next to the bed I slept on, there was a hard glacial window with a bent ledge underneath. On my door there was a small sign encased in plastic giving directions on how to proceed down the hallway in case of a fire.

Where were the pastel pink lace curtains that hung from the windows in my room? The mauve-colored walls? The stuffed animals? The polished burgundy wooden dressers? The walk-in closet full of clothes?

Where was Myrtle? I didn't feel the oppressive heat of her naked body hovering over me. There was no extension cord. No belt. No switch. No smell of perked coffee. No morning news. No gospel music.

Had I lost time? Did I sleep for a decade? Was I finally a woman? Did my breasts get bigger? Was I taller? Was my life just a dream? Did my past—that mean old yesterday—spring from some god's warped imagination?

Myrtle suddenly appeared before me! "Get your triflin' behind up and get ready for school!" she yelled.

Normally I struggled to free my legs from the tight sheets. And then I slipped my feet directly into my slippers in one motion before ducking past her with my eyes still glued to the extension cord, hoping that it wouldn't lash out and bite me.

But not that morning.

After hearing her voice, my legs still wrestled with the sheets, and my body jerked up in the bed, but my slippers weren't in their place. As my bare feet warmed the cold floor, I realized things were different. I looked down at my toes and then up again. Myrtle was not really there. My mind was playing tricks on me. I thought the war was still going on, but it wasn't. Myrtle still had control over me even though she was miles away from me.

As I tried to settle my racing heart and my startled nerves, three dark green bulky trash bags sitting by the door suddenly interrupted the snowy white atmosphere. A yellow sheet of lined paper taped to the middle bag had "Stacy Patton" written in large black letters. When I got closer to the bags and the piece of paper, I could smell the stench from the permanent marker that left the "e" out of Stacey. My name was underlined as if to stress that the contents inside were important and only for my eyes. One of the bags was slightly opened. I pulled the yellow drawstring toward me. As the bag crinkled a bit, I could see my Catholic school uniform folded on top of the other clothes. On top of my uniform was a bar of Lifebuoy soap. To this day I hate the smell of that soap. When I pass it in the cleaning section of the grocery store, I can't help but think of Myrtle.

I dragged the wooden chair from under the empty matching desk and sat down next to my baggage. I felt like a homeless person guarding precious contents that might seem worthless to passersby. Baggage seemed to be a constant theme in my life. It seemed as if plastic bags with yellow drawstrings followed me. I thought about the garbage truck that ate my past when Myrtle threw it away in garbage bags containing my few things after moving from my foster home to their house. I remember she used to tease me by giving me empty bags to put all my stuff in and then wait outside for a social worker to pick me up by the curb. And there I was again, in front of garbage bags feeling abandoned and as if my life wasn't worth much.

Myrtle suddenly appeared before me again! I threw my hands over my head and ducked, waiting for the hit to come. But it didn't. I dropped my hands and scanned the room for her.

"This ain't real," I whispered at the walls. "You ain't real." My voice got louder.

I shook my head and then plunged my hands deep into the middle trash bag to gather my skirt, white shirt, sweater, and long socks. All those colors jumped out at me at once, bringing back the familiarity of my life. Inside that same bag I felt a smaller plastic bag with "Anchor House" typed across the front. There was a cheap square-head toothbrush, a plastic comb, a small tube of no-name toothpaste, and a small bottle of Pert shampoo, a brand I could never use on my kinky hair.

As I made my way to the bathroom just off the corner of the room, I dreaded the prospects of looking at my face. I always dreaded looking at my face. Myrtle hated my face. So did I. She told me I had bugged eyes. She and G gave me a nickname: "Funny Looking." I felt ugly. I felt like some sight.

"Your *real mammy* threw you together in her coochie and pooted you out her behind," Myrtle said to me with the utmost look of disgust crawling all over her face. "She took one look at you and put you up for adoption. Could you blame her?" When I remained silent, she asked, "Could you blame her?"

"No, Mommy," I mumbled back.

"You always been ugly. You ugly and funny looking now and you g'on be that way 'til Jesus comes."

Myrtle once told me that after God made me, he threw away the mold so he wouldn't make that same mistake again. "When you're ugly like you are," she'd say, "you need to smile more often. It makes you look better. It's easier to smile than frown. Takes more muscles to frown. Frownin' keeps you ugly." She didn't stop there: "I put nice dresses on you. Straighten your hair. And that still don't work. Smile!" And then came the hit: pop, right in my mouth. I looked ridiculous trying to smile through hurtful words, a slap in the face, pain, tears.

Standing before the mirror, I leaned in to examine my eye and still swollen face. Suddenly I giggled. I imagined meeting my real mother one day and asking her if she threw me together inside her coochie and farted me out of her ass. After the giggle, a heavy feeling jumped on me. I knew that my birth couldn't have happened the way Myrtle said. But the reality was that my real mother did give me up for adoption. And because she did, I had to live with a monster all those years and I had to face my scars every day of my life.

I buttoned the top button on my white-collared shirt, pulled my wine-colored socks up to the bottom of my kneecaps, and wiped the tops of my penny loafers just as I did each morning. I grabbed my backpack and headed downstairs to the breakfast table. The hallway smelled like a sour mop. The floor creaked under my feet. The Anchor House reminded me of a rectory. I think it was one at some point. As I drew closer to the bottom of the staircase, a mix of voices went from faint to clear. The other kids were finishing up their breakfast at the long table in the dining room. A plastic bag of bagels, Styrofoam cups, a block of cream cheese, and a carton of orange juice lay on the table. I watched from a distance as they all got up at the same time, collected bus tickets, and four dollars apiece for lunch. Before I could say hello, they all cut out the front door to head off to the same Trenton public schools.

"Stacey." A voice jumped out at me from behind. Startled, I ducked and dropped my backpack at once. "It's okay," Michelle, a matronly looking coffee-colored woman, said to me as she bent down to pick my bag off the floor. "It's okay," she said again as I tried to slow down my heartbeat. "Nobody is going to hurt you here," she reassured me.

I knew Michelle wasn't going to hurt me. But she didn't realize that I feared all black women. I thought they were all the same everywhere. Mean. Harsh. Rough. Hostile. Snappy. Sassy. Loud. Unaffectionate. Quick tempered.

"Do you feel safe here?" she asked me in a low voice.

"Yes," I responded like a soldier.

"Good," she sighed. "If you don't feel safe, you need to let one of the counselors know. We are here to help you and to talk with you whenever you need us."

I believed her. But I wasn't the kind to ask for help. I didn't know how to tell somebody that I was scared or wanted to talk. Many times I couldn't find words to wrap around and describe that hollowness inside me.

I reached for my backpack, and Michelle stepped back from me. She moved my backpack behind her legs, as if she were hiding it from me. She looked perplexed. "Why do you have your Catholic school uniform on?" she asked.

"Uhm, 'cause I gotta go to school," I said stroking my shirt and my plaid skirt along the sides of my hips.

"Stacey." The lines in her forehead scrunched together. She reached for my shoulder and began to massage it. "You don't go to Catholic school anymore. Remember? Your parents refused to pay the tuition."

"Why did they do that?" I asked.

"Because you don't live with them. They feel that if you are not living with them, they shouldn't have to send you to an expensive private school." And then that specific morning came back to me as I stood before Michelle.

Two days after Myrtle and G dropped me off at the Anchor House, I woke up feeling cold, guilty, confused, and tired. I wanted to snuggle back into my real mama's tummy. I wanted to wait for a better time to come into the world with the knowledge I now had. Since I couldn't go back into my mama's womb and be born again, I had to accept all my gray feelings. I had to get out of bed, get dressed, and face the rosary-swinging nuns at Incarnation Catholic School and all their talk about purgatory, blessed sacraments, and the blessed Virgin Mary.

Ted, another counselor at the shelter, dropped me off behind the yellow school buses lined up in front of the main entrance. I kept hoping that none of my schoolmates would see me getting out of the huge van with the big white letters, "State of New Jersey for Official Use Only," scrawled on both sides. Ted told me to have a good day. I ignored him and quickly slammed the door behind me.

Sister Margaret, our stocky, wide-shouldered principal, greeted me at the door. "Stacey," her voice pulled me inside. "Come in my office," she said. My heart began to flip around in my chest. Had she heard about me? Who told her? Did everybody else know?

Sister Margaret gently laid her hand on my shoulder, and I flinched.

And then she took it away quickly. "Stacey," her voice was in a whisper. "If-if," she stuttered, "if I had known that you were having such a hard time," she stopped. "I wouldn't have," she stopped midsentence. "I wouldn't have been so hard on you. I'm sorry for being so strict with you. You have so much potential. I thought I was shaping you to live up to it."

She took that same forefinger she had used so many times and pointed it at me. My eyes got all crossed in my head as I watched it slowly come at me. She did the unexpected. She slowly ran her finger across my soft brow, the same brow that she had stretched up to my hairline to punish me so many times.

I was confused. No one had ever apologized for hurting me. I didn't think they had to. Apologies were for adults who couldn't go around hitting each other. Adults were equals. Children were not. We were to be seen and not heard. We were to stay in our place. Nobody owed us explanations or apologies.

Sister Margaret put both hands on my shoulders and looked to the ceiling, as if she was fixing herself to pray or search for the Virgin Mary through the electrical wires. She sighed, and her eyes returned to me. She didn't look into my eyes. Instead she seemed to look through me.

"Your father just left my office," she said.

"He was here?" My chest got tight.

"Yes," she nodded.

"So he told you what happened?"

"Yes, he did." The words came out of her mouth slowly.

"He probably lied. Blamed me for everything. Did he tell you how I got these scars? How she always yelled at me? How she always beat me. How she—"

"Stacey," she interrupted and pressed down on my shoulders to stop my rant. "He didn't tell me the details. We didn't talk about your scars. He was upset, though."

My eyes dropped to the floor. I felt bad even though I didn't want to. Sister Margaret placed her cold fingers under my chin and lifted it gently so I could read her lips. I read her lips well because my ears couldn't believe what she said.

"Your father came into my office and asked for a refund in tuition for the rest of the year." Hard, cold silence came between us. My heart was throbbing in my stomach. She pressed her lips together and breathed hard through her nose. "He said that since you don't live in his house anymore, he refuses to pay for private school. He doesn't feel he should be responsible for your education. That means you can no longer attend Incarnation. You have to go to a public school."

My heart dropped to my stomach. I had heard nothing but bad things about public schools. The kids were roughnecks. They fought all the time. They brought guns and knives to schools. They sold drugs from their lockers. Girls came to school pregnant. No one got a good education. Only the few talented and lucky ones became anything significant. Otherwise, kids who went to public school turned out to be average people who never left their neighborhoods and settled comfortably in the mundane atmosphere of their unchanging environments. That's what had happened to Myrtle and G.

"Ted." She paused. "Ted, the man from the Anchor House, the shelter you stayed at last night," she said, as if I was some drunk who had forgotten where I slept. "He's still waiting for you outside. We all felt it would be best if I told you the news." She grew quiet, and I stood there speechless and feeling powerless. I had been beaten and abandoned, and now they were taking my education away from me. I felt betrayed. "He's going to take you back. The people at the Anchor House will enroll you in a public school."

I simply walked away. There was no need for hugs. No good-byes. No tears. No anger. Nothing. I had to face my cold and unfair reality.

I slammed the door to the big blue van. Ted was quiet for a moment. We didn't bother to make eye contact. Ted was the only person who said nothing about my scars. It was as if they didn't exist. Something about me permeated outward, and that's what he saw. Besides, there were bigger things to be concerned about other than scars that would heal and fade.

"The public schools aren't so bad," Ted mumbled. "You might even like it better than Catholic school. The teachers aren't such stiff asses as those nuns. Nobody tries to scare you by telling you you're gonna go to hell or get stuck in purgatory for not doing your homework. You don't have to recite all those stupid sacraments all the time."

My mind snapped back to Michelle. "Oh, yeah," I said. "I must have forgot."

Michelle was still disturbed. It had been a week since I hadn't gone to school, but I kept putting my uniform on every morning as if everything was normal. But it wasn't.

"You start your new school tomorrow," she said. "Public school will be good for you. It's more diverse. You will get a better sense of the real world. Real people."

For the first few days I spent in the Anchor House, my mind kept leaving me. Sometimes it took me back years at a time. I found myself on my knees picking lint balls off the floor. I sat in the tub with no water and waited for Myrtle to come wash me. Flinched at the sound of creaks in the wall or floor. Ducked when birds flew past. Answered voices that were not really there. Sometimes I sat in a room for hours, replaying every whipping over and over again. I could feel blood dripping from my nose and down the back of my throat. Feel slaps that landed against my face years before. Feel my eyes and lips swelling up. I grabbed my throat and wrestled Myrtle's invincible hand off me. I felt her fingers probing my private parts again. The tips of my earlobes sizzled from the hot comb she used on my hair. I took my clothes off for no reason. I rocked back and forth in my seat. Bit my nails. I could smell the switches, the perked coffee, and Lifebuoy soap. I heard a mixture of church music and the nasty things she always said to me.

"Ugly!"

"Trifling!"

"Stupid!"

"Hussy."

"Good-for-nothin'."

"Dummy!"

"Nitwit!"

"Even God don't love you!"

"Little demon!"

"Pee rat!"

"You ain't nothin'!"

"You ain't g'on be nothin'!"

"You ain't got the sense of a dog!"

"Tramp!"

"You gonna bust hell wide open!"

"That's why yo' mammy didn't want you!"

Myrtle's voice suddenly stopped. There was quiet for a moment. And then, out of nowhere, I remembered Byron. Where did he come from? I thought I had forgotten about him. Maybe my mind had decided that it was time not only to remember my past from my adoptive parents' home but the years in foster care too.

Byron must have been about thirteen or fourteen years old when I was four. He too was a foster child at the same home in East Orange. For some reason, he and I always ended up in a room together—alone. And there he and I were together again, alone in the dining room at the Anchor House.

I heard his voice again: "Look under the table."

I looked under the dining room table, just as I had done when I was a little girl.

"Do you see it?" His voice still sounded the same, deep and smooth. "It's big, ain't it?"

He was stroking his very large dirt-colored penis with one hand. It got bigger and bigger as he talked to me. I snatched my head above the table again, just as I had done back then. I knew something was not right about our interaction, but I never told a soul. Besides, who would believe me? When my head was completely above the table again, I expected to see Byron smiling at me, but the chair was empty. Where did Byron come from? Where was he then? I imagined that he was some pervert feeling up little girls. Maybe he was a rapist or on somebody's sex offender list.

I felt haunted. Those voices and flashbacks made me feel like I had a VHS tape in my head. The recordings came and went on their own. I desperately wanted to find the remote and take control. I wanted to edit scenes out. Press Rewind and be recorded absent. Turn the past completely off. I needed to take back my mind, but I didn't know how.

NINE

Emancipation not only changed the legal status of African Americans; it altered racial identity and representation as well as notions of childhood. Americans began to reconstruct how they understood and saw racial differences to determine how and where they fit after the social upheavals and dislocations wrought by the Civil War, emancipation, and Radical Reconstruction. The color line hardened, and so too did the boundaries between what was an adult and a child. Ideas about childhood came cloaked in the language of evolution, social Darwinism, democratic progress, and race. For whites, black people never evolved and never "grew up." They were frozen children who had no place in the adult business of democracy. This notion that blacks were children served to justify new forms of discrimination that began during Reconstruction and intensified throughout the Jim Crow era.

After the Civil War, black and white children lost their economic value to society in varying degrees. White middle-class children largely became separated from the world of work and the world of adults, deeming them economically useless but emotionally priceless. Children were not supposed to be exploited or exposed to harsh labor conditions. Childhood needed to be prolonged, nurtured, and protected.

In return for their lost economic value, white middle-class children were increasingly romanticized in popular imagery. The white child became the powerful symbol of childhood innocence. The nation figured out that it had to invest in the future of the white child because the white child represented the potential and possibilities of the nation. White children appeared in sentimental genre paintings as vulnerable, angelic, and untouchable youngsters who needed nurturing, protection, and confinement of their sexuality. By the turn of the century, society at large began to reform labor and judicial laws to protect children from various forms of exploitation. Playtime and education became vital aspects of the child's life. White children were taught that the nation's visions of democracy and world power did not include their black counterparts.

In slavery, all black children had prenatal and economic value. In freedom, black children became expendable nuisances whose futurity was always problematic for white society. In return for their lost economic value, black children were further devalued in many ways. They became subjects in racist cartoons, postcards, games, household goods, and visual pornography. Black children were also demonized in black baby tales, nursery rhymes, songs like *Ten Little Niggers*, books such as *Little Black Sambo*, and films like *The Little Rascals*. In freedom, black children represented a new kind of African American citizenry that was never going to be disciplined by slavery. Their potential was unhinged from the peculiar institution, and their potential was unknown and feared by whites. For white racists, the goal in the aftermath of slavery was to undermine the future prospects of the African American race by attacking the physical, moral, and intellectual development of its children by denying them the privileges and protections reserved for innocent white middle-class children.

I remember watching D. W. Griffith's controversial 1915 film *The Birth of a Nation* in my junior high school history class—"a great American masterpiece," my teacher told me. The film depicted two families: the Stonemans from the North and the Camerons from the South. Both families experienced the Civil War and Reconstruction years. The premise of the film was that the Radical Republicans and so-called uppity Negroes were the cause of the country's social, political, and economic problems after the Civil War. My teacher made no mention that African Americans considered the film to be a grotesque distortion of people of color and the facts of history. My teacher did not tell us that the film was a propaganda piece for the Ku Klux Klan and that it advocated the use of violence to put black people back in their place at the lowest rung of society and reconcile the white North and South.

In one scene in the film, Colonel Cameron, a defeated Confederate soldier, is shown pondering the conditions of the South and how to restore white supremacy. He sees a group of black children walking down a path a few yards away from a group of white children hiding under a white sheet. As the black children get closer, the white children jump out to spook them away. Inspired by this scene, Cameron jumps to his feet! The Klan would solve the white man's Negro problem.

Why were children used in that scene? And if white people considered black adults to be children, what then were black children? Why were white and black children crucial to the restoration of white supremacy?

To restore racial order, the nation increasingly turned its gaze to the bodies of black and white children, making them imagined opposites. Ideas about their antithetical differences would be crucial to the maintenance of and justification for Jim Crow laws and customs. The nation not only undermined black children with its perverse racial projections and behaviors, it also undermined poor white and immigrant children by masking larger social and economic problems with false racial ideologies. Ultimately the entire country remained somewhat backward and retarded.

Being at the Anchor House with children of all colors allowed me to see how American society continues to value some children and devalue others. This country has failed, and continues to fail, to realize that all children are not just the future of individual races; they represent the potential and possibilities for the nation as a whole. When we don't invest in and nurture the healthy development of children because of race, ethnicity, class, or gender, we leave the entire nation stunted and backward.

TEN

As more days passed, I began to feel less awkward about my new living arrangements at the Anchor House. Living in the inner city of South Trenton with poor Puerto Ricans and blacks was a foreign experience for me. Folks danced in the street and talked loudly as they hung around dirty bodegas—those little stores that sold pork rinds, ten-cent drinks, and penny candies. There were liquor stores that flashed cigarette signs. Every other block had a check-cashing place. There was a never-ending flow of loud music, cursing children, beeping horns, all kinds of smells, sirens. The streets and sidewalks were littered with broken glass, dirty diapers, chicken bones, cigarette butts, and a homeless person here and there. I couldn't believe that this new world that I found myself in was less than twenty minutes from the quiet, orderly suburb where I had grown up.

For years, South Trenton was a place I had read about in the crime blotter section of the *Trenton Times*. My adoptive parents and I whisked through its chaotic streets with the doors on our car locked down on our way home from church. We held our breath until we were clear out of those zones and were relieved when we returned to our motionless, clean, predictable street where the loudest noises were crickets and dogs.

I was not afraid in my new world. Nothing could be scarier than that haunted house on Hilltop Drive. I simply had to be a chameleon and adapt to my new environment. Though I felt safe with Myrtle nowhere in sight, I still knew not to get too comfortable. I had already survived life in our house on Hilltop Drive, the Pentecostal church, and private school. Living with Myrtle had taught me not to get too comfortable because there was no safe place as long as I was a vulnerable child with little say over my future. My Anchor House stay was to end in thirty days. By the fifteenth day, the staff members still hadn't figured out what to do with me. I was growing weary thinking about my place, my possibilities, and my life. I wanted to move the story along quickly.

Waiting was torturous. It reminded me of all those times the social worker from DYFS picked me up from the foster home in East Orange to drive me on visits to prospective parents. I never sat in the front seat because I was afraid of her. She never told me where she was taking me, and I didn't ask. I just gripped the edge of the back seat and held on tight while she drove.

Sometimes I pressed my face against the window, smearing it with sweat and fogging it with my breath. I looked for skulls, bone fragments, and "Caution" and "Danger" signs along the road. But I never saw any of that. I never knew what was ahead waiting for me. So I sat back, got lost in the black overhead wires and treetops, and accepted the unknown. Today as a grown woman, I suffer from extreme carsickness. Part of my problem is physical—dizziness, nausea, headaches, sweating, vomiting. I believe that at the root of my car spells is the anxiety I had on the road as a child.

A muscular tree's bare twigs, twisted like nerves, scratched at the window I sat next to in the community room. Maybe it was trying to tell me something, give me some sense of direction, and give me some power over my situation. What could I do to save my life? How could I create myself without other people's dirty handprints all over me? Who could I trust not to break me down, control me, lead me the wrong way, murder the little bit of spirit I had left? Did the other kids in that shelter trust anybody other than themselves and their own instincts?

My attention snapped back to the community room and Susan's voice. Susan had pale skin, blonde hair, and a thin frame, all delicately put together. Her eyebrows were the thinnest I had ever seen. She had a gentle mouth, nervous tone, and a fragile air about her. She was leading our Thursday evening group meeting. Group meetings were supposed to be a time when we shared whatever was on our minds, discussed problems we might be having in the shelter, and put our heads together to discuss what to do next. Anything said during group was supposed to remain there. That was my first group, because the Thursday before, some people from DYFS had come by to see me. They told me to strip naked, took Polaroid snapshots of my scars, and asked more questions about my beatings. They also asked me if I was sexually abused. Of course, I said no.

"Okay, residents." Susan crossed her legs and rested a notepad on her lap.

Residents? I frowned.

"We have a few new faces. So why don't we go around the room, say your name, and briefly explain why you are here," she said twisting the cap off her pen.

I watched everybody's eyes shift to the closest person to Susan.

"Me," he poked his finger into his chest. "Why I gotta go first?" He dropped his eyes to his big black untied Doc Martens boots. They looked like war boots. His jeans were wide at the ankles, like bell-bottoms. There was a shredded hole at both kneecaps, as if he put them there intentionally. I could see his striped boxer shorts at his waistline.

"I'm DeWayne," he mumbled shyly. "I spend most of my time dancin' to house music and twistin' my dreadlocks." He giggled, and so did the rest of us. Every time I saw him, he had his fingers buried in his nappy roots. I had never seen a boy who had such a constant love affair with his hair.

"You really like your dreadlocks, huh, DeWayne?" Susan tilted her head and gave him a short smile. "Do you know how many dreadlocks you have?"

"Seventy-one," he answered quickly. "And I have a baby lock growin' behind my left ear," he added.

I was impressed. If that was me with all that hair, I think I would have gotten tired of counting. I wondered what it did for him to know how many locks were on his head.

"They are like little individual people," he said twirling one of those little hair people around his finger.

"Really?" Susan tried to sound intrigued.

"Some are fatter than others. Some shorter. Some longer. Some got their own minds. Some hang and stick out however they feel like. They got little souls. So I gotta touch 'em every day and talk to 'em so they'll grow. And I'm never gonna cut 'em. I want them to get so long I'll have to pick 'em and hold 'em in my arms when I cross the street."

We snickered. I imagined him holding his long hair whips crossing the street with cars almost crashing into each other, people honking their horns, while others tried not to stare.

"They my witnesses," he said in a serious tone. "They seen everything I seen. They even seen things I ain't seen behind me."

I had never met anyone with dreadlocks. The only thing I knew about dreadlocks was Tracy Chapman who sang about how she got a fast car and Bob Marley wailing about Buffalo Soldiers and Rastas. Myrtle said dreadlocks were dirty and smelled nasty. She said they were an abomination to hair and embarrassing to black people.

"God didn't give us hair so that we could make it look all nappy and tangled up like Medusa's head," she said. "They need to cut that mess, comb it, straighten it, perm it—somethin'. I can't imagine what it must be like to sleep next to somebody with all that mess on their heads."

I told Myrtle that Samson in the Bible had locks and they were the source of his strength. When Jesus went into the wilderness to pray before he died, he came back and his hair was locked. Her response was, "I didn't know white people could grow dreadlocks."

"What brings you to the Anchor House, DeWayne?" Susan asked him as she got her pen ready to scribble something down on her notepad.

"'Cause my mama is on drugs." He looked at the floor and ran his fingers underneath his chin. "She don't buy no food. She don't buy me and my brother no clothes. She ain't never home. Sometimes she go out trickin'. She—" he stopped abruptly, like his breath got stuck in his throat and couldn't reach his tongue.

All we heard was Susan's pen scratching the pad. DeWayne gave her an evil stare, and she didn't even know it.

"You writin' this down?" he sneered.

I was still trying to figure out what DeWayne meant by "trickin'." Immediately, I thought about Halloween and circus clowns and magic tricks. But how could that be bad? But then it clicked: somebody who "tricked" was a prostitute.

Susan kept the tip of her pen pressed on the same spot and looked up at DeWayne. "Yes," she answered him and then proceeded to cross T's and dot I's.

"Why?" A wrinkle grew in the middle of his nose.

"Well." She shook the pen between two fingers and struggled with his question for a few seconds. "We like to take notes on the residents so we can see your progress."

Our lives were drama. Susan's job was to document our drama and how we reacted to it. But I could see DeWayne's point. It was arrogant of her to sit there and jot down little notes about our big issues that we couldn't put down on paper in contained lines. That pen, that pad,

Susan's body language suggested that she had a kind of power that we didn't. Somehow she was different from us. I felt that what she wrote down would determine our futures. I wanted to grab the pen and write.

"It's rude, Susan!" DeWayne screamed like a parrot.

Susan stayed calm even with that surprised look on her face. "Can you help me understand what you mean, DeWayne?"

"You can't take notes about me! How you gonna write my name down at the top of a sheet of paper in big letters, underline it, and then write your incomplete sentences about my life? Look, you ain't even spell my name right." He peeked over her hand.

"I'm sorry, DeWayne," she said quickly scratching out "Da" and writing "De."

So the spelling of our names didn't even matter. The three trash bags popped into my head. They had left out the "e" in my name. But why should Susan or any of those other counselors have cared so much about the little intricate concerns we *residents* had? We were there only for a short spell. We came through the door with problems and were going to leave with problems. They knew it even if we had false hopes of believing the system would work for us and that the adults in our lives would keep their promises. Thirty days wasn't enough time to make any real connection with any of us. They would simply watch us, keep us alive, take notes, and then put a number on our file folder and store it in some cabinet when we left.

"You can't take notes about my life," he grumbled and dug through his hair searching for another lock to twist. "How you gonna understand my life through some damn notes? I gotta live this bullshit!"

"Watch your language, please," Susan warned.

"What you want me to call it?" he snapped. "It *is* bullshit! It's bullshit when your daddy ain't a man. When he walks out and leaves you. Leaves you and your little brother and your mama. Don't give us no money. Don't never come around. It's bullshit when you sittin' at the kitchen table hungry. You know you ain't gonna eat 'cause your mama done spent the money on the crack she smokin' in the livin' room."

I kept my eyes down. I could only imagine what his face looked like then. Hard, angry. Angry faces scared me, so I looked away.

"And now I gotta be here. In this shelter. This is bullshit!"

"What's the alternative, DeWayne? The streets?" Susan asked.

How dare she? I jerked my head, surprised and confused. What was she trying to insinuate? I felt lines thickening in my forehead. Something in me began to boil. I couldn't explain why I had that sudden frustrating feeling. But something sounded really wrong with Susan's question. She did not sound like the same woman who had rescued me two weeks earlier.

DeWayne started to say something, but the words didn't come out. The rest of us waited for an answer. He was the most courageous one in the group. He had a fire in him that we didn't have, and he had answers for everything. If he didn't know an alternative, then maybe there was no hope for the rest of us.

The dread-headed boy slumped deeper into his chair. I looked at him closer. Blank. Cut down. Defeated. Speechless. He had hit an impenetrable wall. All he could do was twist the little souls on his head.

"I'm Fatima," said a Muslim girl draped from head to toe in what looked like blue sheets. She reminded me of the nuns at school, only more mysterious looking. I wanted to know what she looked like underneath all that. Looking at her all hidden and covered up made me hot. "I'm fifteen and I'm four months pregnant. My parents found out, so they kicked me out of the house." She rubbed her stomach in circular motions as if she was comforting the child. "I don't have no other place to go. My parents told everybody else I know not to take me in because I am a disgrace to them and Allah. So I came here."

I was glad that somebody other than me asked, "Who is Allah?" I didn't know there were so many names to refer to God. I guess everybody shapes God by giving him names that sound like theirs, and they color him to look like them too.

"Fatima," Susan called out. "Do you understand why it's important to think and act responsibly?" My eyes zoomed in on the girl's face. Her skin was the color of dried tobacco. Her lips were cracked and split. Her teeth were as white as the meat of an apple.

"What do you mean?" Fatima asked.

"Safe sex? Using protection? Abstinence. The fact that you are fifteen and not ready to be a parent?"

I could hear Myrtle's voice in my head when I looked at Fatima's stomach. Myrtle would have said that the pregnant girl has made her bed hard, and now she's got to lie in it. That was her red wagon, so now she had to pull it. The young girl couldn't keep her legs closed. Now she's knocked up. Young girls today ain't no good. They got their legs open for every Tom, Dick, and Harry.

Fatima's bottom lip quivered. "I made a mistake. I wasn't trying to have a baby. I wasn't trying to become a disgrace to my family and to the benevolent and merciful Allah."

"One thing everyone in this room must learn is the importance of being responsible. When you are irresponsible, then you have to live with the consequences of your actions," Susan lectured.

I began to wonder about the consequences of Susan's actions. Wasn't it harsh to talk about a new baby coming into the world as some kind of negative consequence?

Fatima's mouth was buttoned tight. She looked guilty, ashamed. She stopped rubbing her stomach and crossed her arms over her breasts as if to hold back something inside her or hide her pregnancy. She cast sideways glances at all of us.

"So her moms and pops should have kicked her out on the streets?" DeWayne shot at Susan.

"What I'm saying, DeWayne—"

"No." He cut her off and raised his finger. "What you sayin' is bullshit."

Bold, I thought. I had never heard a child correct an adult by telling them what they were really saying. If I did something like that with Myrtle it would be a death sentence.

"Please watch your—"

"Parents shouldn't stop caring for their kids 'cause they trip up. Everybody trips up. That don't mean parents should be allowed to throw their kids on the street like they an empty Campbell's soup can. The consequences for parents who do that should be hard! Hard! You can't blame that girl for being pregnant. People get pregnant all the time. She ain't the first. And she ain't the last. Look at you, Susan. Look at all of us. All of our lives got started 'cause somebody busted a nut!"

We all giggled, even Fatima. Susan's mouth dropped.

"So kids ain't supposed to be bustin' nuts," he shrugged his shoulders.

"DeWayne," Susan sighed, more frustrated with him.

"Still, her baby ain't no mistake. Creating life ain't no mistake. She shouldn't be punished. Her parents should be punished for throwin' her out like a soup can."

"DeWayne, I'm going to ask you to calm down and stop speaking out of turn. If you don't control yourself, then I'm going to have to ask you to leave the group. Have some respect for your fellow residents."

Susan annoyed me. I wanted to hear DeWayne speak out of turn, and

I'm sure everybody else in the room wanted to hear him too. He made the meeting more stimulating.

I looked at Susan closely and waited for her to say something. I wanted to tell DeWayne that he was right. Maybe he shouldn't have been so loud, cursing, and cutting her off while she was talking, but I think he made sense. Susan looked away from DeWayne. I could tell by the way her cheeks were getting all flushed that she didn't know how to deal with him and was growing tired of his presence.

"Moving right along," she sighed and directed her attention to the Puerto Rican girl sitting next to Fatima. DeWayne rolled his eyes and twisted harder.

"I'm Marisol," she said nervously. She was searching her fingers for another nail to bite. She couldn't keep her leg still. "I'm fourteen. I'm here—I'm here at this place 'cause my uncle, Poppy's little brother, touched me and don't nobody believe me. They let him stay in the house, and he keeps doin' it when nobody's around. So I left. The police found me and took me back. I left again. So they brought me here. I swear to God!" Her voice cracked: "I told Poppy I ain't goin' back there 'til he's gone. But they don't wanna believe me." A tear began to roll down her face. She quickly wiped it away and tried to pull herself together. I thought I was the only kid on earth who wiped tears before they could finish falling.

Marisol's confession hit a nerve inside me. Was I supposed to tell them that Myrtle touched me too? There was no way I could do it. I saw the way everybody was looking at her, feeling so sorry for her even in the midst of their own problems. Perhaps they were thinking, *Well, at least that didn't happen to me.*

I knew exactly what it felt like for somebody to touch my private parts as if they didn't belong to me anymore. But I didn't want anybody feeling sorry for me and looking at me weird and wondering what it must be like for somebody to play with your private parts when you don't want them too. So I decided not to say anything about Myrtle touching me.

"My name is Liz. I just turned sixteen two days ago." That's all she said, like she didn't want us to know why she was there.

"Why are you here, Liz?" Susan asked.

She hesitated. The look on her face said that she didn't think it was any of our business. "'Cause I drink too much." She spit it out.

"Too much?" Susan's eyebrows raised. "How old are you?"

"Sixteen." Liz sucked her teeth as if she knew where Susan was about to go.

"Should you even be drinking at all?"

"Should my mama be drinkin' at all?" Liz gave Susan attitude.

"Your mother is an adult. You're a minor," Susan reminded her. "This brings us back to my point about responsibility." Susan began to lecture again, but that time she wouldn't get the chance.

"Lady, you can't tell me shit about responsibility." Liz jerked her head back and forth.

"Watch your language, please," Susan ordered. DeWayne had started something with all that cussing. Or did he? Maybe real children cussed. Maybe children with nothing to lose cussed. I was too scared to let anyone else hear me say such words. I wondered how I would sound.

"No, *you* watch your language!" Liz sassed her.

I held the bottom of my seat. My heart sped up. I just knew Susan was going to lose it and end up slapping Liz for her smart mouth. Even though Susan was not her mother, she was still an adult, and there was no way an adult was going to let her get away with that kind of disrespect. In the world I had grown up in, other adults who caught you acting up were allowed to whip you. And then you had to go home and tell your mama that somebody had to whip you, and you got whipped again for bringing embarrassment to your family. I guess that's what they meant by it taking a village to raise a child. Everybody in the village had switches and the right to give you an ass whupping.

"I am responsible! My mama ain't! Won't you tell her to stop drinkin'. She the one that gave me my first shot of Hennessy when I was seven. How you gonna give a seven-year-old Hennessy? You ever tasted Hennessy? Ya'll ever tasted Hennessy?" Liz looked to us. We shook our heads. The closest thing I had to alcohol was Martinelli's sparkling cider. And I had the nerve to pretend I was drunk off it simply because it came from what looked like a wine bottle. "That stuff burns the shit out your chest. It's strong enough to grow hairs on your titties!"

We laughed hard. I imagined Myrtle's baggy breasts with those raisin-colored nipples and my new breasts covered with patches of hair.

"My mama used to put dollar bills in my hand and send me to the liquor store to buy her forty-ounce malt liquors. And she always gave me a sip. And now I like gettin' lifted. So what? At least I ain't smokin' crack. Don't call me irresponsible. My mama is the irresponsible one."

"Your mother doesn't get into street fights," Susan noted as I watched the air go out of Liz. "Your mother didn't get arrested for stealing. For public drunkenness. Did she?"

I felt that Susan could have left those details out. We didn't need to know the girl's crimes. Liz couldn't say anything. She couldn't even look the rest of us in the face. She was broken and reduced to a sinner, and she knew it.

A honey voice broke the silence: "Kaya Horton." He was pretty—too pretty for a boy. He had a soft, dark-almond complexion and intricate glossy cornrows. I wondered whose girl's legs he sat between to get his hair done like that. He was knife-blade lean and so calm he didn't seem real. He looked as if he never got mad at anything and didn't take life too seriously. "I'm sixteen. I'm here because my father said he doesn't know what else to do with me." He sounded smart. His voice didn't match the way he looked.

"Why is that, Mr. Horton?"

He smirked and shrugged his shoulders.

"Do you think it's cool to be rebellious?"

"Everybody's got to defy something," he said.

"Don't you think you're headed down a destructive path?" Susan suggested. Kaya toyed with his fingers.

"Destructive path? Is this place, the Anchor House, a stop along my destructive path?"

I could tell that Susan was searching for the right way to answer him. "Keep going this way, Mr. Horton, and you're going to end up in jail or dead."

Myrtle always said the same thing to me: jail or death. What a thing to say to a child. People shouldn't put such negative words out into the universe like that. Don't they realize that they have the power to put our minds in jails and graves with their words? Don't they know that they kill our little spirits over and over again with that kind of talk about the worst kind of fate for us? They should tell us that we have infinite possibilities and that it is important that we try to do all we can to touch them before our lives end.

It was my turn to speak. "Hi," I cleared my throat and diverted my eyes from Kaya's pretty black face. "My name is Stacey Patton. I'm twelve. I'm here because my adoptive mother beat me all the time." How was Susan going to find fault with me?

"She did that to your face?" DeWayne frowned.

I gently brushed the side of my face. It didn't hurt anymore, and the scabs were just about dried up. But clearly I still had more healing to do before the scars faded. I tried not to look at anyone else. I felt embarrassed that they knew I was victimized. I was somebody else's prey. I was weak and had the scars to show it.

"Yo, we should find that bitch and tie her up and do what she did to you so she knows what it feels like." DeWayne punched his fist into the other palm.

"Word up," Kaya added. His smile arrested me.

I smiled back and then quickly dropped my eyes to my lap. Funny, so many times I had thought of tying Myrtle up and doing everything to her that she had ever done to me. But sometimes just thinking about all that drained me. I'd have to find every weapon she ever used on me: rolled-up newspapers, switches, the Bible, extension cords, metal hangers, hard combs, belts, broomsticks, and shoes. I'd even have to use my own hands and feet. And then I'd have to look through my file of memories to pull out every incident and every hateful thing she'd ever said and done to me. I didn't have that in me.

"Now that we've all gotten acquainted, we need to talk about this program. How can the Anchor House help you?" Everyone's eyes focused on Susan because this was the part we had been waiting for.

Susan explained to us that we would all be assigned a social worker from the Division of Youth and Family Services who would be in contact with us and work with our parents. Everyone would be involved with working out a plan that was in our best interests, she assured us. While we were in the shelter, we were expected to continue our lives by going to school, attending groups, going on outings, and meeting with our counselors every day.

"Anchor House is a temporary shelter," she explained. "Each of you has thirty days to stay here."

"What happens after thirty days?" Marisol asked.

"Well." Susan paused. "Hopefully you will return home. That's our number one goal."

"Back home?" DeWayne sighed. My body weakened. A sudden sick feeling came over me.

"Yes," Susan nodded. "Back home. It is not the goal of the system to break up families. We want to preserve families. Keep them together. Families are the cornerstone of our society."

"So a crackhead mama, deadbeat daddy, perverted uncle, drunk mama, a beat-the-shit-out-your-daughter mama, and a daddy that gave up on his son . . . that's family? That's the cornerstone of society?" asked DeWayne.

Kaya put in his two cents: "Children are the cornerstone of society. What's done to children determines what kind of society there's gonna be."

"How you gonna have a society with fucked-up kids that's gonna run the society one day?" DeWayne asked.

"Our hope," Susan continued, ignoring Kaya and DeWayne, "is that we can sit down with everyone in the family and work out a plan so that when you return home, things will work out."

"Do you think people can change in thirty days, Miss Susan?" I asked in a small voice.

"People can make a commitment to change," she responded. "It takes work on all sides."

"What if it's a person that has beat you and called you names for eight years? Do you really think they're gonna stop?" I asked.

"With professional help." She sounded so sure. But Myrtle was beyond professional help. Besides, she wasn't the kind of person who would seek somebody else's help. She would tell people that I was the one with the problem. All I had to do was do what she told me to do exactly the way she wanted, and she wouldn't have to beat me.

"With a miracle," Liz mumbled. "If they beat you once, they ain't gonna stop. They are gonna beat you again and again. They can't help it."

Liz was right. Myrtle would have to die and be born again with different chromosomes in order to change her ways. Myrtle listened to nothing but the fireplugs inside her. She was not going to stop to think before hitting me. She was never going to find anything positive to say about me. That demon inside her was just as old as she was, and I knew it was not going to leave in thirty days.

Suddenly I felt like I was in some swamp with heat hanging over it. The thought of having to return to 123 Hilltop Drive scared me. My stomach grew weak, and my bowels began to churn.

"It won't work out. It can't." My eyes teared.

"How do you know if you don't try?" asked Susan.

How could she save me from that place and then later suggest that returning was a possibility? Obviously she had seen something very wrong with those people. She didn't think it was a safe place for me to be. That's why I was at the shelter.

"I've tried. For eight years, I tried. I tried to live with beatings. With hurtful words. With somebody that doesn't love me. With somebody I have to call mama when I know she shouldn't be a dog's mama. You don't know what it's like to live with fear shut up in your bones every day of your life. You don't know when the next hit is coming, but you know it's gonna come. You don't know what it's like to have to peek around the corner before you turn it. And sometimes when you go to peek, the hand is right there, slapping you for peeking. You don't have to go home with me. You come to work and leave. What I go through every day doesn't stop."

"What if she promises never to hit you again?" Susan asked.

Was she really that naive?

"I can't remember how many times she's broken that promise," I answered. "And it's not just getting hit. It's all the mean things she says and does. I got scars on the inside of me too. Miss Susan, I can't go back there. I refuse to go back." My voice hardened. "If y'all send me back, I'll run away again."

I knew Susan couldn't take care of me. Nor could any of the other counselors there at the Anchor House. And neither could the social workers at the Division of Youth and Family Services. They couldn't possibly act as parents and nurture all of us who came into the system. We had too many problems, too many needs. But I was looking for new parents. I wasn't looking for the system to nurture me. I wanted them to listen to me and keep me safe, provide the necessary things for me to stay alive until I was old enough to do it for myself. I knew that system would fail me if they sent me back to Hilltop Drive.

"You have to give your parents another chance, Stacey," Susan urged.

I was frowning at her green eyes by then. "Another chance? For what? Another chance to say something mean to me? Another chance to break me down? Another chance to beat me?"

Susan's face darkened. She turned her wrist over to check the time. She had had enough of group for that day. "Okay, time's up. Group is over. Next Thursday. Same time. Same place." Everyone but me jumped up from their seat, glad that it was over. My eyes were still stuck on Susan's face.

"We don't need another chance, Susan. She doesn't need another chance to kill me. And I don't need a chance."

"You don't need a chance for what, Stacey?" She gave me a serious look. Now she wanted to listen.

I wanted to say, "A chance to kill her if she ever hit me again or tried to break my spirit." But I didn't want Susan to think I was dangerous, so I got up from the chair and left the room.

"A chance for what, Miss Patton?" Susan's words followed me out the door and around the corner.

ELEVEN

D uring slavery, black sexual activity was encouraged and even rewarded. The more sex the slaves had, the greater their chances were of producing offspring who would sustain and perpetuate the white man's cheap labor force. Slave women were often given incentives for producing children: lighter workloads, material benefits, and sometimes, freedom based on the number of children she bore. But the black female's sexuality was also demeaned on the plantation. Whites described black women and girls as hypersexual and jezebels.

Some white plantation owners alleged that black females solicited sexual attention from black and white males. To justify their sexual violations of slave women and girls, white men invoked such claims and stereotypes. In freedom, stereotypes of black sexuality helped justify new forms of discrimination and sexualized racial violence, including lynching and rape. Black sexuality became increasingly demonized and criminalized, and white society put black children's bodies under an erotically coded and ubiquitous gaze.

By the 1890s, politically minded white physicians began to publish a multitude of studies regarding the health and fate of black people. White male physicians, mostly from the South, argued that since the demise of slavery, the health of blacks had declined. They predicted that the black race would eventually become extinct because freedom had made them disease ridden, insane, criminal, and sexually deviant. But despite such grim forecasts coupled with the genocidal violence following Reconstruction, black people did not die out. They continued to live through desperate and trying times, and they continued to bring babies into the world.

While white racists committed themselves to preparing their progeny for the future, they demeaned and marginalized, and even attempted to exorcise the black child from society. The Darwinian concept of survival of the fittest was the language of the day. Whites became increasingly concerned with their own procreation and deterioration and protecting and purifying the race. The good breeding of "others" they deemed to be unfit and degenerate. Eugenicists and social scientists blamed blacks and other so-called inferior groups for a multitude of the nation's social problems, so they advocated marriage restriction between the races, social segregation, sterilization, and even castration of black men and boys. For African Americans, black babies represented a beacon of hope—a sign of racial survival. But for white society, the black child represented the antithesis to all ideals that whites celebrated: kindness, Christian compassion, purity, innocence, prenatal obligation, and custodianship of the future.

To justify their crimes against black humanity, whites used the language of social Darwinism and projected stereotypes of black sexuality. In most white minds, blacks were savages, beasts, rapists, oversexed, jezebels, harlots, and hypersexual. Unlike civilized whites, they embodied a sexual energy that they could not repress. Black children were not much different from black adults. Black boys and girls were denied a place in the powerful Western category of childhood innocence. Their bodies, including their genitals, were read as a terrain of meaning in American race making. In the minds of many whites, black bodies—their sexual nature, and sexual activities—were problematic.

Throughout the twentieth century, black parents tried to create a counternarrative about their children's character, bodies, sexuality, and destiny. What white people thought, said, and wrote about black boys and girls spilled over into black child-rearing practices. White people's gazes and ideas often motivated actions that had consequences for black children. In slavery and freedom, black parents kept secrets from their children largely to protect them so they wouldn't grow up too fast. Secrets would keep menstruation, bodily changes during puberty, childbirth, sex, incest, and rape closed subjects. Black parents wanted to keep their children innocent for as long as they could. This silence has had intergenerational consequences that have led to many sex-related pathologies in black families and communities, and it has also kept them from viewing their bodies and sexuality as sacred and beautiful. More important, blacks haven't learned how to view their sexual bodies as key to the survival of the black race.

When I was a little girl, Myrtle ordered me to keep my legs closed and

TWELVE

M y first day at my new public school wasn't as scary as I had expected it to be. For years, Myrtle had pumped my head up with stereotypes about kids who went to public schools. "They're fast," she said. "They grow up before their time. They ain't got no discipline. They're all roughnecks. Public schools don't help kids get ahead, especially not black kids. Public schools are just another way the white man helps to keep us down." She said that she sent me to private school all those years because private schools were the best. I would come out leaps and bounds ahead of my peers who went to public schools.

During my first day at the local high school, I kept some of Myrtle's pieces of advice in the back of my mind: "Keep your mouth shut. Speak when spoken to. Don't stick your two cents in where it don't belong. And keep your eyes down." That's how I was taught to deal with strangers in this big mean world. When I did lift my eyes, I saw fights break out of nowhere, a pregnant girl, and big black girls giving me hard, cold stares. In class, though, I was able to fully open my eyes and lift my head to absorb my lessons.

School was always a safe place for me, even when I felt odd and left behind. No one was going to whip me for a wrong answer. School was the only place where things seemed logical. But Catholic school was much different from Ewing high school. Incarnation was predominantly white with a handful of black students. Everybody wore uniforms. Everybody had to be smart to stay in the school. And everybody followed the rules and feared the school authorities.

There were all kinds of kids at my new school: black, Asian, Indian, Hispanic, and white. All kinds of dress styles and colors jumped out at me. I wasn't used to such nonconformity. There were rich kids, working-class kids, and welfare kids. Some were brilliant, others were smart but didn't want others to know it, and there were kids who would always have a hard time putting two and two together. Some kids didn't look as if they belonged in high school. They looked like men and women, old and experienced in things they shouldn't have been at their age.

The only places all those different groups of kids mixed were the cafeteria, hallways, and gymnasium. Classes were designed by a level system from one to five. Level 1 was for the Advanced Placement students—those who were likely going off to college. Level 2 was for the above-average kids who worked a little harder and still had good chances for college. Level 3 was for the average students who struggled a bit. Level 4 was below average, and level 5 was Special Ed. A large majority of the black students were in levels 3 and down. The level 1 and 2 classes were small and mostly all white and Asian. That's where I was placed, since I had transferred from a private school.

For the most part, I found my teachers to be helpful and geared toward helping us learn. The students in and outside my classes were curious about me. They wondered how I had lived in the same neighborhood with them all those years, but none of them had ever seen me before. They were also curious about my scars.

When I returned to the Anchor House at the end of the day Susan had a big Kool-Aid smile on her face. "Stacey." Her voice rang just as she put the phone back onto the receiver. She was sitting behind the big wooden desk in the main office when I checked in. Maybe she had some good news for me. "How was your first day at your new school?"

"Different," I answered, sounding blah and disappointed.

"Oh, I'm sure you'll adjust fine. You always do," she said. "You're one of the strongest people I know."

Maybe I did have a way of adjusting, being a chameleon. But Susan didn't know that I didn't want to spend my life changing my colors and adjusting to fit into situations that circumstance had placed me. A chameleon is always trying to survive. But you never really know what its true colors are. I wanted to change my world, not be changed by it. I wanted to decide my next move and pick out places that were tailored according to my needs and desires. As it stood, the world was the way it was, and I was simply in it.

Just as I turned to leave, Susan stopped me. "Oh, Stacey, we won't be having a session tonight."

"Good," I mumbled in a low and broken voice.

I didn't understand why Susan always thought we needed to talk. Maybe talking was a white thing. White people seemed like they always wanted to discuss something, drudge things up, figure things out, get things off their chests, and go to therapy. The way I had grown up, black people left things unsaid. There was no such thing as going to therapy. The folks I knew went to church and took whatever was on their hearts and minds to God in prayer. And if you didn't go to church, you drank. People laughed or they cried. Many times they laughed to keep from crying. People called on God in prayer, or they used God's name in vain to curse at the people in their world or at life itself. It was that simple. But there wasn't a whole lot of verbal analysis. Sometimes silence made the most sense.

"I have to leave early tonight. But Lydia, the night shift counselor, will be here if you need to talk. Right now I'm the only staff here, so I have to man the telephone," she said. "Everyone else went out for recreation. Kaya is the only resident who stayed behind."

Kaya. His name made my heart speed up. I quickly left Susan in that office with the phone ringing and followed the warbled sound of the television down the hall. As I stepped inside the community room, I saw Kaya sitting with his legs and mouth opened wide, fighting sleep. He looked funny. I thought he was going to snap his neck. When I giggled, his half-open eyelids lightened and registered that I was not part of his dream.

"I wasn't 'sleep," he lied, trying to collect himself. "I knew you was there."

"No, you didn't," I grinned. "I could have stuck somethin' in your mouth."

I dropped my backpack on the floor as he sat up straight, wiped the corner of his mouth, and threw me a delighted look.

"You're back," he said fixing his shirt.

"Yep." I sat down next to him, leaving a wide space between us on the couch.

"How was school?" His eyes still looked dazed. "Was you scared?"

"A little bit. But it was all right. Just different from what I'm used to. How was school for you?"

"I didn't go to school."

"You were sick today?"

"No." He paused. "I feel fine. I don't go to school," he said looking away from me like he was talking to some invisible person sitting next to him. "I got kicked out of school."

I leaned toward him. I wanted to know more. I had never met a kid who didn't go to school or one who had gotten kicked out of school. Getting kicked out of school was only something I had heard about. It seemed like the worst sin a kid could commit.

"Why?" I licked my lips, wanting to drink all his thoughts and words to come.

"I used to go to a private school." He scratched his cheek. "My dad wanted me to go there. I told him I hated it. So I stopped going, and they kicked me out."

"How come you didn't like private school? Was it because your daddy wanted you to go and you didn't?"

"Maybe that was part of the reason. I just didn't like the environment. The kids were uppity and fake with each other. The teachers got on my nerves. They can't teach me nothin' no way. I can stay at home and read books. All they teach you in school is about white people. What the fuck do I wanna learn about their asses for?"

I looked around the room to see if anybody was listening. I smiled because I had never heard a black youngster say such things.

"Shit," he huffed. "The world is black. The world is mostly people of color. Black people. Brown people. Yellow people. Red people. The world ain't white. White people are the minority. Not us! But we got to go to school to learn about their asses. To celebrate them. I'm sick of white man lies."

I said nothing. I didn't know what to say. He was right. All I had been taught was about white people. It seemed as if everybody else was invisible. Nobody else contributed anything to the world.

I saw the arrogance and defiance flying out of Kaya's mouth. But there was something appealing about that coming from him. Maybe I liked that aspect of Kaya because it didn't exist in me. I was too busy being humbled and broken down by people, to the point where I disobeyed my true self to be obedient.

I couldn't imagine not going to school. Not learning. If I didn't have something new to learn, I think my brain would have just atrophied and eventually crinkled up like a leaf in autumn. I needed school to escape the madness in my life, not to mention the fact that I had heard those "stay in school" speeches. How else was I going to make myself into something and redefine myself other than through my education and finding my real family?

A sense of worry loomed over me. If Kaya didn't go to school, he might not become anything. Didn't he know this? Didn't he realize that he was a black boy in America? Didn't he know he had everything against him? He was going to need every ounce of education he could get. Nobody respected a black person with no education. So what if it was all white man lies? Those lies were key to getting ahead in a country ruled by white people.

He abruptly changed the subject. "Your mama must be crazy. She must be crazy to do that to a pretty face like yours."

Pretty? Fireworks went off in my head. I felt uncomfortable the second that word came out of his mouth. He wouldn't stop tracing me with his heavy eyes. He had to be tired, I thought. But suddenly I was drawn into his eyes, like he was working magical powers with his pupils. The look he gave me made me feel like no one had ever looked at me directly before then.

"She's not my *real* mama." I tried to bring him back to the subject. "I'm adopted."

"Where's your real mama?" He kind of snapped out of his stare.

"I dunno." I shrugged my shoulders.

"Do you know her name?"

"No." I shook my head, wishing I did know her name or a thread of something about her. Was she tall? Short? Skinny? Fat? Did she have long or short hair? Was she dark, fair, or medium complexioned? Big eyes like mine? Just some minute detail would have made my dreams and imaginations of her a bit less incomplete.

"My mama is dead," he said, as I felt my heart drop in my chest. "My mama was the only somebody on earth that could tell me anything. Now she's gone. When she left me, something inside me died."

What dies in a person who's still alive? And how does the rest of their body compensate for the loss? How long can they go on living with that lifeless part of them just decomposing into dead weight?

"How did she die?" I asked.

"Cancer. She had a tumor in her brain. I watched her bones come through her skin. She lost all her hair. She had to wear diapers. They let her come home toward the end. There wasn't nothin' else they could do for her. And she didn't wanna die in some hospital. She wanted to die in the home she had made for me and my dad. I thought I could handle it. I knew it was gonna come soon. But then she started stinking before she finally died. I could smell her leaving me."

I tried to imagine what it smells like when somebody is dying. I tried to think of all the foul odors I had come across in my life. In my imagination, I mixed them. We both stared straight in front of us. When I looked over at Kaya, I could tell he was looking at his mama, maybe in her bed, her casket, or just standing in front of him dressed in something pretty. I wanted to ask him to ask his mama if she could see my mama walking around on earth somewhere.

"I felt her die, you know."

Something shook inside my chest. I swallowed hard. It got hot in there all of a sudden. I didn't think that kind of thing was possible. I knew you could see a person die; everything just stopped moving. You could hear their last words. But how could you feel their life stop?

"How—"

"My hand." He stopped my question and raised his right hand. It was trembling. He spread his fingers as wide as he could and turned his hand slowly, showing me the black and white side. "My hand was on her chest. And when she left, I knew. Her body went limp. And her eyes." He stopped. "They didn't blink no more. They was just frozen open. You never forget somethin' like that."

A voice startled us: "Just checking in on you two." Lydia, the night shift counselor, popped her head in the doorway. "I'm in the office if you guys need anything."

We acted like she wasn't there. I listened to her hard footsteps, each one loud and distinct. They quickly became slight taps and then faded altogether. I stole a glance at the rap video playing on the television screen. Myrtle would be mad that I was watching rap videos. Kaya's eyes were looking at me again. I felt them and tried to ignore him.

"You got a boyfriend, Stacey?"

"No," I said plainly. I was still thinking about his mama stinking up the house before she died and him feeling the life go out of her.

"Why not?" he sounded surprised.

"Am I supposed to have one?" I raised one eyebrow.

"Hell, yeah," he answered, looking at me like I was strange for thinking otherwise.

"Why?" I threw him a smirk.

"'Cause you pretty." He licked his lips. I liked the way his tongue left a shine on them.

"What about ugly girls?"

"They have boyfriends too." He smiled. "There is somebody for every-body."

"I don't have time for a boyfriend. I have to focus on my schoolwork."

"Who told you to say that?" he asked.

"What?"

"Somebody told you to say that," he insisted. "Did your mama tell you that?"

I held my breath and told the truth: "Yeah, she did."

"Brainwash," he huffed. "They say that kind of stuff because they don't think kids know what love is. They think the only kind of love we are sup-posed to know about is between our relatives and between God. Any other kind of love is supposed be the love of school and play. But I know better." He poked at his chest with his thumb. "Truth is, life ain't no good without lovin' somebody else, whether you thirteen or a hundred."

"I never had a boyfriend."

"You don't like boys?"

"No, it's not that," I said nervously. "I wasn't allowed to have a boyfriend or even talk about boys."

"That's too bad, 'cause you too pretty not to have a boyfriend."

Too pretty? He definitely hadn't fully awakened. I didn't believe him. Boys had always teased me about being bony. My flat chest. My little booty. Boys had always admired my strength—the fact that I could run as fast as they could, catch balls, shoot baskets, and even box with them. It was as if I was one of them. They didn't talk about me the way they talked about other girls. When I stood among other girls, they didn't notice me. Plus, boys I knew liked light-skinned girls or white girls—girls with big breasts and girls with big asses.

Myrtle never told me I was pretty, even when she put me in nice dresses and took me to the hairdresser to get my hair permed. When my school pictures came back, she always commented about a strand of hair being out of place or about that smile looking like a smirk. She didn't allow me to try on makeup or paint my nails. She didn't want me getting too grown or cute. All she ever called me was ugly, skinny, and funny looking. And when she constantly blackened my eyes, opened up my lips, made my nose bleed, I felt even more unpretty. And since I had permanent scars, I believed I could never be pretty, just disfigured.

But whenever Myrtle called me stupid, I didn't believe her because I was an A student. In fact, I knew much more than she did, and she knew it. That's probably why she started to say, "You got book smarts, but you ain't got good common sense." Common sense, if she really had any, was all she'd ever acquire. I didn't believe her when she said I wasn't going to amount to anything without her and G. Deep inside me, there was too much drive. I can't tell you where it came from, but I had it. I had refused to let her be right. But when she said I wasn't an attractive girl, I believed her. As I sat there with that beautiful brown boy telling me I was a pretty girl, I couldn't believe him because I was certain that Myrtle was the only person on earth who knew the truth about how I looked.

"Are you a virgin?" Kaya looked at my lap. Something pierced the middle of my body. I was uncomfortable with his question. I felt vulnerable. Put on the spot. But I couldn't let him see that. So I answered his question with a question.

"Are you?"

"No," he answered quickly. I felt like I was missing out on something. I was still a little girl.

"Yes," I answered shyly, looking down at my lap.

"Have you ever kissed a boy?"

I looked away from him and shut my eyes. I remembered feeling prickly stubble and mustaches on my soft skin. Hot breath. Coffee. Double Mint gum. Cough drops. Peppermint candy. Slimy wet lips covering not only my lips but my nose too, all at once. I hated the way their juices stayed on my lips, even after their kisses ended. My uncles, adoptive grandfather, and adoptive father made me cringe each time they pinned their lips on me without my permission. They kissed their wives, sisters, and my cousins the same way. There was something sick about that kind of close interaction between family members. I couldn't figure it out then, and I still haven't. I just know it didn't seem right.

"No," I said softly.

I knew Kaya wasn't talking about the kind of kisses I grew up with. He was talking about something more intimate. But there was that little boy from East Orange.

———

I don't remember his name or what he looked like. Today he is just a little brown blur in my mind. He lived next door to my foster home. "Lady," was what he called me, even when I didn't know that little girls grew up to become ladies. I thought kids stayed kids forever and big people just came out the way they did. The little boy told the other kids I was his girlfriend. We had play weddings through the fence separating our back yards. My ring was something we found off the ground and bent into a little circle around my finger.

My foster mother would throw bags of lollipops down from the window as we played. I was in charge of giving everyone candies. If I had a cherry lollipop and he had grape, he refused to eat it. He traded the grape lollipop with somebody else. It was never a problem with the other kids because they realized his obsession over me. He wanted his world to be like mine.

"Lemme taste yours, Lady."

I always frowned. "That's nasty. I got spit on mine. There's germs. You can't share a lollipop."

"Sure you can," he insisted.

"Why do you wanna lick my lollipop?"

"To see if it tastes like mine."

I stared at his juiced-up lips and then back at my lollipop. And then I held my lollipop in front of my face and looked at it and then at him. I reluctantly slid the glossy candy through the opening in the gated fence and watched it disappear into his mouth. I never wanted to put it back in my mouth knowing his juices were now on it.

"Oomph, it tastes good," he swore up and down. There was too much of the lollipop to throw away, so I just popped it back inside my mouth, hoping his juices didn't drastically change the taste or that I'd catch cold or turn green or, worse, die.

Days before I left the foster home for good, he held onto the gated fence for dear life and begged me for a kiss. I thought it was the nastiest thing to kiss boys then.

"Please, Lady. Please," he whined and pressed his whole body against the fence. "Please, just one. Just one little kiss."

I looked at his sincere face and felt sorry for him, so I pushed my lips through a space in the fence and quickly touched my lips against his. When I backed away, his lips were still puckered out in the same spot and his eyes were still shut. It was like he tried to savor what we had just shared for as long as he could. He slowly opened his eyes, returned his lips back to the rest of his face, and said, "Thank you, Lady."

I remembered how we would sit with that gated fence between us for hours. I listened to him talk about Spider Man and the Incredible Hulk. I'd ask him why he thought they never showed us Charlie's face from that show *Charlie's Angels*. He wanted to know if Tom and Jerry or Sylvester and Tweety would ever be friends.

Sometimes we just sat quietly, wishing we could be on the same side of the fence. When he was on punishment, which he always was, he couldn't come out to play. He'd hang from his bedroom window and call to me. I'd watch him roll up his sleeves and show me the little knots in his arms he called muscles.

"Look, Lady." He'd poke out his chest and flex his arms. "Do you like them? I did push-ups for you."

"Yes," I'd say. "They are bigger than they were yesterday." We'd giggle, and he'd ask me to marry him again. We had a play wedding sometimes more than once a week. It was always just as exciting each time.

I should have asked his name. I wonder if he remembers me, our kisses, cherry lollipops, Spider Man, the Incredible Hulk, Charlie's Angels, Tom and Jerry, the push-ups he did for me? The way he tried to impress me with the little knots in his arms that he called muscles? Where is he now? What kind of man is he now?

"No," I opened my eyes and looked at Kaya. "I never kissed a boy like you."

His body heat jumped on me. I could smell the coconut oil sheen in his cornrows. I sat perfectly still, watching him inch closer and closer to me. I could smell soap around his neck. I heard him breathe. He sounded as if he wanted to inhale me.

My palms got sweaty and trembled. His lips softly pressed against my cheeks. Again, and again, and again. Each time his peachy lips touched my skin, I felt little electric impulses traveling to other parts of my body. Though I felt so good on the outside, I felt as if I was sinning. His small breaths tickled my ear. I sat on my hands thinking what kind of magic this was. Kaya stuck the tip of his tongue in my ear. It sounded like a wet swab cleaning out my canal. I jumped at first, but then I wanted more.

Our eyes met. He knew he had touched a nerve in me. I was caught up in some rapture, someplace I had never gone before. I wasn't even thinking about Miss Lydia down the hall, my algebra homework, the short time I had left at the Anchor House, or the slight ache underneath my left eye. All my problems and worries began to fade from my consciousness.

Kaya kissed my cheek again. Then he wet his tongue and dragged it behind my ear, inside the lobe, and down that long curve between my ear and shoulder. The tip of my nose brushed his. His silky fingertips traced the outline of my lips, and then his hungry mouth collided with mine. I wasn't sure how I was supposed to do that right. I thought about how they do it in the movies. They usually shift their heads in all directions, press hard against each other, and breathe all heavy. Sometimes they look as if they are going to swallow each other whole.

And then he did the unexpected: he slipped his tongue in my mouth. I drew back, shocked. I was thinking germs. Nasty. I gave him a crazy look, wanting to spit his juice out of my mouth. But he was smooth.

"Tongue kiss," he whispered. "This is what people do. This is part of the kissing game." He drew into me again.

I loosened my lips and then the muscles in my jaws. I tried not to think about the exchange of spit going on. Instead, I focused on his tongue and pretended it was some chilled piece of fruit. Cantaloupe.

Still sitting on top of my hands, I started to get used to that tongue-kissing thing. Those electric impulses got sharper and more intense. Kaya's hands got involved. He slowly unbuttoned my shirt. My heart was racing. I wanted to stop him. I didn't want to stop him. I didn't want him to see my breasts because I thought he'd be disappointed. But when his entire hand cupped one, he shoved his tongue deeper into my mouth and let out a moan. I guess he wasn't disappointed. Still, I couldn't lose my feeling of disloyalty. No one had ever felt my breasts—no one other than myself and Myrtle. They belonged to her, my master, not to this black boy.

Kaya's slender fingers grabbed the inside of one of my thighs. I felt like butter, melting in his hands. I shouldn't have been letting him touch me like that, I thought. This was a trick of the devil. I was acting irresponsibly.

Kaya grabbed my wrist and freed my hand. Slowly, he moved my hand to his lap. His pants were unzipped. I was baffled. When did he unzip his pants?

He stopped kissing me. I couldn't move my hand. I didn't know what to make of all that or what I was supposed to do. I had never touched a penis or seen one up that close—that long, that hard, that ugly-looking, smelling weird.

"You wanna suck it?" he asked coolly.

Had he lost his mind? "What?" I frowned.

"You wanna gimme some head?"

First he stuck his tongue in my mouth, and now he wants me to put my mouth on his prick?

"Nigga, please." I frowned as he showed me his teeth. "I ain't puttin' my mouth on that. Nasty boy."

"You might like it." He smiled harder as I still held on to it like some thin pole. "You don't have to do that," he said. "Just touch it nice and soft."

As I stroked his penis up and down, I waited for it to change color or something. I was getting bored, but he seemed to like it. He kept raising his hips and telling me to go faster and saying, "Yeah, just like that."

Kaya's breathing got staggered. His right hand left the back of my neck and found its way to the inside of my pants. He softly brushed my vagina. He wasn't rough like Myrtle. I felt his hands inch lower, my heat warming his cold fingers. A gasp escaped my mouth as he touched that secret place. I opened my legs wider. His fingers were wet now.

"There it is," he whispered. "So wet. So tight."

The coconut oil sheen in his hair was heavy in my nostrils by then. His middle finger slipped past the folds of skin and entered me so gently that at first I didn't feel it. Then he pushed against me hard. My mouth tried to scream, but he covered my lips with his. He swallowed what I tried to say. I jerked my head away and pushed his shoulders back.

I took my word back out of his mouth. "Stop!"

I grabbed his strong, stiff wrist and pulled his wet fingers away from me. He looked confused, like something went terribly wrong. "What?" he asked.

"I can't do this," I mumbled. "I just can't do this."

"Are you scared?" he gave me a half-smile.

"Yes," I answered in a shaky voice. I stood up to fix my clothes. He was still sitting there with his legs wide open, his penis standing up and poking its head out of his pants.

"It's okay," he said in a reassuring voice. He looked at the same fingers he tried to thrust inside me. I paused and looked at them too. I watched his mouth meet his fingers. He wrapped his lips around his fingers and slowly slid them out again.

I frowned. "You're nasty."

"Why am I nasty?"

"Do you know what goes on down there?" I cringed.

"Yeah. And? I just wanted a taste of you," he said swallowing hard. "I wouldn't hurt you. And I wouldn't make you do anything you didn't wanna do. There's many girls out there, you know."

"And?" I shot at him.

"Most of them are too nasty to taste." I expected him to say something totally different. "I don't mean just tasting what's between your legs. Or your lips. Or the cocoa butter you use on your skin. I mean tasting who you are. Tasting what it's like to be in your world. Tasting what's inside of you. I'm picky about what I put in my mouth. I only like sweet things on my tongue. And sweet things in my life."

"What?" I smirked. "You think you're a black Shakespeare now?"

"No." He gave me a serious look. "I'm just trying to get my point across. You shouldn't be so defensive. Not everybody in the world is out to do you wrong."

I looked down at his lap again. His penis had curled up. I focused on the chiseled muscles in his stomach and the trail of hair leading from his navel down to his crotch. "Why don't you put that away," I said, walking out of the room.

I felt like a scared little girl. It wasn't Kaya's fault. He did nothing wrong. Truth was, I couldn't allow myself to enjoy that experience. There was a ghost sitting between us cracking her knuckles the entire time. It was Myrtle.

She seemed to rise up out of the floor like a witch. I saw her face before me, smirking and frowning. The rough timbre of her voice, and the tricks of her speech blew up in my ears. That Lifebuoy smell overtook Kaya's sweet coconut aroma.

And I got scared. Scared of all the unknown and unsaid things about sex. Scared of being called a baby having a baby. Scared of becoming a statistic that the white news media talked about all the time. Scared that people would think I was some kind of loose black girl. Scared to embarrass myself, Myrtle, and my race.

How was I still so scared of Myrtle during that intimate moment with Kaya? Myrtle was across town in the suburbs. I was there in the heart of the inner city. And yet she still had her hands on me. How was I going to free my body from what she thought of me? How would I free my body from what she thought white people thought about me and from what I thought of me?

THIRTEEN

I often wondered what it meant to be a black father during slavery and freedom. How did notions of black fatherhood change over time? For black fathers and their children, notions of fatherhood were elastic. During slavery, white slave owners denied black men authority over their wives and children, as well as the ability to exert their manhood in various ways. Still, many black males maintained strong familial bonds by trying the best they could to be protectors and providers. Emancipation elevated black men to a new status. They could now assume the role of provider and protector in their homes inasmuch as racial segregation and terrorism would allow.

Irresponsible. Lazy. Uneducated. Uncaring. Hypermasculine. Hypersexual. These are some of the negative stereotypes of black men. These traits, however, are not genetic or cultural attributes of African Americans, and they do not apply to the vast majority of these men. They represent fundamental problems within American society on the whole. The challenges and struggles of black fatherhood cannot be discussed out of the context of slavery, serial poverty and discrimination, Jim Crow terrorism, and African cultural values and gender roles.

As a little girl, I did not have intense longings for closeness with my adoptive father. My longings were for my biological mother rather than my father. G had fulfilled at least some of my expectations of a father, whereas Myrtle satisfied nearly none. The most courageous and heroic black men presented to me as a child were all dead—men like Martin Luther King Jr., Malcolm X, Huey Newton, Booker T. Washington, George Washington Carver, and Langston Hughes. Other larger-than-life black male figures were men like Muhammad Ali, Michael Jordan, Magic Johnson, Jesse Jackson, and other entertainers. But I didn't know real-life black men like those in my world.

My favorite movie, Alice Walker's *The Color Purple*, was inspirational to me for so many reasons. The main character, Celie, struggles with self-esteem, family relations, racism, and physical and sexual abuse. She is strong and resilient. The black men in the film are abusive. Ignorant. Buffoons. Emasculated. After seeing that film and seeing black men like those in my own world, I gave up on black males. I didn't respect them. I feared them, even looked down on them. I felt they were useless. They simply made babies. They didn't act like fathers. They seemed better off absent. The film seemed to intersect with my real views of black men.

During my late teens, I began to listen to rap music. The artists began calling black women bitches, tricks, hoes, and all kinds of other degrading names. They called each other niggas. They glorified illicit drug selling, gambling, hustling, pimping, and black-on-black violence. Yes, I danced to the music because it sounded good. But I was always troubled by the consequences that such popular expressions would have on black boys and girls, women, and black men themselves.

On the whole, my view of black fathers and black men in general was largely shaped by the negative imagery provided by whites and black women. The black women in my world were constantly critical of absent and present black men. They often cut black men down. Sometimes they did not allow black men to be fathers. I felt that black mothers often expected more of their daughters and less of their sons. Perhaps they believed that black women and girls had better opportunities than black men and boys. Maybe black females are less threatening to white society. Nevertheless, I would have to come to know black males on their own terms.

FOURTEEN

Life in the Anchor House made me feel that I really was at the bottom of the ocean, where the big fish eat the little fish. At any moment, I expected to be crunched, chewed, swallowed up, and forgotten. Time continued to flow indifferently above my head. Some days moved slow as a snail. I hated sitting idly by waiting for the State of New Jersey's child welfare system to work for me. My case was important and of the highest priority, I thought. But little did I know that I was merely one among so many other caseloads sitting on my social worker's desk. As the seconds ticked away, it became increasingly hard for me to fight my urge to get up and run from that place. I had no idea where I'd run to or end up. But at least I'd be satisfied knowing that I was going somewhere other than from one room to another in that shelter, only to sit on my hands and wait for change to come.

I watched the faces of the other children around me harden, break out with pimples, give in, and crack. The once-dim lights in their eyes slowly turned to specks. Their speedy and defensive lips grew silent. DYFS, that almighty New Jersey child welfare system, didn't seem to care. Black kids. Puerto Rican kids. Arab kids. Poor white kids. We had no individual identities to our social workers. To them, we were just case numbers, statistics, and problems. Their persistent goal for us was to find a placement.

With eight days left at the Anchor House, I faced the possibility of being placed in a permanent foster home or group home situation. I also risked being sent back to my adoptive parents' home. I found it hard to breathe during all that waiting. I felt like I had man-sized fists lodged in my chest. Sometimes I even lifted my shirt to look for knuckles poking out. Instead, I saw my ribs through my skin. I began to look more and more like that plastic skeleton sitting in the back of my human physiology class. With each passing day, I lost more and more weight. Worry, anxiety, and fear robbed me of my appetite. I feared that if I kept losing weight, my new breasts would suck inward or deflate. I needed my breasts. They were the only sign that I was slowly progressing toward being a woman, leaving childhood and powerlessness behind.

I hadn't heard from my social worker at DYFS in weeks, but I knew her name. Helen something. And I knew she had been in contact with my adoptive parents and Susan. Susan kept hinting that they had come up with a plan. Before my time was to end at the shelter, my adoptive parents, Susan, Helen, and I would have a meeting. Myrtle would agree never to hit me again. If she got angry, she would promise to walk out of the house. Picture that? Would the devil ever walk out of his hell? And how did they expect me to trust her promise never to hit me again? I had heard that so many times throughout the years when nobody else made her utter the promise. Susan said that G promised to be responsible for making sure we all went to family therapy once a week. I didn't want promises. I didn't want therapy. I wanted to be cut off from them.

"Our goal is not to break families apart," my social worker would tell me. "Our goal is to keep families together."

"Even families that don't work anymore?" I asked.

She said that I had to work harder and be patient. Time would make things right between my adoptive parents and me. Did they really think I was going to change my mind about going back to 123 Hilltop Drive? Did they think I was stupid? Didn't they know this was how kids ended up dead? DYFS was always quick to close abuse cases and move on to the next without having solved the problems. I had read those stories in the papers about kids who died while social workers and neighbors knew what was going on. It wasn't until the child was dead that people acknowledged there was something wrong with the system. I couldn't allow that story to be written about me.

I didn't know what rights I had as a minor in my situation, and no one would tell me. People just kept saying that I needed to be cooperative, to work with the system. They even threatened me with talk about being put in a detention center for running away. But I knew better: detention centers were for kids who broke rules, and I was just trying to protect myself. Regardless, the people from DYFS and the Anchor House made me feel that I was being left out of my own life. They made decisions for me without asking what I thought. They defined what my best interests were.

In the system, my peers and I were treated as if we didn't possess a clear and precise notion of our own situations and feelings. We were simply impartial players in the drama of adult relationships or mere bystanders waiting for our destiny to be shaped by those bureaucratic hands. That was the plight of being a child, a third-class citizen with no voice. I knew that then, but I couldn't articulate it the way I just did. Ten years as an adult with a great deal of reflection has helped me explain that era of my past. I just knew it was unfair being a twelve-year-old child in a world where adults failed me and weren't held responsible.

Susan closed the door behind her. It was time for another one of our daily sessions. She plopped down on the couch in front of me and lifted her legs one at a time, snuggling them into her Indian style. She threw back her hair and let out a long breath before giving me a cheerful smile. I couldn't understand how she seemed so calm. All the molecules inside me were still jumping up and down.

"So, Miss Patton," she toyed with the top of her shoe. "What do you want to talk about today?"

I looked at her and said nothing. I didn't want to do the talking. I wanted her to tell me what was going to happen tomorrow.

"How do you feel?" she asked plainly.

I lied: "Fine."

She looked at me as if she was expecting me to say more. My eyes moved away from her and fixed themselves on the pearl-colored wall. There was silence for a moment, interrupted by somebody laughing down the hall.

Susan didn't know what to say. She probably didn't even want to have that session. Meeting with me every day was merely part of her daily requirements so she could write down in the logbook that she had done her job. She looked at the wall and then back at me repeatedly, as if she was trying to see what I saw, trying to figure out why I found its blankness so interesting.

I hated those games that counselors and social workers played. They wanted to see what we saw and know what it was like to live in our minds. Why? I didn't know. Maybe they were trying to play social minstrelsy. Maybe they had some sort of imagined connection with us. They wanted to know what it was like to be confused, powerless, and silenced so they could say they understood our plight. They wanted us to believe that they were on our side, but they couldn't be, because they were adults. Maybe they expected that through their imagined connection with us, they could figure out themselves or explain things about their own childhood.

"You have trouble looking people in the eyes, don't you, Stacey?"

I was offended. She made me feel that something was wrong with me.

"No." I felt my chest rise and fall again, the fists still poking somewhere inside me. "I can look people in the eyes." I proved it to her by looking at her eyes for as long as it took me to answer her. I searched for that spot on the wall again. And then I picked some place on the floor to stare at.

"You know, the eyes are a dead giveaway to the soul," she said. I really should have been given a dollar for every time someone said that to me. I would have gotten enough money to get out of that shelter on my own.

"Perhaps you're afraid of showing people your eyes because you think they might see through you. Those eyes might tell people that you're really not fine. That you're scared. Sad. Lonely. Angry."

I kept my eyes on the floor because I wanted to, not because I didn't want to look at Susan and listen to her talk about what she saw in my eyeballs. While she was wasting time trying to read my soul, she could have been working on a solid plan for my future.

"Stacey." She massaged the arm of the couch. "Do you ever talk about your feelings or what's on your mind?"

"No," I mumbled, and shifted in my seat.

"Why not?" Her head tilted to one side.

"Nobody ever asks me how I feel or what's on my mind."

"Don't you think they'd like to know?"

"Nope." I watched her draw her head back against the wall behind her.

"What makes you think that?"

"People got their own problems. Why would they want to hear about mine?" Myrtle had always told me that I shouldn't complain about the bad things in my life, even though she would have sworn I didn't have a bad life. She said that just when I thought I had it bad, there was always somebody else out there who had it worse.

"But it's still important to express what's on your mind."

"I'm a child. A child ought to stay in a child's place, right? A child should speak only when spoken to. A child should keep her two cents to herself. A child should be seen and not heard."

Susan didn't realize that I had grown quite comfortable with those rules about my place as a child. For years, I sat among grown folks watching their manners, listening to their gossip, soaking up their perspectives, living through their memories as they recalled them, stealing some wisdom. But I was smarter than they thought, even though I was not allowed to comment. I had answers sometimes. Though I was expected to keep my lips pinned shut, I knew that what I had to say was worth more than two cents. I held on to every spoken syllable. In my mind, I decided who was wise and who was absurd. In my head, I'd say, "I will grow up and make more sense than these people."

"Do you ever feel scared, Stacey?"

"Yes."

"When?"

"When I see lightning or hear thunder," I said, thinking of all the times Myrtle would turn off the lights during a storm and tell me to be quiet. She said we were supposed to shut up and be still during a storm because God was at work. I usually hid under my bed and prayed. Sometimes I cried with each boom that shook the windows and walls. I took back all the bad things I ever thought about Myrtle.

"When else are you scared?"

"When I'm about to get a beating."

Susan's blonde hair gathered behind one shoulder now had a brown tint. Her mouth was turned down. I glanced out the window at the crooked corner across the street heavy with Puerto Ricans.

"What makes you sad, Stacey?"

"Why would I wanna think about what makes me sad? I don't feel like being sad right now," I frowned.

"It's important to get in touch with your feelings so you'll recognize them and get control over them."

I didn't feel that I was ever out of control. But just to cooperate with her, I reached into myself and pulled back layers, like peeling a raw onion. I never thought about sadness. It's not someplace I wanted to be. I knew physical pain. I knew fear. It all made me cry. But I never really stopped to think about how sadness was different from those feelings that came as a response to physical pain or fear of danger.

"Sometimes my adoptive mother beats me so bad that she leaves big, open welts on my skin. They don't close up right away. I have to go to bed and try to find some way to sleep right. It's hard though. It's hard to find a space on my body where there are no welts. The sheets hurt me so bad."

"The sheets?" She looked confused.

"The juices oozing out of my welts stick to the sheets."

"Ugh," she gasped, as if she was feeling sorry for me. I didn't want her to feel sorry for me. I didn't want her to be sad for me. I wanted her to be angry. I wanted her to realize my plight. She needed to hear the gruesome details so she could understand me.

"I just lie there looking up at the ceiling until I know she's asleep and it's safe for me to cry. That's when I'm sad. It's not the beatings or the clingy sheets that make me sad. I'm used to all that. I expect it to happen over and over again. I get ready for it. I don't quite feel normal if she's not yelling, in a bad mood, or beating me. I expect to face a war every day of my life. What makes me sad is missing my real mother. I get sad because I can't see her or touch her. I don't know where she is or if I'll ever find her. The thing that makes me saddest is not knowing if she loves me."

I saw water in her eyes. Now she picked a spot on the floor. When she lifted her eyes again, the pearl-colored wall behind my head looked quite interesting to her.

"Anger." She gritted her teeth. "Do you ever get angry?"

"No."

"Never?" She didn't believe me.

"Never."

"Impossible." She gave me a half smile.

I gave her a cold stare back.

"Everybody gets angry," she insisted.

"I'm not everybody."

"Yeah, but you're still human. It's a natural human reaction to get angry," she said. "I get angry," she added.

"Not me," I insisted, shaking my head. "I never yell. I don't curse at people. I don't hit people. I don't say mean things. I don't break things."

"Those are not the only ways to get mad, Stacey. People can get angry without hurting others, without being violent, without losing control. You have to find positive ways to channel your anger. There's nothing wrong with getting angry. If you don't let it out, then it turns inward into depression. Eventually you'll turn on yourself."

Susan said that anger is like a flame. It gives us energy to fight back when someone is trying to hurt us. All the times Myrtle hurt me, I had no choice but to let the incidents go and forget about them. I had to act like what she did to me didn't harm me on the inside. I made excuses for her.

"You ever watch nature shows?" she asked.

"Yeah," I answered, with hyenas, giraffes, elephants, and rhino humping scenes flashing across my head.

"You know the lion is the king of the jungle, right?"

"Uh-huh."

"The lion has a powerful roar," she said. "It roars to send out a message that it is protecting its territory. The lion roars because it senses danger coming. He has to send his enemies a message. So he shows his big teeth. Sometimes deep down inside, he may really be afraid, but his enemies will never know. All they see is the lion's strength and they hear that roar. He shows his power and that he will stand up for what is his. He will protect himself, and he is certain he will not be defeated. His anger at a potential threat to his existence allows him to be assertive and stand up for himself. You have to learn how to do the same thing, Stacey. You have to hold your head up. Look people in the eyes. Speak up for yourself. You can't be passive. You can't be a victim for the rest of your life. You can't let people abuse you."

Susan made a lot of sense, but she confused me sometimes. One minute she seemed like she was on my side, telling me to stand up for myself and that I shouldn't let anybody do me dirty. And then the next minute, she sounded like the other folks who were part of the system. I didn't know if I could trust her fully, because she too was part of the system when the hour ended and the office door opened.

Susan was the only person who had ever told me that I had the right to roar, to get angry, to stand up for myself when I think somebody is doing me wrong. Most adults in my life regarded that as disobedience and rebelliousness. I always doubted myself and thought that I had something to do with people mistreating me. The way I grew up, I had been made to think that anger couldn't occupy anyplace inside a child's body. Any sign of it meant that the devil must be beaten out.

"I ain't no lion, Susan."

"What are you then?"

"More like a little fish," I said.

"A fish?"

"Uh-huh."

"Why a fish?"

"I'm a little fish swimming around fish much bigger than me. Big fish eat little fish, and the ocean don't care."

"Don't be so hopeless, Stacey. You must survive," she insisted. "You have a purpose. You haven't come this far for nothing. You have amazing strength for someone so young. I know that right now, you can't see beyond your situation. You have to learn to free your mind and transcend these walls, your adversaries, and the odds in front of you."

I tried. I really tried hard to see past my situation at that moment. I wanted to find some patience and hope, but uncertainty was blinding me. That panic made me wonder if there was any meaning or worth in this life. I felt like a mixture of tiny bits and shards trying desperately to piece myself together.

During my session with Susan, I began to feel needy, like an infant crying out to be held and loved. I had this intense need to reach out to Myrtle and G for some of their brand of love and nurture. Where that feeling was coming from, I couldn't tell. It was strange. I was an abused child yearning for my adoptive parents' love. Why was that happening?

I started hearing Myrtle's voice in my head again. She was saying, "No one will love you like me or your father. You cannot survive in this world without us. Your life won't be worth two cents without me or your father."

I began to doubt whether I could survive without Myrtle and G. For eight years, my hopes for the future and need for love had been solely invested in them. But the reality was that I could never realize my hopes and dreams with them. And I could never find the real meaning of love through them either. So there I was, feeling like I did when I was five. I was alone again. I felt like I didn't belong anywhere or to anybody.

Our session ended promptly at the end of the hour. Susan left me there in the room, alone. My thoughts shifted away from my problems to the pretty brown boy—Kaya. Where was he? What was he doing? Was he happy?

The pretty brown boy had left the shelter the day before. My nostrils still sifted the air for traces of coconut oil sheen. I kept expecting to hear his laugh, to see him smile when I entered the room, for him to beg me to sneak in the bathroom with him so he could steal a quick kiss. His father had come to pick him up. Kaya looked like a younger version of his dad. The older Mr. Horton had bushy eyebrows like Kaya, only thicker. He was about five inches taller. He too had that calm, smooth, soft-spoken manner. They both looked tired. Tired of fighting. Tired of worrying about each other. Tired of being stubborn. When they greeted each other in the community room, Kaya's dad put his strong hand on his son's shoulder and looked deep into his eyes as if he was looking for his son's heart through his pupils.

"My boy. I-I mean, my little man," he corrected himself.

I guess his father figured that when a child leaves home and then returns, that child is no longer a boy or girl. The time spent away from home, away from the parent, turns a child into a little man or little woman.

"Me and you are gonna work this thing out together," Mr. Horton said, both hands gripping Kaya's shoulders. "We gonna lead and follow each other."

Lead and follow. I couldn't believe his father was willing to follow his son. How could a child lead a grown man? Mr. Horton essentially swallowed his pride to acknowledge that he too made mistakes and didn't know everything despite being a grown man, a father. He was asking for his son's help while promising to be there to support him into manhood.

"Son." He cleared his throat. I knew Mr. Horton was about to say something else profound, so I tuned out the rest of the room. "People say that kids today are a handful of trouble. They say children are a liability to society. But I been thinking. Children are in trouble because their parents are in trouble. While you was away, I had to think about how I was in trouble and how I let my trouble affect you. And I put my foot down. I decided that I'm not gonna let some institution raise my son. There ain't no substitute for my love, son. I brought you into this world, and I'm gonna do all I can to keep you here and make sure nothin' takes you out."

Myrtle used to say, "I brought you in this world, and I'll take you out." Stupid. She didn't bring me into this world. She wasn't my real mother. But I did fear the fact that she was perfectly capable of taking me out. It was a power trip, I guess. They gave life, so they had the power to take it away.

"I felt helpless, son," Mr. Horton continued.

"Me too." Kaya dropped his eyes to the floor.

"But now we can be men." Mr. Horton grabbed his son's face with both hands. "We can help each other. Your mama is gone. We can't bring her back, son. And God knows I wanna bring her back so bad sometimes. It hurts you that she's gone. Hurts me too. 'Specially 'cause I know she won't see you become a man. We can't do nothin' for her except be strong men for each other. That's what she would want us to do. Be strong." He gave Kaya a mild shake.

And then Mr. Horton did something I had never seen a father do with a son: he kissed him on his cheek. Even Kaya seemed stunned. But I think that right then, Kaya knew his father loved him. Love lets a child know that nothing in this world could destroy him, and though I didn't have a father like Mr. Horton who had the capacity to articulate his feelings and express them, it was important for me to see that interaction between Mr. Horton and his little man. I was inspired.

Before he walked out the front door, Kaya came over to me. He didn't say a word, and I didn't know what to say to him. There was nothing I could say to equal his father's words. I surely didn't want to say good-bye, but I had to. I wouldn't have minded crossing paths with that pretty boy any day. But I certainly didn't want to do it in a place like the Anchor House or someplace worse. I wanted him to go with his father, be happy and become a beautiful man. He gave me that smile but was acting kind of shy, like it was our first time meeting each other. Kaya held up a folded sheet of paper between two fingers. He gently grabbed my hand and placed it in my palm.

"Miss Patton." He licked his lips the way I liked. "You are a pretty girl."

He leaned forward. I thought he was going to kiss my face. Surely that would get me in trouble with the night shift counselor, who was standing in the corner. No physical contact was allowed between the residents.

When his lips passed my cheek, they pressed gently against my earlobe. "Any motherfucker who tells you different, lemme know and I'll beat their ass."

I giggled, and he walked away without giving me a last look. I watched his father push the door open and walk out with his son. I immediately opened the piece of paper. It read:

FOR A TASTE CALL ME 393-1791 KAYA HORTON.

The next evening I held that little piece of paper in my hand as I sat in my room. It was slightly wrinkled. I had folded and unfolded it many times, trying to figure out if I should call him. I studied his handwriting. It was neat for a boy. I saw his pretty face again, the way he half-smiled at me, the way his eyes went through me. And I remember how he walked out that door, leaving me behind in that ocean. I didn't like the way that cold air slapped me in the face when the door slammed behind him. I didn't like standing there in the middle of the floor, alone.

"And so it goes again," I mumbled to the walls, and pinched the piece of paper into a small ball, aimed it at the trash can next to the pile of dirty clothes, and threw it.

I had opened myself up. I let down my guard. I thought I made a connection. He left me. He walked out the door and left me. Just like everybody else, he left me, cold and alone. How could I have been so stupid to think that in a shelter full of kids with problems, I could have found someone to stay in my life? I had almost forgotten what that place was. It was a shelter, a place to take cover until the storm was over. All of us in there had a different kind of storm, and when the storm passes over, we all were supposed to leave and go back to our worlds. Teens came there, and they went. Life there was temporary.

"Stacey!" Somebody's screaming voice just about broke something inside me. My first response was to get nervous, like I had done something wrong, like I was in trouble or about to be whipped by Myrtle. "Phone!" the voice yelled.

My heart was still beating fast like a snare drum. I wondered who could be on the phone for me. Who could be calling me? Nobody had called me for the past twenty-six days I had been there. The only contact I had with people outside this shelter had been with classmates and teachers at school.

The drumbeat in my chest slowed as I approached the black receiver dangling from the silver body of the pay phone. There was a sign above the phone that read: "15 MINUTE TIME LIMIT PER PHONE CALL. THANKS, STAFF."

When I picked up the cold receiver and pressed my ear against it, I was still thinking that maybe somebody made a mistake. No one ever called me. No one called me at the shelter. No one ever called me at 123 Hilltop Drive. I wasn't allowed to talk on the phone. I suddenly heard Myrtle's voice enter my head as I parted my lips to say hello to whoever was waiting on the other end: "You ain't got nothin' to be talkin' about on my phone. You ain't got no business."

"Stacey," the voice rattled my nerves. I almost dropped the phone because it suddenly got heavy.

I remained silent. Anxious. Guilty. A little sad. I didn't know what to say. I felt like a scared kitten.

"Stacey, it's your dad," G said, his voice crackling.

I took in the deepest breath I think I had ever taken in my life.

"I know who it is," I said clearly into the phone, trying to sound unmoved. "But it's not my father."

"Don't be like that." He sounded like he was begging. "I am your father, Stacey. I am the only father you know anything about," he reminded me.

My foster father flashed across my mind. He was lying in his bed watching football. I saw those long feet covered in black polyester socks. I could see his postal uniform. I saw his hands breaking ice cubes to put in the mouth of a child who wouldn't stop crying. Closing my eyes, I tried to erase my foster father and G. I tried to imagine my real father, but my thoughts turned black and red. I guess those are the colors of absence.

"I tried to treat you as if you were my own," G continued. "Like my own flesh and blood."

"Was it different?" I frowned and reached down for the chair underneath me.

"Different? What do you mean by different?" he asked.

"You make it sound as if things would have been different if you didn't have to pretend I was like your flesh and blood but actually your flesh and blood. Your real daughter."

His voice raised. "How can you say that, Stacey? I never treated you bad. Why you gonna make me suffer? For the last eight years, I tried my best."

"That was your best?"

I could hear him pacing the floor and the phone cord getting twisted around his phone receiver. I was wondering if Myrtle was sitting in the room listening. I was also wondering why he had decided to call me after all that time.

"Listen, Stacey, I know I got to do things different—"

"Just you?" I cut him off.

"We," he stressed. "We got to do things different. Me and your mama. I don't like comin' home at night and walkin' past your room and I don't see you there." His voice sped up: "It ain't right. The other night I got home from work and I went in your room. I curled up on your bed. I cried. I cried and cried 'cause I miss you. I want you to come home."

"It's all about what you want," I whispered away from the phone. He didn't hear me.

I listened to him sniffle and struggle to speak to me. I had never heard or seen G cry, and now that I knew his tears were for me, my heart began to melt.

I felt so bad. I wanted to wipe his tears away, even though he had never been there to wipe my own tears and reassure me that everything was going to be fine. I wanted to believe him. I wanted so badly to believe that he had changed or had some great awakening. I so desperately wanted to believe that things were different. He was sorry for everything that had gone wrong those past eight years. I could hear it in his whimper and feel it in the echo of his staggering breaths and soupy sniffles penetrating the phone waves.

"Your mama and me have been talkin'. We talk about you every day. She cries. I cry. Sometimes we cry at the same time. She's sorry, Stacey. She's real sorry. We both realize that we got to make some changes. You're thirteen years old. You ain't no little girl no more. You need freedom. We can't be so tight with you. We can't be so strict. Myrtle can't be beatin' on you every time you make a mistake. She can't be beatin' you all the time."

"All the time?" A firecracker went off in my head. "All the time? No time! Never! Not one hit! Never again!'"

G said nothing. His silence let me know that he hadn't changed. Myrtle hadn't changed. I was twelve, and I knew that change was revolutionary. To change things didn't simply mean that you just shifted something to the other side of the room to make things look different. You had to throw everything out and start over with just the bare walls. And then you had to paint those and tear up the floor.

"So y'all are sittin' around the house cryin'! Y'all don't know nothin' about cryin'. You gotta cry almost every day for the next eight years to know what it feels like to be me. You gotta cry hard! You gotta cry 'til no more tears come out your eyeballs. You gotta cry loud like thunder. Cry like rain drizzling. You gotta cry without lettin' a sound come out your mouth. You gotta cry 'til somethin' in you won't let you cry no more. Then you can tell me somethin' about cryin'."

I couldn't allow G to make me feel guilty for his tears or Myrtle's tears. I had to make myself believe that I did not make them cry. I realized that their tears came from different places. G missed me. My absence was tearing him up inside. And once again, he was helpless and weak because he felt he had lost me. The only way he could try to get me back was to cry, because he knew his tears would break me. I knew he loved me, real child or not. But he was not a real father, and I don't mean in the biological sense.

Myrtle's tears were a different story. Let her cry! Let her weep! Let her make that boo-hoo sound. Let her cry until she got migraines. I didn't care. Her tears came from her own guilt. She did me dirty. Maybe she cried because she couldn't undo the pain, the scars, or unsay all the bad things she had uttered to me. Maybe she wanted to correct it all but didn't know how. Perhaps she cried because she had lost another child.

I once looked Myrtle in her face and said, "Everything happens for a reason. And you couldn't have children for a reason. You weren't supposed to be anybody's mother."

Even though she was incapable of physically bearing a child, she still could have given birth to me outside her womb. Her love could have inspired me, given me strength, and helped me grow into a woman.

"You never did without," G said. "You had a roof over your head. Clothes on your back. Food."

"I'm wondering what it would be like to have no home, to be naked, and even hungry sometimes but have all the love you need," I say. "Material things can't be a substitute for love," I said. "You got to make it come out of you. You got to make me feel the love. All these years I didn't feel special. I felt ugly. Different. You both called me 'funny looking.' You let her beat me. You didn't protect me. And you would always say, 'You know daddy loves you, right? You know your mama loves you. Right Stacey?'"

"I love—" he started to say.

"No, George Jenkins! It's too late for that," my voice shook. Anger was running through me like an army of men. Yes, anger. "You can say those words for days. But you got to show it."

"Will you let me show it, Stacey? Give Daddy a chance to show it," he pleaded.

"No," I said coldly.

I couldn't be around Myrtle while she tried to revive her heart. I couldn't wait for him to build up strength and finally become a man. I had to grow. I had to do what they couldn't do. I had to give birth to myself.

I hung up the phone with G still talking. I studied the pay phone—the thin slot for coins, emergency numbers, directions on how to make a collect call, the shiny buttons, the snakelike phone cord. That was the first connection I had lost because I wanted to.

As I walked away from the phone, I suddenly realized something. All the other kids in that shelter had biological parents, and they were in that place with me because their parents did them dirty. They faced the same kind of struggle for love and nurture as I did, yet they knew their genetic link. All that time, I believed my abuse stemmed from being an adopted child. But it wasn't true.

Every day parents do their children dirty: foster children, adopted children, orphaned children, and children of flesh and blood. Love comes from the heart—not flesh, not blood, not genes.

I knew I was cutting off my ties to Myrtle and G, but I still realized that I would need love and nurturing. But for that moment and near future, I knew I had to find some love inside of me. But I didn't want to live in a bubble. I didn't want to be alone in this universe. I was still a child in need of direction, discipline, guidance, protection, nurturing, and love. I needed the guidance and love of a black mother, and the protection of a black father.

Where would I find it? I didn't know.

FIFTEEN

There is a stately-looking photograph of civil rights doyen W.E.B. DuBois sitting on my windowsill among a stack of books. Taped to the top edge of the small bronze-colored frame is a yellowed piece of paper with a few of his own poetic words printed in small type:

Free, free as the sunshine trickling down the morning into these high windows of mine, free as yonder fresh young voices welling up to me from the caverns of brick and mortar below—swelling with song instinct with life, tremulous treble and darkening bass. My children, my little children are singing to the sunshine.

DuBois wrote these words in his prophetic 1903 book *The Souls of Black Folk*. He declared that the songs, lore, and other expressions of black people represented the singular spiritual heritage of America. Through song, dance, music, and various other forms of vernacular culture springing from the soul, African Americans were able to articulate certain messages to the world about death, bondage, suffering, resistance, hope, faith, and the meaning of freedom and democracy. For DuBois, black people's words—spoken, chanted, sung, shouted, or written—have been the greatest gift of black folks to this nation and to the rest of the world.

During my own bondage as a child, Myrtle stifled my curiosity and my voice. I was not allowed to question anything, to be creative, to assert my individuality, or to have a voice. Dancing was not allowed. It was sinful. Sexual. Improper. "All black folks know how to do is shake their butts," she said. "And white folks stand back and watch them. They laugh. They say, 'Look at them fools.' They call them clowns and niggas."

According to Myrtle, black people were only supposed to dance for

Jesus by shouting during church services. And that kind of dancing was reserved for the saved, sanctified, and filled-with-the-holy-ghost Christians. By forbidding me from dancing, Myrtle was assured that I would not divert my little self from her control over my body. To assert my individuality and raise my voice was considered rebellious and dangerous. I wanted to be able to wrap words around my pain, hopes, fears, tears, and anger and speak them. Some black parents realized that the mouths of black youth could be powerful weapons that could get them into trouble. To keep black children in line, they silence them by curbing their curiosity and beating the spirit out of them with swift backhands to the mouth.

Exorcising silence from my soul would be the first step to claiming and defining freedom for myself. Only then would I be able to find the courage to unhinge myself from Myrtle's control over me. To look people in the eyes. To be rebellious. To buck the system. Challenge the status quo. Only then could I be seen and heard and move myself beyond my relegated child's place to grow, evolve, and progress. The music, poetry, literature, art, and dance of the slaves and their descendants would provide substance for my own healing as well as stimulate my mind. The words of African Americans would give meaning to my life and help me find strength, a sense of identity, and a connection to a past and family of people.

SIXTEEN

S usan told me that I needed to find a healthy outlet before all my feelings boiled over and destroyed me. I had basketball. But she said I needed something that exercised my mind. Basketball allowed me only to exert physical energy.

"You've got to find some other way to channel your all your feelings," Susan urged. "Fears. Anger. Years of stuff you've packed away. All your life you've been told that you're not supposed to feel anything. You've survived because you didn't allow yourself to feel. You have to unlearn this behavior. You've got to let all that stuff inside of you out."

That bit of Susan's advice planted the seed in my head, and I decided to join the Creative Writing Club at school. Every Tuesday for two hours, seven of us met in the East Wing of the school for two hours to write poetry and short stories that we read out loud.

"By reading our work out loud, by sharing our deepest feelings, we can free ourselves," said Mrs. Hughes.

Mrs. Hughes was a fifty-something-year-old white woman with thick, bushy brown hair and bushy brown eyebrows to match. Her eyes never missed a trick. She didn't look like she ever slept. Mrs. Hughes taught English and called the Creative Writing Club her "baby." She said it helped her bring out the best in students. After my first few weeks at Ewing High School, she stopped me in the hallway.

"You look like a creative soul," she said, startling me. She had appeared from behind me like a gray ghost out of nowhere.

"No," I shook my head. "I ain't no creative soul," I mumbled and searched my locker for my algebra book. "I'm just a tiny sack of bones with a voice nobody listens to."

"See!" she clapped her hands together twice and then put them over her mouth. Then she pressed one hand against her chest as if she was trying to keep her lungs from bursting through. "I was right! Only a creative soul could be that articulate."

Strange woman, I thought. She scanned my face and drew her head back as if she could see something in me that I was either trying to hide or didn't know was there. I snatched my eyes away from her. One of her chilly hands gently grabbed my chin.

"Miss Patton," she whispered. She knew my name. How did she know my name? "You can bring everything to this club. Bring your fears. Bring your anger. Bring your frustration. Bring your madness. Bring your dreams. Bring your confusion. Bring your power. Bring it all. It is wanted here. There are miles of pen and paper."

"Miles." I looked perplexed.

"Miles and miles," she said in a singsong voice.

I shrugged my shoulders. "I don't have much to say."

"You'd be surprised, woman!"

"I'm not a poet. I'm not a writer." My voice dropped.

"Stop it!" she demanded. "Stop telling lies! Of course, there is a writer in you. You just have to find her."

Mrs. Hughes reached into the pile of folders snuggled underneath her armpit and pulled out a small black and white poster of a white man with hairy forearms sitting over a typewriter. His hair was slicked back, and he had a serious and determined expression on his face.

"Do you know who that is?" Her hands trembled a bit as she held the poster in front of my face.

For a second I felt dumb, like I didn't know anything. I felt I should have known who he was. Besides, he was on a big poster in school.

"No." I shook my head. "I don't know who he is."

"That," she paused, "is Ernest Hemingway, one of the greatest literary figures to have blessed the earth with words. You'll come to know his work well," she assured me. "I pointed him out to you because he said something very important that stands in my mind when I work with young writers like yourself. Someone once asked him, 'What is the best early training for a writer?' And do you know what he said, Stacey Patton?"

"No." I raised my eyebrows and shrugged my shoulders. I didn't even know the man, so how could I have known what he said?

"He said that the best early training for a writer is an unhappy childhood." She gave me a look that told me she knew everything about me.

Maybe she had heard about how my scars got on my face. Maybe she knew about the Anchor House and how they were planning to send me back to hell.

"Old eyes, Stacey Patton," she sang softly. "My dear, you have a child's face, but you've got old eyes. Happy children don't have old, soulful, searching eyes like yours." I dropped them to the floor, like I always did. "The first time I saw you walking in the hallway, those eyes told me a story," she said.

The day after Susan's suggestion, I found myself creeping down the East Wing in search of Mrs. Hughes's classroom. I found Mrs. Hughes hovered over a pile of papers with an old-fashioned feather pen in her hand. Some hypnotic space-age music was playing in the background.

"C'mon in, Miss Patton," she said jovially. How she knew it was me, I'll never know. She hadn't looked up from her papers. "I've been waiting for you."

I inched closer to her desk, massaging my hands nervously. "I'm interested—"

"I know," she cut me off and grinned at the papers. She lifted her head and slipped off her bifocals all in one motion. They fell against her chest as they hung from a lackluster chain. "You want to write! You have mountains of things to say! And they will listen. You need an altar," she rambled.

"An altar?" I frowned. I didn't want to sacrifice cows, start a fire, or pray.

"You need to slay ghosts." Her eyes stretched like she was telling a spooky story.

"Ghosts?" My lips twisted.

"Of course. But ghosts have bones," she said, like she knew for a fact.

"Bones?" I didn't believe her.

"How do you think they move around?"

"They float," I shrugged.

"Ah! Only in the cartoons, my dear. Ghosts are real. They eat, sleep, and die. They wreak havoc and cause chaos."

"They sound like humans," I said.

"They are." She reached up and gently squeezed my cheek. "Look at those dimples." She smiled and reached up to my face.

"So why are they called ghosts?" I quickly changed the subject.

"Because that's what we make them," she said. "Ghosts are the people we hate, love, fear, feign for, and want to forget. They are the people we want to die, to push into exile, or even dig up from the grave. Ghosts are the things we want to remember and the things we choose to forget. They haunt us. They control us. They distort our reality. You have to slay these ghosts and lay down their bones," she said in a serious tone.

"How?"

She held up her feather pen. I watched a speck of ink drop onto her paper like black blood. "They say the pen is mightier than the sword, my dear. But that's not true. If someone is holding a gun to your head while you've got a pen in your hand, what do you think you will write, Miss Patton?"

"The end," I said, as we broke into laughter.

"My point exactly," she said, returning the pen back to the jar of ink. "But the pen still is mighty, and you can use it like a sword. It works very well on ghosts every time. Writing gives you power over the worlds that you create. You win arguments. You have the last say. You control the characters. You expose their beauty and their ugly. But—" She stopped, then started again. "Before you can create worlds and characters, you have to go inside yourself and write what you see. And that can be frightening because you don't know what you might find lurking behind your soul."

When she stopped talking, I felt that she was searching me again through my eyes, so I picked objects on her desk. "Why do you divert and hide those marvelous treasures?" she asked. "Some people have six fingers, are cross-eyed, crippled. Some people have faces that have been melted by fire. Others are just outright ugly! Look at you," she said, still holding my chin. "If I had a face, a smile, and eyes like yours, I would think I had done something really wonderful in my former life."

I didn't know how to respond. Instead, I fought the urge to look into her eyes.

"Silence is a sin, Miss Patton."

Three days before I was to leave the Anchor House, Mrs. Hughes stopped me in the hallway again on my way to my algebra class. Her timing was always perfect. Sometimes she'd slip quotes into my hand or tape them on my locker. Sometimes she'd just whisper wise words into my ear. But that Friday, she had a gift for me, she said. I watched her hands anxiously as they disappeared into that big burlap shopping bag she always carried. When they reemerged, she held a thick blue book in her hands, smiling as if it was some great treasure.

"This is a book of poems written by Langston Hughes," she said tracing the gold letters on the cover with her fingertips. I had never heard of Langston Hughes. There was a bookmark sticking out. She opened the book to that marked page and took a long glance at me. "This is my favorite poem," she smiled and gently placed her hand against her chest. "My favorite line, 'Life for me ain't been no crystal stair,' says so much. It's the perfect metaphor."

Right there in the middle of that hallway, she began to recite the poem as loud as she could. I listened to the poet's words about the harshness of a life full of tacks, splinters, torn-up boards, and bare steps. Still, the poet talked about not giving up, about climbing despite the roughness and pain under the feet.

"Mrs. Hughes is crazy," some girl passing by remarked.

"That lady is bugged out," somebody else snickered.

"Naw, she real deep," a boy with an out-of-control Afro said.

"Mrs. Hughes, you're in the wrong profession," another teacher whispered in her ear and tapped her shoulder gently. "You should be in theater."

The whole time she ignored them and focused on me. I knew she wasn't acting. She was for real. She felt every line in that poem. Every word meant something to her, and she wanted that poem to mean something to me. She put the marker back in its place and closed the book, smiling affectionately. I stood there imagining crystal stairs, the pain of splinters in my feet, and an old black woman climbing a staircase. And then Mrs. Hughes handed me the book.

"That poem is about hope and courage. It's my favorite. Every writer should have a source of inspiration. Maybe Langston Hughes will inspire you."

At lunch I sat at a corner table alone with my greasy fries, cheeseburger, and a carton of orange juice. I stepped into Langston's world and began to live everything. I felt as if I had left my body, escaped my troubles, and gotten lost in the adventures he wrote about in jazz clubs, the streets of Harlem, and churches. I could feel the pain and beauty of being black in America then. I was amazed at how he captured the human experience and wrote about it in a way that was simple yet powerful. I was also intrigued by how an old white school woman like Mrs. Hughes had such a connection with that dead black poet.

When school was over that day, I stood at the corner of Parkway Avenue and Lower Ferry Road waiting for the bus to go back to South

Trenton. The number 34 bus crept up the street belching out black smoke into the air. Its engine sighed when it came to a stop in front of me. As I entered the bus, I handed the driver my red school ticket and headed straight to the back where no one else was sitting. I flipped through the book and came across a poem about death not ringing doorbells or knocking. Death just comes when it wants to. It comes through the walls and the television. And it doesn't announce itself. I had never thought of death being like some rude person just finding you wherever you are, not caring about what you're doing or what you have to do. It just steals you away like some thief in the night or daytime. Scary. On that note I closed the book and peeked over at a copy of that day's *Trenton Times*. I read the headline: "Four Teens Die After Joyride Ends Tragically."

My eyes moved slowly down the page to the four small square photos of black boys. The photo on the end arrested my eyes, and I stopped breathing. My bowels felt like they were going to drop to my ankles. My throat got dry, like it always did when I was about to cry. *This can't be*, I thought. His photo had to be part of another news story, not that one. He can't be one of the four who went joy-riding in a stolen car. He couldn't be dead.

I picked up the paper and held it close to my face. Those eyes. Those same glossy cornrows. That slick smile. I could even smell coconut oil sheen in the air. And then that name: Kaya Horton.

The story didn't say that he had just returned home to his father after a short stay at the Anchor House. It didn't tell the readers that his mama was dead and he and his father were still having a hard time dealing with it. The writer forgot to say that Kaya was a smart kid, a good kid, and a kind kid who often got pulled into the wrong crowd.

The car was a 1991 Honda, stolen from West Trenton. I convinced myself that Kaya didn't know it was stolen. The other three kids probably drove up to him, honked the horn, and asked him if he wanted to go for a ride. The police saw them: four young black guys riding in a nice car. When they ran the plate number through their computer, it turned up stolen. They flashed the lights and turned on the sirens. The chase began. Eventually three cop cars chased the car down John Fitch Way, a highway right next to the Delaware River.

At some point in the chase, the driver lost control of the car, and they veered off next to a small section of the river, about fifty meters wide. They got out of the car and started to run from the police, who were close behind. The boys thought they could escape the police by crossing the Delaware and Raritan Canal from the Jersey side into Pennsylvania.

The police stood on the shoreline and watched all four of them form a human chain by holding hands. The boys didn't know there was a forty-foot drop in the middle. They all went down and didn't come back up. Early the next morning, they dragged Kaya's 170-pound body out of the frigid November water.

I made a big wrinkle in the newspaper because I gripped it so hard. I couldn't believe what I had just read. Kids aren't supposed to die before their time. But time infected children just the same as it did adults. Still, I had this notion that children were immortal. Death was not something they were supposed to consider. How unfair Kaya's death was! How was I to make sense of that loss?

I wanted to cry, but the tears wouldn't come. I wanted to scream, but I didn't have the strength. I wanted to press Rewind and record Kaya out of that scene. I needed to edit the tape, enter it, and breathe life into him. I felt helpless. There's no feeling more powerless than wanting to resurrect the dead and knowing you can't. So, I wrote a poem right there on the back of that bus expressing how I felt.

Midnight.
Trenton Makes the World Takes Bridge.
No wind.
No stars.
The moon looks like a slice of orange.
Miss Delaware's cool pretty black face asks me for a kiss.
My body puckers up.
I jump.

When I stepped inside the Anchor House, I didn't hear any crying or anybody talking about the sad news. Everyone looked unaffected, like the day had been perfectly normal. Did they read the paper? Did they care?

My body was still trembling. I was scared. Shocked. Still too sad to cry. My palms were sweaty. I finally found Susan in a back office sitting next to a computer holding a mirror up to her face. She had just spread dark red lipstick on her lips to match her heavily rouged cheeks. I watched her pat her hair to make sure it was still in place. She moved her hands to her breasts, adjusting her bra up. For a second, I imagined the day when I would be able to do that.

"You killed him, didn't you?" I grumbled at her. It was a defiant and accusatory statement.

Susan put one hand in between her breasts because she was startled by my voice, by my coming out of nowhere.

"Stacey," she grinned and tried to catch her breath.

"You killed him!"

Susan just looked at me for a moment, then asked, "Killed who?"

I threw the newspaper down on the desk in front of her and let it roll open to the front page on its own. Stepping back, I watched Susan lean over the paper and pick it up to read. When she finished reading, she looked up with a guilty face. It had turned chalky pink, like Pepto-Bismol.

"Stacey, I'm sorry—"

"You killed him!"

"It was an accid—"

"No, Susan! You killed Kaya!"

She defended herself. "They stole a car. They drowned. It's written right here in the newspaper, Stacey. He was in the wrong place at the wrong time. Kaya never thought about his actions before he did them. He didn't value life. He never took anything seriously. And now, unfortunately, he's dead."

I wanted to bite her for being so cold and judgmental.

"What's not written is what you told him a few weeks ago before he left here. You told him he was gonna end up in jail or dead. You told him that! You put those words out into the universe. And now Kaya is dead. You killed him, Susan!"

"Stacey." She stood up. I walked out on her, leaving her there to call my name. I stormed out the back door and searched for the basketball. Susan didn't follow me. I guess she figured she'd give me some space and we'd work it out in a counseling session later.

She didn't give Kaya any hope when she said those words, like some kind of prophecy. Even if she thought it, she shouldn't have said it. Susan confirmed for him probably what countless others had said. If Susan had told him that he was going to live and become some great man like Langston Hughes, then maybe he would have thought twice about getting into that car, before running from the police, before crossing that river.

Kaya Horton might have been a bit more careful with his life because he would have had some hope for his future.

Now, there I was, missing every jump shot I put up. Even my lay-ups rolled out of the hoop. I wanted that pretty black boy to whisper something sweet in the wind, though he was dead. I wanted him to tell me he was okay. I wanted to hear him say that he'd wait for me wherever he was.

I was nervous, scared, and vulnerable in a way I had never been before. Was death going to pay me a visit? When? How? Where? Kaya's death had brought a new fear to me. I couldn't make bad decisions. I couldn't get caught up in the wrong crowds. I couldn't be in the wrong place at the wrong time. I had to cling to some kind of hope so that I wouldn't lose my life. Most important, I had to stay away from people like Susan who had negative prophecies.

That Saturday, I found myself sitting in a doctor's office somewhere in Princeton. Ted was sitting next to me, flipping through some homemaker magazine. He had to be bored. Why else was he reading about potting plants, sewing curtains, and choosing the top ten desserts for the holiday season? He wasn't that kind of man.

There were no stethoscopes, blood pressure cuffs, cotton swabs, needles, gurneys, or paper gowns in that doctor's office. He wasn't going to take my pulse or temperature or check my reflexes. That doctor wanted to get inside my head, a place I didn't allow anyone to enter. Besides, what did he expect to find? Did he want to pluck the emotional bone out of me and pass it around like some kind of specimen?

When the psychiatrist called my name, I jumped up. At that same moment Ted grabbed my wrist and pulled me into him. "Wait a minute, kiddo." He motioned for me to come closer.

"You comin' with me, Ted?"

"No, kiddo. I can't go."

I was disappointed. Throughout my short stay at the Anchor House, Ted always had a way of making me feel strong. He always knew what to say.

"Just remember somethin.'" He paused and moved his head slightly past my body to see where the doctor was standing. His voice got low: "Shrinks are more fucked up than the people that come to see them. They take on all that sickness. So don't let him make you feel like something is wrong with you."

Ted gave me my wrist back, and I put my defensive wall up. I was prepared for the good doctor. He wasn't going to penetrate me. I wouldn't let him read me.

The shrink gave me a psychotic smile as I walked into the office. He closed us in and bent down next to the door and flicked on the switch of a small apparatus that made a humming noise to muffle our conversation so no one outside the office could hear us. I felt like I was preparing for confession.

He picked up a manila folder with my name written in black marker. The "e" was missing in my first name, as usual. He sat, crossed his legs, opened the folder, and gave me a more manic-looking grin before he cracked his lips.

"Miss Patton."

I tried to figure him out. White male. Smart looking. Fifty maybe. Strange acting. Married? Children? There were no photographs on his desk. No books other than a DSM-V manual, dictionary, calendar, tape recorder, and a pen. The clock hung right over my head. I guess he had put it there so that I couldn't see it but he could. That way he had total control over time in his world. He knew how much had gone by, how much was left, and I couldn't be preoccupied with it.

"I understand you've been living in a shelter for almost one month now. Am I correct?"

"Yes." I gave him a quick answer.

Was he normal? Did he ever get pissed off? Did he ever cry? Was he a shrink who got into the business to try to figure out his problems through his patients? Did he figure it all out? I wanted to know.

"You're supposed to return home on Monday," he said, my heart jerking a bit in my stomach. "How do you feel about that?"

For a split second, I thought about DeWayne as the shrink aimed his pen at his pad. I didn't mind so much that he was going to take notes. He wasn't on the same level as Susan. This interview with the psychiatrist was important. He was going to decide my future based on what I told him. It was a last effort by DYFS to make a decision as to whether it would be healthy for me to go back to Hilltop Drive based on my psychological state. So I wanted him to write it all down.

"I don't want to go back there," I said bluntly as he began to scribble.

"Can you tell me why?"

"Because she beats me."

"What if she agrees to stop?"

"She won't stop," I answered.

"How do you know?"

"She's sick. She can't help it." I thought that was a good answer. He was a psychiatrist. He knew about sickness. He knew it took longer for mentally ill people to get better. "She is a like a husband who beats his wife. Once he starts, he ain't gonna stop."

He wrote more.

Myrtle couldn't be fixed, I wanted to tell him. And then I wondered about the good doctor again. What was broke inside him? What did he need to be fixed? I started thinking about other kinds of doctors: heart surgeons, brain surgeons, and orthopedic doctors. What if they had broken hands or eyes? Then they wouldn't be able to fix people properly. But what about shrinks? Were they ever people who were emotionally intact enough to fix people?

"How do you feel about your parents?"

"They're not my parents," I said defensively.

"Oh," he paused and gleaned through the papers in the folder. "You're adopted." His eyes returned to mine. He asked the question again but differently. "Do you love them?"

"No."

He looked surprised at first. I could tell that he wanted me to elaborate, but I didn't know how. When I gave him that quick answer, I had no feelings running through my little body. I had been required to say it because that's what children were expected to say of their parents. But for me it was like saying thanks. Thanks for putting a roof over my head, feeding me, and putting clothes on my back. Those were the reasons I was supposed to love them. But when I set all those things aside, I was left with complicated thoughts about my adoptive parents.

"Share a memory with me, Miss Patton," he almost begged. I watched his hands relax.

"A memory?"

"Yes. Anything. Something that comes to your mind when you think about your adoptive parents."

I looked across the room, searching as if my memories were plastered on the walls. For a few seconds, my eyes were glued to the reproduction

Monet hanging above the couch where he sat. I looked at my lap, closed my eyes. I opened them again, and the first thing I saw was the shrink's untied shoelace. At that moment, he became human to me, and at that same time a memory came to me.

"When I first came to live with my adoptive parents, I wasn't good at tying my shoes," I said, still looking at his brown laces. "She taught me how to tie them. But the way she taught me was different from how most people tie their shoes. She showed me how to make two bows and then bring them both together into one knot. Most people make one bow and wrap the other string around it and pull it out into one bow. The way she taught me was hard. She got mad at me and kept slapping me until I got it right." My eyes were still pinned to his lace. I wanted to know who taught him how to tie his shoes.

He didn't respond to my memory. He showed no emotion. He just kept writing. And then suddenly he put his notebook on the opposite end of the couch next to a stack of cards.

"Do you get good grades in school, Stacey?"

"Yes."

"Do you like school?"

"I love school," I said, giving him a grin.

"What's your favorite subject?" he asked.

"I have two favorite subjects. I like English and history."

"Why do you like those subjects?"

"I like English because we get to read stories, write, learn new words. I like history because I always want to know what happened in the past. History helps me make sense of right now."

"Do you plan to go to college?"

"Yes."

"Have you given any thought as to what you want to be when you become an adult?"

"Alive," I answered.

He looked thrown off. He slid his glasses off his face and laid them on the stack of cards closest to his leg. He held his pen perfectly still for a few seconds and then crossed his legs the opposite way.

He cleared his throat. "Most young people say something like they want to become a doctor, lawyer, firefighter. Something of that nature. Why did you say alive? Alive is not an occupation."

"Well, I have to be alive first," I said.

"This is true," he nodded. "But why alive?"

"'Cause I can't think that far ahead to tell you what I want to be when I grow up. I can't see beyond right now. I really don't want to see past right now if there's gonna be bad stuff waitin' for me to go through. Right now, the only plan I can make is to get through today and the bad stuff I gotta deal with today. I hope to still be alive when I've gone through all this."

He scratched the rough stubble on his chin and wrote for about a minute. "Stacey, I'm going to show you some pictures now. I want you to tell me the first thing that comes to your mind when you see each one. There is no right or wrong answer."

The first picture looked like somebody stood back and threw black ink at it and watched it drip down the page until it dried that way. At first I had no words. I knew he said there were no right or wrong answers. But I wanted to try my best to make sense, to get it right. I looked closer and began to see a form.

"A butterfly." I nodded. "Yeah, a butterfly." He said nothing, just scribbled on his pad. The next card looked almost the same as the last. The shrink stared at me, waiting. His look tells me that it's not exactly the same image as the last. So my eyes zoom in. "A uterus," I smile.

The shrink showed me about ten more ink blot cards and I gave answers like *snot, tree branches, kidneys, fallopian tubes,* and *spider webs.* Slowly the pictures became clearer.

He held up a card with a woman sitting alone in a room. She was staring out an open window with her arms folded across her chest. Nothing was outside the window—no trees, grass, and no picket fence.

"She might be thinking about something," I said, squinting to look at her face. "Maybe she's trapped. Maybe she wants to go outside. She could be lonely. She could be sad."

"How about this one?"

The card showed a little girl sitting naked in a bathtub. The water was up to her belly button with her undeveloped nipples showing. Her arms were in the water too. A man was kneeling down next to the tub. His sleeves were pushed up, and his hands were in the water. I couldn't see a towel. I couldn't see his hands. I couldn't see the expression on his face. My heart jumped into my mouth. That scene was too familiar, too close to home. How did that doctor know? Why did he choose that picture to show me?

"What do you see, Stacey? What's happening in this picture?" he asked.

I needed a minute to really look at the picture. I didn't want to say the wrong thing to give the doctor the wrong impression. My eyes zoomed in on the little girl's face. She wasn't smiling. She wasn't frowning. She looked blank. She might have known the man. She might not have known him. It could have been her father giving her a bath. But her father shouldn't have been giving her a bath. She looked too old for that. Maybe she asked him for help.

I could tell my silence was troubling the shrink. He turned the card toward him and looked at it for himself. When he turned it back to me, still waiting for an answer, my eyes dropped to the untied shoelace.

"I don't want to play this game anymore," I mumbled. "I'm tired now."

"Okay. Fair enough," he said slowly stacking the cards and laying them down on the couch again. I heard the rough stubble again and knew he scratched it without looking at him.

I knew the question was coming. So I wasn't surprised when he asked, "Stacey, were you sexually abused?"

"No," I shot at him, shaking my head hard more times than needed for him to get the point.

He didn't believe me. He wrote down more words than *no* on his notepad. "Did anyone ever touch your genitals in a bad way? Did anyone ever look at you without your permission? Did anyone ever make you touch their genitals?"

"No." My chest tightened. "Never."

He didn't ask me any more questions about being touched in a bad way. Instead, he changed the subject. "Have you ever tried to hurt yourself?"

My heart jerked in my chest again. "Once," I answered him. Weird. I could easily admit that I had tried to hurt myself but found it hard to share that dirty secret about how Myrtle sexually abused me. I didn't view self-hurt as another kind of victimization.

"Once?" he looked up from his notepad.

"Yes," I sighed deeply. "I tried to kill myself once."

His voice dropped. "Tell me about that time."

The first time I was in the third grade. That day it hurt especially bad when I sat in my chair at school. Myrtle had beaten me twice the night before. First, because I turned my head too fast and she thought I had rolled my eyes at her. The second time, she called my name and I answered by saying, "What?" instead of "Yes, Mommy." My skin was cut up something kind of bad. I kept asking to go to the bathroom to put cool, wet paper towels on the welts and to cry.

At 2:00 that afternoon we went to the playground across the street for recess. I walked in slow motion over to the swing set. The boys begged me to play touch football with them, but I ignored them. My little hands gripped the thick link chains and wouldn't let go. I didn't swing back and forth. I just sat there limp, staring straight ahead of me.

Out of nowhere the sky got dark. The wind picked up and lifted leaves off the ground. Then came the thunder. Two girls screamed when they saw lightning split the sky. Everybody but me started running for the gate.

"Stacey Patton!" my teacher yelled. "Let's go! The storm is coming! Stacey Patton! Line up now, or there'll be no recess for you tomorrow!"

I ignored her. I couldn't move. I didn't want to move. My classmates began to scream my name and get mad at me. They were getting drenched because of me. They were all just as scared of thunder and lightning as I had been until that day.

The rain pelted down onto my face and mixed in with my tears. My teacher left me there on that swing and walked my classmates into the building. When she returned minutes later, two other teachers and the principal were with her. The storm had gotten worse.

As they tried to peel my fingers from the chains, I screamed, "Leave me alone! I wanna die! I wanna die! I wanna die!" I kicked and screamed the entire time they held my legs and arms in their hands.

"How did you try to kill yourself then?" the shrink looked confused.

"I wanted to stay on the swing. The swing had metal chains. I wanted the lightning to strike me so I would die."

He took a long pause and looked at me as if he didn't understand me. "What happened when you went home that day?"

"She beat me."

"She beat you?" He sounded surprised.

"Yes. She beat me for getting my clothes, shoes, and hair wet."

Silence sat between me and the doctor. He didn't write anything. I didn't look at his face. I could hear the minutes ticking away on the clock that I couldn't see behind me.

I interrupted the silence: "I didn't know how to kill myself the right way."

"Did you really want to die? Or was it a cry for help?" he asked.

"I never said help," I answered him. "Besides, who was gonna help me?

I wanted to die. To get off this earth. To end my pain. To get away from her so she could never hurt me again."

"Do you feel that way now?"

"Like what?"

"Like getting off this earth?"

"I look up at the clouds sometimes and wish I had wings."

"Do you want to end your pain?"

"Who wants pain?"

"Do you feel like dying?"

I looked him right in his eyes. "I'd rather be dead than go back there with those people."

The shrink gave me a hard look. Our eyes locked, and silence hung above our heads for a moment. I didn't flinch. Neither did he. I almost didn't breathe.

"Stacey, I don't think it's a good idea for you to live with your adoptive parents, do you?"

"No."

"But I don't think it's a good idea for you to be in foster care either. You're too old for that kind of situation, and you've been through too much already. I'm going to recommend that you be placed in a group home setting where you can be a bit more independent. You can go to school, play sports, and get some much-needed psychotherapy. Maybe you can work things out with your adoptive parents in the future. But right now, you need to be in a safe and stable environment. I will type up my report and give it to the counselor before you leave."

The tension left the room and my body all at the same time. I felt that somebody had opened a window and let fresh air into my life. I could breathe. I could finally breathe. Freedom was finally going to have meaning for me.

PART III

REDEMPTION

ONE

November 1992

A winter, spring, and summer passed. I was fourteen. I had been away from my adoptive parents and the Anchor House for a little over a year. My social worker from DYFS had placed me in multiple youth shelters and foster homes over that year. Finally, she got me a placement at the TRIAD Group Home, only minutes from Hilltop Drive. On the surface, the group home seemed like the perfect placement for me.

It was a huge yellow house situated on Pennington Road directly across from a Lutheran church called Abiding Presence. There was a winding driveway, with a backyard and basketball court. Inside the home, a large recreation room sat adjacent to the living room. A wooden staircase separated the dining room from the kitchen. Behind the kitchen were a staff office and bathroom. The sign on the office door that said, "No Residents Allowed," along with the locks on the refrigerator and cabinets and the exit signs over the doors, were the only signs that it was a state-run institution.

At first, I had a sense of calm and stability. I wasn't going to be shuttled from one place to another unexpectedly. But I still remained on my toes, ready to defend myself. And it didn't take long for me to develop the initiative to get out of the program and try to move on to something better. I resented being a ward of the state, so I had no intentions of staying long at the group home or in the State of New Jersey child welfare system.

About one month into my stay at the group home, I found myself staring out the square window of the television room. The leaves outside the house lay dead and brown on the hard earth. A short woman who lived down the street walked by with a dachshund on a purple leash. The dog barked at something I couldn't see through the streaks in the window. When the woman and her pet disappeared, I looked at my hands and proceeded to clean my index fingernail with a toothpick I had gotten from the kitchen.

This toothpick made me think of Myrtle and how she was always rolling one around in her mouth. I started wondering what changes my adoptive parents had made in their lives now that I was no longer part of it. Did they still go through their same routines? Did she still prepare a bowl of cornflakes for me in the morning? Did she still fry fish on Saturday nights? Did G still set out a plate for me at the table, forgetting I wasn't there? Did he still come to the table in those musty undershirts? Who said grace now? Did Myrtle move her clothes to my empty closet? Did she still spend hours picking lint off the laundry? Did they miss me?

I hadn't seen or spoken to my adoptive parents in all that time. But sometimes I picked up the phone, dialed their number, and listened to them say, "Hello ... Hello. ... hel-lo." And then I'd hang up. Sometimes G would say hello twice and then breathe into the phone. I think he knew it was me calling.

Once in a while I got angry about all the beatings I had gotten and the scars all over my body. No one had taught me how to channel my anger because anger was a feeling I swore up and down that I didn't have. My survival strategy as a child was simply to let things go and make excuses for the people who had hurt me.

It wasn't until I came to TRIAD that I began to express my anger in an intense way. I'd punch the walls, hurting my fists. I'd kick trees in the back yard. I'd nearly injure myself trying desperately to dunk basketballs. I truly believed if I could dunk the ball, then all that rage I had pent up inside me would leave.

Sometimes I tore up my room searching for a quarter. And then I'd ring my adoptive parents' home and slam the phone down as hard as I could when they answered. But I stopped doing that when somebody told me that the click doesn't sound any louder on their end. It only hurt my ears.

A few times I dialed their number and left off the last digit. I said every cuss word in the book and wished death on both of them. Just when the cuss words started flowing, I'd hear, "If you'd like to make a phone call, please hang up and dial again." But as time went on, I found myself calling them less and less. More and more I wished to strengthen my distance from Myrtle and G. I told people I didn't have parents. In essence, it was true. They had not given me life. And though they had been my legal guardians, they did not fulfill their duties, so they didn't deserve the title of parents or guardians. I wanted nothing from them—not their money, not their permission slips, not their apologies. Nothing.

In my new environment, I didn't look to others to assuage my feelings of emptiness and frustration that stemmed from my broken ties with my adoptive parents, so I found ways to gratify and soothe myself. I chose to be alone and found comfort and healing in my solitude. I didn't feel I was condemned to be a lonely soul for the rest of my life. But at the same time, it was hard for me to believe that I could make connections with or become attached to any new people who came into my world. My fear of abandonment and abuse made me repel people who sometimes had the best intentions.

I spent most of my time in my room reflecting on my past and imagining my future by idealizing the most important people in my life—the people I didn't know but should have. My biological family would be the only people, I thought, who could help me feel whole and important. There was power in their absence from my life. I had an intense hopeful anticipation of our reunion. I knew it was going to happen. When? Who knew? But I was going to make it happen. It had to happen. Something in my life was going to turn out right. And it was going to be my ultimate dream of my family reunion. Everyone was going to welcome me back with open arms and love me. We'd promise never to leave each other again. Nothing but death could tear us apart.

Still, I was at an emotional disadvantage because I was still a minor and had no right to search for my biological family until I turned eighteen. Four more years of waiting seemed unfathomable. So I passed the time alone, swimming around in my illusions. In my mind, I put those anonymous family members on a pedestal way above myself.

Everything I did—getting good grades, being the best athlete I could be, writing poetry and stories, winning matches on the debate team, staying out of trouble—was to one day share with them. I wanted them to be proud of me. To admire me. To accept me. To love me. To validate my existence. This hope helped me stay focused while I was in that group home. That hope was going to help me make TRIAD Group Home and that entire child welfare system a stepping-stone to a successful life that I would share with my family.

As I walked away from that living room window, I took a quick glance at Sharon, a sixteen-year-old black girl who wore her hair in Afro puffs and sucked her thumb and toyed with her earlobe whenever she watched television. Sharon was one resident I stayed away from. She was deceitful and made trouble among others in the house. She smiled in your face one minute and the next stabbed you in the back. None of us knew her story, why she was in the group home. She never talked about her past.

Eight girls and four boys lived at TRIAD Group Home. We had all been physically or sexually abused, and in some cases both. The youngest kids were twelve, and the oldest was seventeen. We all were required to go to school and psychotherapy once a week. Everybody had a chore that changed each week. We got ten dollars a week for allowance and sixty dollars a month from the state. Once a year we were given $200 for clothes.

The rules at TRIAD were simple: no drugs, no alcohol, no sex, no skipping school, no leaving the house without permission, no stealing, no disrespecting of staff, and no fighting. Anyone who broke the rules got kicked out of the house and ended up back in some shelter. The rules were pretty straightforward to me. I never had a problem with rules. I just couldn't live with people setting limitations on me, like the directors of the program, Sisters Lorraine and Mary.

Sister Lorraine and Sister Mary came rolling into the room like two slopping elephants. They had an evil aura about them. I couldn't explain it or figure it out at first, but the first time I met them, I felt it. When you're somebody who has been abused for a long time, you develop a certain sense about bad people.

Sister Lorraine and Sister Mary said they were nuns, but I saw no sign of religion in them. They weren't like the nuns I had known at Incarnation. They didn't wear those itchy penguin suits or carry rosaries around with them. They never spoke of God or the Blessed Virgin Mary. They cussed and smoked, and the staff members said they were lovers. Certain staff members and residents referred to them as "fat dykes" behind their backs. I simply tried to imagine those two women rolling around together in the dark, and I cringed at those two bodies—short, stubby, over 200 pounds, never-ending breasts, wide butts, and all that evil—in one bed. Outside of that sexual context, just looking at them in their normal state was something I avoided doing. Both were hard on the eye.

Sister Lorraine asked Sharon to leave the room because they were going to have a meeting with me. "Hello, Stacey," said Sister Mary, as she turned off the television. When Sister Lorraine plopped down on the couch, I heard the plastic covering on the seat sighing as it lost its air.

"We meet with all the residents after they've been here at TRIAD for at least a month," said Sister Lorraine, scratching her armpit. Sister Mary's eyes studied Sister Lorraine from head to toe as she spoke to me. "We want to make sure you are adjusting well here at TRIAD."

"And—" Sister Lorraine put up a finger, "we want to discuss your future."

I didn't know if a kid was supposed to adjust well to some state-run program. How did a kid adjust well without parents? Did adjusting well mean becoming comfortable or satisfied with arrangements that somebody else had made for me? How was I supposed to adjust well to my new title as ward of the state? That alone made me feel thrown away and unwanted. I was some statistic, part of some social worker's caseload, a burden on society.

The neighbors hated our house. It was always kept neat and clean, there wasn't loud music, and we didn't run around terrorizing other people in the neighborhood. The problem was that the house was in an all-white upper-middle-class neighborhood, and there were twelve troubled black kids living under the same roof. They didn't want that kind of "element" around their children.

Truth be told, I felt nervous living around them. The neighbors threw us hostile looks. They pulled their children close to them when they saw us walking past or playing in the backyard. They made me feel odd, as if I had done something wrong to be in that house.

Sister Mary and Sister Lorraine explained to me that I was supposed to live in the group home until I turned eighteen. Once I turned eighteen, I would move into the Independent Living Program in Trenton. The state would find me an apartment, which I'd share with someone I didn't know. They'd pay for me to go to Mercer County Community College if I chose to continue my education after high school. Every month I'd receive a check for food and other expenses.

"And," Sister Lorraine's eyes got big as she glanced at Sister Mary and then back at me, "every six months you get $200 for clothes instead of just once a year."

"The Independent Living Program lasts until you turn twenty-one. By then the state expects that you'll find a job and be ready to support yourself," Sister Mary said.

Sister Lorraine gave me her social rhetoric: "This system is like a safety net for young people."

"Not a springboard?" I asked, trying to be cynical.

They looked at each other awkwardly.

"A springboard?" Sister Lorraine stretched her eyes.

"You can get stuck in a net," I said. "A safety net will stop you from fallin', but it doesn't help you get anywhere. You want us to end up somewhere, right?"

They ignored my comment and question. Perhaps they didn't like my metaphor. Maybe they just didn't want to acknowledge that mine made more sense than theirs. They really thought they had a solid plan mapped out for me. They probably really thought that TRIAD Group Home, the Independent Living Program, and the resources from the State of New Jersey Division of Youth and Family Services would be the keys I needed to help me reach my full potential as a productive citizen.

"If you are smart, you will work the system. You will take the resources we offer you and make it work for you. This is a great opportunity for you being here at TRIAD," said Sister Lorraine.

I gave them a slight grin and dropped my eyes down to my fingernails and the toothpick so they couldn't see my grin turning to a silent laugh. I heard Myrtle's voice in my head: "Nobody will give you the kind of life that we can give you."

I took in a deep breath and let the words come out: "I want to go to boarding school."

They were stunned.

"Excuse me?" Sister Mary's eyebrows crunched together.

"I want to go to boarding school." I repeated myself louder and clearer that time. They looked at me as if I had taken leave of my senses.

The idea seemed to come out of nowhere. But boarding school was something that I had been thinking about for over a year. At one of the youth shelters I had been placed in before TRIAD, I met a counselor named Cornell Manning. He told me that youth shelters were no place for a kid like me. He said I would waste away in the system and fall through the cracks. He didn't want to see that happen to me. So he told me about a better way out.

Cornell had grown up in the inner city of Trenton. He was smart, a track star, and had a charming personality. He applied to The Lawrenceville School, a prestigious boarding school down the road from Princeton University. He won a full scholarship, got his education, and went to college.

One evening he brought a colorful brochure from the school. That world looked so comfortable. Stable. Rich. Green. Sunny. Privileged. Cornell kept encouraging me to apply to the school, but I didn't have the courage. He said I was smart, athletic, black, and female—something they didn't have much of at the school. Though I had all those advantages, my biggest disadvantage was that I was a ward of the state. The kids at Lawrenceville, I thought, came from perfect homes. I wouldn't fit in there.

I stumbled across the brochure one evening during one of my temper tantrums. That time I looked through it closely from back to front cover. The kids looked happy, confident, and intelligent. In their eyes, I could see that they knew they were going somewhere in life. I wanted to be part of that. One way I was going to be able to truly define myself was through a stellar education.

Every Tuesday night, students from Lawrenceville Prep came to TRIAD for two hours as part of their community service program. They tutored us, played games, or just hung out with us. So while the students were there, I watched them interact with the other kids. I listened to the way they spoke, the way they wove their sentences together into smart ideas. They didn't seem snobby or spoiled like prep school kids are often stereotyped. Still, I was a bit intimidated by them and yearned to be in their shoes with the opportunity they had. Though they were my age, they didn't seem like children. They had old souls and adult minds.

I was afraid that one of the kids from Lawrenceville would look at me and laugh when I said that I wanted to apply to the school. I figured they'd patronize me with talk about how I could make possible anything I put my mind to, even if they didn't think I had a chance in hell of getting into the school. But that wasn't the case. One of the boys, George, a white kid from Connecticut, gave me the 800 number to the school and told me to ask for Charlie Williams. Mr. Williams was the guy to talk to about scholarships, he said. George told me he was a scholarship kid. I was shocked because on the surface he looked like and sounded like one of the rich white boys.

"Are you not happy here at TRIAD?" Sister Lorraine asked me.

"Stacey, this is the best program for kids like you," Sister Mary cut in.

A kid like me? How did she define that? I wasn't like other kids. I was an individual with needs and aspirations.

"There is a long waiting list on my desk of other kids who would appreciate being in this program," she reminded me, as she did so many times with the other residents.

"I'm not unhappy," I assured her. "I do appreciate being here. But I want something better."

"Something better?" Sister Lorraine frowned, insulted.

"Something better?" Sister Mary echoed a split second later.

"Yes." I paused. "I want something better. I don't like your plan for me. I don't want to sit in this system. Waste away. Fall through the cracks. I want to go to an Ivy League school, not Mercer County Community College. I don't want to run to the mailbox every month for a check from the state. I don't want to have to wait six months to shop for clothes when I need them. I don't want people telling me what I can and can't do."

"What's wrong with your public school?" Sister Mary asked, annoyed.

"Nothing," I smiled. "I like my school. I like my teachers. I like the other kids there. I just want more."

"Why do you think you deserve more?" Sister Lorraine smirked.

"Because I deserve it," I shot back at her. "I've been through a lot and I just want to take control over my life."

"Why boarding school?" Sister Mary shifted in her seat.

"Because it's the best. I can go to school, I can live on campus and better my chances at getting into an Ivy League college, and I won't have to live in some group home or shelter or worry about where I'm gonna be the next day."

"Ivy League," I heard Sister Lorraine mutter under her breath.

"Do you realize," Sister Mary started to say something. "Do you—" she started again.

"It costs over twenty thousand dollars a year to go to one of these prep schools," Sister Lorraine finished for her.

"I can apply for a scholarship," I suggested.

Sister Lorraine raised both hands in the air. "Do you know how competitive it is to get a scholarship?"

"I can compete," I said.

Sister Lorraine's voice hardened. "Let's be real, Miss Patton. You're a ward of the state! You're in the system. Those kinds of schools only take the cream of the crop. You are not the cream of the crop!"

I felt as if she had just thrown a dagger at me. "Why not? Why am I not the cream?" I got defensive.

"Must we point out why, Stacey?" Sister Lorraine asked.

"Yes," I insisted.

"Number one," she tapped one finger. "You don't have parents taking care of you."

"You have deeply rooted psychological problems stemming from your past," Sister Mary added.

"You don't get straight A's," continued Sister Lorraine. "You're an A and B student."

"You don't have money."

"And you're not white," Sister Lorraine put the icing on the cake. "How do you expect to survive in an old-boy school network like that?"

"Well, then, I don't want to be part of the crop if I have to be white, some boring nerdy straight A student with nothing else to offer the universe. So what if I have no money, no parents, and I have some psychological problems. I think that all makes my application a bit more interesting because despite all this, I'm still here and still trying to make the best of my life!"

"Really, Stacey, I admire your courage," Sister Mary sighed. "But you have to be realistic."

"In the twenty-five years I've been in this business, I've never seen this sort of thing happen," said Sister Lorraine.

Sister Mary's voice got low. "Stacey, we don't want you to set yourself up for failure."

"Everybody fails at somethin'. You have to fail to get some place great and to become something worthwhile. Failin' is not tryin'," I said in a rigid voice, looking them directly in their eyes. "What's worse is not trying to set myself up for anything."

Trying and trying again is the purpose of being on this earth. If I don't try to better myself, to prove folks wrong, to beat the odds, then I will always be some little girl or, worse, some walking corpse.

"No boarding school is going to waste twenty thousand dollars a year on a ward of the state," Sister Lorraine said as she got up from the couch shaking her head hard.

Sister Mary and I were left alone in the room. She rubbed her thighs slowly with her fingertips. "Stacey, you may get better grades than the other kids here. You may be smarter. You might be a good ball player and have other hidden talents the other kids don't have. But you are no different from the rest of them. You are a ward of the state, and you can't change this fact."

I looked down at my kneecaps. She was right. Ward of the state. That was my label. Maybe I was being too ambitious. Twenty-five years was a long time to be in that business, so I guess Sister Mary should have known best. But she didn't know Stacey Patton.

"I've never met someone so young and so conceited," she frowned at me.

"What's wrong with being conceited?" I asked.

"You think you're better than everybody else!"

"No. I think highly of myself for the first time in my life. I realize that I have the power inside me to turn things around. I am important. If I don't think highly of myself, then who will? You and Sister Lorraine obviously don't think highly of me. You guys don't think highly enough of me to believe that I can achieve this goal despite my circumstances. So it looks like I'm gonna have to do this on my own."

"Good luck." Sister Mary grunted and laughed at the same time. She motioned her hands as if she was washing them of me. "This reality check will be good for you."

"We'll see," I smiled back at her. "It might be good for you too." I watched her leave the room, my heart still racing in my chest.

That little attack was good for me. It taught me not to back down or be deterred by somebody else. I knew I was going to have to do a lot more of that to heal myself and get respect. I couldn't allow myself to be defined through the eyes of others. Still, I had a lot of work to do if I was going to beat my odds and prove Sister Mary and Sister Lorraine wrong.

Of all the odds I had facing me, my greatest was my own fear. I was afraid to fail. I believed that if I put my mind to getting into The Lawrenceville School and I failed, then somehow that failure would say something about me. People wouldn't consider all that I had lived through and had facing me. I lived in a world where people were ahistorical. They didn't acknowledge that some people were born with nothing and came from nothing. People don't always create their own dysfunction. History creates it for them, and that history is always linked to the present. Nothing was ever going to be handed to me. I knew I had to set my eyes on what I wanted. I had to decide that I wanted it more than I feared it. That was the only way I was going to aspire to greater things.

Otherwise I would continue to view life as survival and constant struggle.

It took me nearly two weeks to pick up the phone and dial the school's 800 number. Fear had locked up my fingers. All I kept thinking was how those people were going to laugh at me when I asked for an application to be sent to a group home. I must have dialed that number three or four times a day and hung up. But each time I dialed the number, I got more and more courage. Finally, I called and spoke to the receptionist who patched me through to Charlie Williams, the man George said I needed to speak to about scholarships.

Mr. Williams had a loud and energetic voice that shook in my ear like thunder.

"My name is Stacey Patton," I said nervously.

"Any relation to General George Patton?" he asked. His question threw me off.

"Excuse me, sir?"

"General George Patton? Old blood and guts? War hero? Any relation?"

"No sir," I grinned into the phone. "No relation."

"What can I do for you, Miss Stacey Patton?"

I took a deep breath. I didn't want to sound nervous or intimidated. I had practiced over and over again what I needed to say and how I needed to say it.

"Mr. Williams, I know it costs a lot of money to go to your school. I can't pay for it. I live in a group home. But it's not my fault that I'm here. My adoptive mother beat me all the time." I spoke so fast I ran out of breath. "I want to come to your school to get out of the system so I can go to a good college and have a better life. I get good grades, and I play sports. I'm involved in other activities: the debate team and the creative writing club."

He giggled. I tried to catch my breath and slow down my thumping heart. Why was he giggling? This was no prank call. My attempt to reach for a way out of my situation was nothing to giggle about. Couldn't he hear the desperation in my voice? Couldn't he tell I wanted and needed that opportunity more than anything else?

"Well, Miss Stacey Patton," he paused and giggled again. "It's not every day that I get a call like this. I admire your courage. Can you come here next Monday for an interview?"

I almost choked. "An interview? Um, yes. An interview. I can come. I'll be there, Mr. Williams."

"Let's say ten o'clock," he said. "You're going to come to the admissions building. It's a big campus, so just ask someone if you get lost."

"I'll be there! What should I wear, sir?"

"Just be you," he said before I thanked him over and over again and hung up the phone.

I took one small step and moved forward. I had been on the brink of letting Sister Mary and Sister Lorraine discourage me from imagining myself beyond the child welfare system. I was ready to accept my reality as it had been thrown at me. But I made one phone call and found hope. I once heard an old black man say that hope was a song in a weary throat. At that moment I felt like singing.

One of the girls in the house let me borrow a skirt suit and some stockings for my interview. Though I had never stepped foot in a world like Lawrenceville, I knew that appearances were important. I had to look like I could get along and belong at that school. I couldn't go there looking like a ward of the state.

That Monday came, and Sister Mary agreed to drive me to the campus. At first, we were silent as we rode down that five-mile stretch in Princeton that snaked southwest toward Trenton. We passed Princeton University, Bristol-Myers Squibb, the governor's mansion, and Jasna Polana, the most expensive house ever built.

Just a block away from Rider University and farther down Route 206, I started to see the 200-year-old campus, which stretched for about a mile behind high brick and wrought-iron fences. Across the street there were a few shops, restaurants, and big old houses. My mouth dropped when I saw the golf course and dozens of turn-of-the-century buildings, mostly built of a dark-red-brown hewn stone.

"I can't believe this is a high school," I mumbled.

"Yeah," Sister Mary replied. "Hard to believe." And then she muttered, "Cream of the crop."

She was trying to irk my nerves by being sarcastic. But I didn't waste my breath on her. I had to save my energy and focus for my interview.

The trees, flowers, grass, colors, organization of everything, the students' faces—none of it looked ordinary. The whole scene was breathtaking, like something out of a magazine. It all seemed like it was flowing from immense wealth and privilege. I wanted to be part of that simply because it was another world, a perfect place for me to escape.

We drove slowly through the main entrance, allowing students to cross in front of us with their lumpy backpacks. The dorms had names like Cleve, Griswald, Woodhull, Dickinson, Kirby, McClellan, Stanley, and Dawes, among other names. I wondered who those people were and what they did to get their names on the front of the buildings.

Two boys wearing khaki pants and polo shirts were throwing a little white ball back and forth with long white sticks that had nets at the ends.

"What's that?" I asked Sister Mary.

"Lacrosse," she answered. "It's a sport rich kids play."

"Maybe I'll try that sport some day," I said.

"It takes a lot of skill and coordination. You have to do a lot of thinking," she said.

"So does basketball. So does track and field," I said shooting her a dirty look.

Sister Mary parked the car in front of the old gray chapel. I straightened the small pile of documents in my lap. I had my transcripts, creative writing pieces, and sports clippings from the *Trenton Times*. When I opened my door, I heard a bell chiming, and less than a minute later all the students disappeared into the buildings. Sister Mary opened her door. I watched her get out. When her eyes met mine, she could see there was something wrong.

"Problem?" she sneered. "Are you having second thoughts about doing this? Do you want to turn around and go back?"

"No." I felt the chilly wind across my face. Even the air smelled cleaner there. "You don't need to come with me," I looked straight into her eyes.

She looked insulted, cut down a peg or two.

"And may I ask why?"

"Because I want to do this on my own. I don't need your help or your presence. If this gets messed up, I want it to be because I messed it up. I don't want anyone else to have anything to do with it. Anyway, you and Sister Lorraine don't think I'm gonna get in. I don't need to bring that kind of negative energy into my interview. So please don't come."

She toyed with her keys, pointing one of them at me like she was going to say something. She got back into the car and told me she'd be waiting for me and slammed her door.

The admissions building was just past Memorial Hall and Father's Building. I couldn't walk right. My butt and inner thighs could hardly breathe in this skirt. I never felt natural in dress clothes. As I made my way up the white marble steps and through the big green doors, I looked down at my ankles and noticed a run beginning to form in my stockings.

"Miss Patton," that thunderous voice boomed as I walked in the building. I couldn't be concerned about the run in my stockings.

A tall, jolly-looking white man with rosy cheeks, khaki pants, blue blazer, red tie, and battered penny loafers reached out his huge hand to me. "Come on in," he said as everyone in the lobby smiled at me. I kept wondering how he knew it was me walking through the door. I hadn't described how I looked over the phone.

I wanted to jump right in and get serious with Mr. Williams. "Lay down what I have to do to get in," I wanted to say to him. What kind of job do I have to get to pay for my tuition? Instead, he told me corny jokes to break the ice again. I laughed.

"So you want to come to Lawrenceville?" He leaned back in his seat.

"Yes sir," I smiled, massaging the top of my pile of documents.

"Why?" he asked.

"Because I can do well here," I said as I handed him the documents.

He didn't look impressed. He said nothing about my grades, the stories, or the clippings.

He ran his finger across his forehead. "I don't know how this can be done. We're talking about a significant amount of financial aid for three years. We're talking about a full scholarship."

"I can work." I threw the idea at him to let him know how serious I was about attending the school. He smiled and shook his head. "None of our students work. Gone are the days when students serve in the dining halls. We want our students to focus their attention on their academics and make the most of their Lawrenceville experience. At Lawrenceville you can't tell the scholarship kid from the kid who comes from millions. Money is not what earns you respect around here. A whole slew of other things matter. You are measured by your character, intellect, and what you add to this community."

Mr. Williams stacked my papers and handed them back to me. Something in me sank. I watched as he picked up a sterling silver Cross pen off his cherry wood desktop. He licked the tip of his finger and reached for a form of some kind.

"This is a waiver for you to take the Secondary Schools Aptitude Test. Every kid who applies to prep school has to take it," he explained.

"What do I have to score?"

"Higher than zero," he laughed. I didn't know if he was joking or serious. "When you complete your application, send it directly to me. Don't worry about the application fee. You will receive an acceptance letter or rejection letter by March 4. I'll see what I can do to make this work. I can't promise you anything, though, so don't put all your eggs in one basket."

He shook my hand again, and I left his office.

A senior black girl named Michelle from Brooklyn took me on a tour of the campus. Mr. Williams told her to show me all the sports facilities: the squash courts, the Olympic-size pool, the ice hockey rink, the indoor track, and both basketball courts. As I walked with her, I was envious of her opportunity. I could visualize myself in that picture. The whole time I kept hoping it wouldn't be the last time I set foot on that campus.

At first it didn't cross my mind how I would fit in with the other students. I knew that most of them were rich and white and had important names and connections, even though Mr. Williams said all that didn't matter. Even in poverty-stricken worlds, names and connections mattered. But I would come out of nowhere and make them know my name. I wouldn't tell anyone that I was a ward of the state, that I was a foster child, adopted, abused, a scholarship kid. All they would know was that I am Stacey Patton, that interesting smart girl from Trenton.

"So you're really going through with this?" Sister Mary asked as I locked my seatbelt across my waist. Her eyes looked over the brochure and application I guarded with my life.

"Yeah, wouldn't you? Look at this place."

I couldn't wait to get back to the house and start on my application. It was due in three weeks. I was going to have it done by the end of that week. I had to fill out information forms, write three essays, and get teacher recommendations.

"I still don't understand why you would want to put yourself in this situation where you're so different from everybody else." She turned the key in the ignition, and the car coughed itself awake.

"I'm already in a situation where I'm so different from everybody else. You just don't see it. I'm just a number to you." I opened the brochure and melted into the colorful panoramic shots of the campus.

"We'll see if you're so special," Sister Mary said as we drove off the campus. She was right. We would see.

That March day didn't come quick enough. I couldn't concentrate on anything but getting back to the group home and checking the mail. That afternoon, the long yellow school bus came to a slow halt two blocks from the TRIAD House. That school day seemed as if it would never end. I couldn't concentrate during class. I didn't want to be there, and that bus didn't seem like it moved fast enough. That day it seemed that every red light on Ewingville and Pennington Road stopped us. I hustled down the school bus aisle and jumped off without saying good-bye to anyone. But they understood. Many of them knew how important that day was for me. I had been talking about it and counting down the days since the fall.

I swung my backpack onto my shoulder. I heard my feet slapping the sidewalk. My arms pumped hard. The wind blew through the newborn trees, allowing their leaves to give me a soft applause. I ran past a bare trunk on a neighbor's front lawn and twisted myself around stubs of broken limbs left over from fall. I smelled azaleas that had opened early. As I willed myself to run faster, my strong athletic hands trembled. At times I felt that my body was going to get stuck in midair. But I couldn't think about stopping.

When I finally got inside the house, I dropped my backpack at the bottom of the staircase in the hallway and darted toward the back office where the staff put the daily mail. It was as if everything around me got dark. There were no colors, no shapes, no smells, no sounds other than my breathing.

My eyes narrowed when I saw it, sitting there waiting for me next to no other mail. I remembered what George had told me. "If you get a small, thin envelope that means you didn't get in. If you get a small, thin envelope and a big envelope, that means you got in."

Something in me broke when I scanned the entire area surrounding the thin envelope and didn't see the big one. Where was it? "Is this all the mail?" I asked in a weary voice.

I dragged my finger along the envelope and then picked it up. I studied the face of the envelope. "The Lawrenceville School" was typed in big red block letters. The seal in the corner had "Virtus semper viridis" etched on it. It was addressed to me, Miss Stacey Pamela Patton. I tried to read into whether it was a rejection or acceptance letter by how they typed my name. Would they have wasted time writing my name like that if it was a rejection letter? Still, where was the big envelope? Oh, my God, I thought. I didn't get in. I was heartbroken before I even opened the envelope. "That's all the mail that came for you, Stacey," I heard a voice in the back office say to me.

Some sick feeling began to stir at the pit of my stomach. I didn't want to face the prospects of being stuck at TRIAD until I turned eighteen. I couldn't imagine facing the "I told you so" I knew I'd get from Sister Lorraine and Sister Mary.

I couldn't imagine failure. It wasn't the kind of thing I had ever prepared myself for. For me, failure equaled some kind of internal death. And I didn't want the lights to go off inside me. I didn't want to become a walking corpse before I left childhood. I was already an old woman.

I pulled myself out of the kitchen, through the narrow hallway, and up what seemed to be ten thousand wooden stairs. I kept holding the unopened envelope up to the light so I could see the big red REJECT letters through the folded paper inside.

Each step I climbed, I kept thinking of Langston Hughes and the crystal stairs in his poem. Sighing dramatically, I slammed my bedroom door and searched out the chair to my desk. I wanted to be alone. I didn't want anybody to be around trying to console me when I knew they had doubted me from the beginning. I didn't want to hear, "It's okay," because it wouldn't be okay. It would be the end of the world. I stared at this envelope, studying every small corner and crevice while thinking about how it reminded me of linen when I ran my fingers across its surface.

My future was in that envelope. Not only was it super-thin, it looked unpromising. I had put all my eggs in one basket because I didn't apply to any other schools. I didn't have a backup plan. I would have to stay in public school, graduate, go to the Independent Living Program, and then Mercer County Community College. I'd just have to hope for the best.

I sat there quietly breathing more evenly as I lifted the envelope and turned it over. I picked at the top left corner until a space was torn. I picked and picked; listening to the tearing sound that felt like it was piercing my eardrums. The envelope was finally open. I slid out the ivory-colored letter and watched the envelope hit my desktop. I swallowed hard as I unfolded the paper and read. My eyes didn't miss one detail. The date. The return address. The school seal raised in the middle of the letter. I even recognized that old building smell I had smelled that day I went to my interview with Mr. Charlie Williams. Finally, I let my eyes take in the words:

Dear Miss Stacey Pamela Patton,
It gives me great pleasure to inform you that you have been

admitted to The Lawrenceville School for the Fall semester of 1993.

I stopped right there. I couldn't read anymore. The letter slipped out of my hand. I jumped up from my chair, clinching both fists and raising them in the air, like I had scored the winning shot in a championship game. I didn't believe it. So I picked the letter up off the floor and read the line again, more carefully to make sure I wasn't hallucinating. I dabbed my finger on the tip of my tongue, wetted it, and then dragged it lightly across the signature of the director of admissions. When it smeared, I confirmed it was real and official.

"Yes! Yes! Yes!" My chair hit the floor, when I banged against it. "Oh, my God! I got in! I got in! I'm going to prep school! I'm going to boarding school," I hollered.

For the first time in my life I cried happy tears. At that very moment I believed that saying I always heard at church: "Trouble don't last always."

I heard somebody knocking. Before I could say "come in," the door opened. It was Sister Mary. She leaned against the door frame and crossed her arms. My excited face turned to a simple smile.

"I take it you got your news," she said, sounding bland and unaffected, almost unhappy.

"Yeah, I got in," I held the letter high. "I'm gonna frame this." I wish I had a camera so I could have taken a picture of the expression on her face and framed that too.

"Well, congrats. Just make sure you graduate," she uttered as she closed my door.

"Why can't you just be happy for me?" I yelled at the door. "She can kiss my ass," I muttered.

If I was the director of that place, I would have been joyous if a kid did something like I had done to get out of the system. She should have been thinking that I was one fewer case she had to deal with. I was going on to bigger and better things. Wasn't that the goal of the system? Didn't they want and expect us to reach our full potential?

I wanted to call Myrtle and G to throw my good news in their faces. I wanted to tell them they were wrong about me. It was official. I was never going to come back to them crawling, on drugs, pregnant, in trouble, needing and wanting them. My life was worth more than two cents. I had proven that by earning a $24,000 a year scholarship to one of the finest prep schools in the nation. What would they think about that?

But then I realized how immature that would be even though I would have loved to see the dumbfounded look on their faces. So I simply let my success be my greatest revenge all on its own.

When I finished reading my acceptance letter, I picked up my chair, sat down, and gazed out the window in front of my desk. I watched the sky for hours. Eventually the sun melted below some trees behind the Lutheran church across the street. It left behind long butter-colored fingers in the sky.

Myrtle and G didn't matter anymore. Yesterday didn't matter. My loss of self-esteem had been a barrier to loving and asserting myself. It had stunted my courage. But my acceptance to Lawrenceville sparked something inside me that would never burn out. All that had happened to me before that day had humbled me and brought me to my knees. But it didn't vanquish me. From that day forward I promised never to doubt myself or let anything bring me to my knees again. I would never allow anybody to define me or my possibilities. I would shape my own destiny.

TWO

Some things change, and other things stay the same. And some things simply repeat themselves. We call them cycles. The people in my life were like cycles, repeating and hardly changing. That's how it was in the world I was leaving behind.

There I was, riding down that road again as I sat in the front seat of my social worker's car. I wanted to scrape off those words on the side of the window: "State of New Jersey for Official Use Only." You could hear a pin drop in that car each time we stopped at a traffic light, just as you could years before when a different social worker took me on visits from the foster home in East Orange. I'll never forget that one visit she took me on where a woman and her husband took one look at me and shook their heads.

"She's too old," the woman said to her husband. "I want a baby. Babies don't know. Babies don't have as much baggage."

We never stepped foot in their house. The social worker turned me around by my shoulder, and we left. Did she think that foster kids were tailor-made to order like dolls?

I smiled to myself as I remembered that trip. My eyes moved past the letters on the window and got lost in the emerald-colored trees and the black ropy telephone wires. Six lumpy green garbage bags were piled up in the back seat, and one sat on my lap. Thoughts of Ted crossed my mind. I hadn't heard from or seen him since I had left the Anchor House, but I remembered what he told me about emptying my baggage and looking at it. Eventually I got rid of all my material possessions I had from my adoptive parents' home. Slowly I recreated the stuff of my baggage. The problem was that I still had the same bags. One day when I got some money, I would get suitcases, I promised.

My other belongings were packed in the trunk: brand-new sheets, a matching gray comforter, towels from Macy's, alarm clock, stereo, mesh basket, stocks of soap and other toiletries, snacks, laundry basket, a jar of quarters, and the Ernest Hemingway poster Mrs. Hughes had given me on my last day of school at Ewing High. I promised her I'd put the poster directly over my desk in my dorm room at Lawrenceville.

I was so excited when move-in day arrived that last day in August. I felt like I had firecrackers in my head. The night before, I couldn't sleep because I was up thinking about how I was going to organize my new room. I was assigned to Kirby House, the dorm closest to the dining center and the field house. Thirty tenth- and eleventh-grade girls lived in that same dorm. Three other dorms—Stanley, Stevens, and McClellan—also house tenth- and eleventh-grade girls. Our dorms were part of what was called the Circle Houses. It was designed to look like a small community where there would be unity, camaraderie, competition, and pride.

"Wow!" my social worker blurted out as we turned into the main gate. "This is a high school?"

"Yep," I giggled. She saw what I knew: Lawrenceville was an extra-special place, a completely different world.

"Unbelievable," she gasped. "This looks like a college campus. Better looking than most college campuses. And they gave you a full ride?" her voice jumped.

"Yep, a full ride," I said proudly, straightening my body in the seat.

"Well," she smiled. "Miss Stacey Patton. You've certainly been given a lot of rides in your life, but none quite like this one," she said. "You done good, kid. I sure hope you make the most of this opportunity. I don't want to get any calls saying I need to come get you and find another place for you."

We looped around the campus through limousines, BMWs, SUVs, Volkswagens, and mini U-Haul trucks. The license plates were from all over: New Hampshire, Maine, Rhode Island, Florida, Nebraska, Texas, Virginia. I saw two boys struggling to get a long busted-looking couch into the front doorway of one of the dorms. Some kids were out playing lacrosse and Frisbee in a section of the campus called the Bowl. That field, about half the size of a football field, separated the lower school boys' dorm from the lower school girls' dorm. Just as we passed that section, I saw a mother fighting back tears as she held her son. I could tell he probably couldn't fully understand her tears. She was probably feeling a whole confluence of emotions: pride, fear, and loss.

"Don't park right in front of my dorm," I pleaded with Helen. "And don't tell anybody you're from DYFS."

"Okay." She dragged the word out of her mouth. "I don't have a problem with finding some other parking space. But who am I supposed to be if I can't be your social worker?"

"Tell them you're my aunt," I said.

She almost choked on her laugh. "You sure about that?"

"Sure. Why not?"

"Look at me, Stacey. Do you really think people are going to believe I'm your aunt?" She turned to give me a better look at her blue eyes, long dirty-blonde hair, pointy nose, and thin lips.

"Why not? Black people have white relatives. Just tell them you married into the family."

She chuckled. "Okay, this is your day. I'm not going to do anything to mess it up for you," she assured me.

There were girls everywhere when I stepped inside the Kirby House. I heard a mix of Led Zeppelin, Red Hot Chili Peppers, the Beatles, and the Blues Travelers. I didn't know those groups and didn't listen to that kind of music before I came to Lawrenceville, but it slowly grew on me. At first I was tortured by it. I called it head-banging music. I wondered how they danced to it. Ultimately I found myself singing along at times.

I can't say the same about the gospel, rap, hip-hop, reggae, soul, and R&B music I played in my room. I constantly got complaints and was told to "turn that shit off." At one point, my housemaster confiscated my speakers for one month. My crime was playing black music too loud. I had never known any black people who played or listened to music softly. We had to feel the music and become part of it. I almost went crazy without Mahalia Jackson, 2 Pac, Cassandra Wilson, Tracy Chapman, Buju Banton, and Brian McKnight.

There was a constant flow of traffic up and down the three flights of stairs. All the girls dressed the same: Teva sandals or Birkenstocks, khaki shorts, plain white T-shirts and V-necks from stores like J Crew, Abercrombie & Fitch, Banana Republic, and the Gap. They all talked alike. Even the Asian girls sounded like Valley Girls. They were cookie-cutter people with first names like Paige, Amy, Mokey, Fletcher, Ally, and Emily and last names like Van Deusen, Van Ness, Nelson, Bunn, Penske, and Hearst.

Helen unloaded my belongings while I met my housemaster, Mr. Rousseau, who was a French native, and my assistant housemaster, Mrs.

Werner, an Asian woman from Hawaii. Mr. Rousseau taught French and coached the Ultimate Frisbee team. Mrs. Werner taught chemistry and coached the cross-country team. They both welcomed and congratulated me on getting into the school. They were happy to have me in Kirby House, they said. Mr. Rousseau handed me my class schedule, school ID, and a key to my room.

"You have your own room," he said pointing me in the direction of the second floor. "I thought you'd feel more comfortable in your own space."

He was right. I needed my own private space. If I was going to keep up appearances and keep my past hidden from everybody, I didn't need a roommate getting in my business and asking questions.

When Helen dragged my last bag upstairs, she wished me luck and said she'd be in touch. I knew I wouldn't hear from her again. DYFS never put real closure on cases. Quite frankly, it didn't matter to me. I didn't want to ever see that blue car on the campus again, and I didn't want to be associated with the system.

The first thing I did was put Hemingway on the wall. Despite a few wrinkles, the poster hadn't changed much. I began to wonder about Mrs. Hughes. How was she? What was she doing at that moment? Did she think of me often? Were there teachers like her at Lawrenceville?

"Hi." A chipper voice with a deep southern drawl startled me as I unloaded my bags. "I'm Perry," the girl said, reaching out her hand.

"I'm Stacey," I said, shyly reaching for her hand. I wasn't used to kids shaking hands like adults. Where I had come from the kids touched fists, threw peace signs, or gave each other quick nods.

"What form are you in?"

"Form?" I looked confused.

"Form means grade. They do it like the English school system here," she said.

"I'm in the tenth grade, whatever form that is," I said.

"Third form," she said. "So am I."

"Where are you from?" I asked.

"Texas. And you?"

"Trenton."

"So close. Why are you boarding? You could easily be a day student."

"I'm going to be playing sports. It'll be easier for me as a boarder."

"True," she agreed.

I couldn't take my eyes off her T-shirt. I tried not to be offended by it and searched my mind to find some rationalization for why she was wearing it and why she was standing in front of me acting like I didn't notice it. Plain as day, that Confederate flag was stitched across her chest. At the bottom were the words: "Southern Pride Sweet As American Pie."

"If you need any help, lemme know," she said as she walked out of my room. At that moment, I made up my mind that I would stay away from her. Later I discovered that three other girls had wall-size Confederate flags hanging on their walls. Didn't they understand the history behind that symbol? For them it represented pride. For me it represented a nightmare for my ancestors and predecessors.

As Perry left, I stood there more concerned about whether she saw through me. Could she tell I had just come from a group home? Did my eyes give away that I was a ward of the state? Adopted? Abused? Scholarship kid?

"Hi." Another chipper voice. "I'm Rebecca," the brunette said as she poked her head into my room. "You can call me Becca."

I didn't know if I should have been making rounds to all the rooms to introduce myself, but I didn't have to. Everybody seemed so eager to come to my room, curious to see the new girl. I was one of two new girls to the dorm that year. Everybody else already knew each other.

"Cool poster," Becca said, flinging her hair behind her shoulder. "Who is that?"

"That's Ernest Hemingway." I looked at her, surprised that she didn't know who that great man was. But then I remembered that I hadn't known either.

"Stacey." She leaned closer to the wall to read Mrs. Hughes's handwriting: "There are miles and miles of pen and paper awaiting your words. Write young woman! Write!"

"A teacher at my old school wrote that for me," I explained. Someone down the hallway called for her.

"Nice to meet you," she said and rushed out.

Once I settled into my room and organized it the way I had been envisioning it in my head for months, I left the dorm to run errands. There were lines everywhere: the bookstore, the comptroller's office, and lines behind the syllabus on each classroom door. We had assignments to complete before our first day of class. I was looking forward to getting started with classes. The only major adjustment for me was going to be going to classes on Saturdays.

I saw a handful of black students when I went to the comptroller's office. That's where they handed out stipend money for scholarship kids. We were all there to get money for our books and supplies. They had first names like Tiffany, Sasha, Corey, Derek, and Dipo and last names like Williams, Washington, Owens, and Johnson. They smiled when they saw me and even gave me hugs, like they had known me all along.

"What house did they put you in?" asked a girl named Patia who was from Brooklyn.

"Kirby," I answered.

"Ilk, Kirby." Kathy from St. Louis frowned.

"Why did they put her in Kirby?" Jamilla, also from Brooklyn, gave everybody else a distorted look.

"That's the ho house," Tiffany snickered.

"You ain't hear about that house before you came?" asked Jamilla.

"No."

"Them girls be givin' up the coochie," said Tiffany.

"Raunchy tricks," said Patia, the tall girl standing over Tiffany. I wondered if she was on the basketball team.

"Y'all," Jamilla covered her mouth. "she's the only black girl in that house."

"Damn," said Tiffany.

"That's foul," said Patia.

The boys were silent, just looking on.

"You requested to be in Kirby?" asked Jamilla.

"No," I said. "I didn't request a dorm. That's just where they put me." They had no idea that throughout my life, I had never requested a placement.

"They put all the black girls in McClellan," said Tiffany.

"All five of us," said Patia as everyone snickered.

"You can come visit the sistas whenever them hoochies get on your nerves," said Patia.

"Yeah, come chill with us," Jamilla urged.

"Ladies." A white teacher bowed his head as he walked by us as we made our way across the campus. "What are we doing here?" he smiled. "Are we having some kind of revolution?"

Everybody got quiet for a second. "Yeah," said Jamilla boldly. "We lookin' for massa."

We all snickered and stepped up our speed. "They fuck with you like that here," she said. "I fuck right back with 'em."

When I got back to Kirby shortly before our six o'clock house meeting, I had my school books and supplies in hand, my assignments for the first day of class, and had eaten my first bland semiwarm meal at the dining center. Mr. Rousseau was knocking at my door just as I turned the corner.

"Stacey," he smiled. I loved how the French intonation of my name sounded when it came out of his mouth. "I wanted to speak with you earlier today, but I thought now would be a better time."

"Okay, just let me put this stuff in my room," I said, juggling my bags and reaching for my key.

He followed me inside, gazed around the room, and told me I had fixed my room up nicely. He said it had character.

"I want to make sure you feel comfortable here, Stacey. I realize you come from a different kind of background, and it may be difficult adjusting, especially since there are no other African American girls in the dorm. I complained to the admissions office and told them they should at least send two instead of one by herself. You have to understand that many of these girls see black people only on TV, so they may come across as curious and ignorant. Try to be patient and understanding, but if you have any problems, my door is always open."

I told Mr. Rousseau that contrary to my difficult past, I had grown up in a predominantly white neighborhood and had gone to school with white kids. But I didn't live with those white people, and I didn't know rich white kids. They were a different brand of white people.

At our first house meeting, I picked a comfortable spot in the corner next to the piano, away from everybody else. Finally, all thirty of us were together in the same room. We all introduced ourselves one by one. It was then that I realized just how different I was. The other girls knew each other and had the same things in common. They went to the same country clubs and ski resorts. They traveled to different countries. They salivated over the same blond-haired boys. They laughed the same. They said *like* every third word. They played in each other's hair and laughed at jokes I didn't find funny. Most of all, they didn't have to think about being white.

At first, it wasn't my blackness that made me feel so different. I had come from a different culture and class of people. Theirs was one of money, privilege, and conformity. In mine, people had to struggle to hold on to the little bit of something they had. There were no silver spoons or platters.

I sat there looking at that sea of whiteness and decided I wanted no part of it. I did not come to Lawrenceville to be bleached or whitewashed. I was simply there to soak up the best education and use Lawrenceville to get me into a good college. But that same evening, my attitude on our racial differences changed when I walked into the television room just as one girl asked another to pass her "the nigger stick." I watched as the other girl passed her the long black remote control so she could change the channel. They never saw me because I quickly turned around and went to my room seething with shock and anger.

I heard Myrtle's voice in my head, "You can't trust white folks. You can't trust them no further than you can see them. And then you better not get too close. They may let you into their worlds, but that don't change nothin'. You will always be that nigger. They might smile at you. They might act like they like you, like they accept you. But the minute you forget that you ain't nothin' but that nigger, they gonna remind you. So don't get too big for your britches, girly."

All those years I thought Myrtle was just talking crazy. But after that little incident, I pulled out that file in my head that I had kept with all of her lessons about race and racial etiquette. I started thinking about how she told me I had two strikes against me because I'm black and female. I was going to have to be just as good as the white man and better if I wanted to be anything. I thought Myrtle had racial paranoia, but it was a sort of intuition that was slowly becoming mine. But at the same time, I had been abused, so I was already paranoid. I didn't know who I could trust. I didn't know who was out to get me, black or white.

For me to survive in that white world at Lawrenceville, I was going to have to develop a double-consciousness, that twoness that W.E.B. DuBois talked about in the *Souls of Black Folk*, one black and one white. I would not talk like a Valley Girl, but I would speak their language and read their literature in the classroom and open spaces on the campus. Behind closed doors, I would spend time with my black peers, speaking our language, watching black comedy and films, reading black books, and listening to black music. I would sing in the gospel choir and join the Black Students Union.

I couldn't be too radical or too threatening. But at the same time, I would not celebrate or seek to immerse myself in white culture. Many times

I resented it. Every day whiteness was thrown in my face: their history, their poetry, their songs, their philosophy, like nobody else existed in the world or contributed to the making of humanity. There was no pluralism. There was eurocentrism, ethnocentrism, and white over everybody else. When we talked about black, red, yellow, and brown people to promote diversity, that kind of talk was met with hostility. They asked, "Why? Why should we learn about that? Why should we have that thrown in our faces?"

"Nigger stick." I laughed to myself as I lay on my bed. What other things did they say about us when we weren't around? But then I reminded myself that black people said things too. Racism works both ways. Growing up, I heard names like *cracker, honky, whitey, devils,* and *ofays.* But the way I understood it, black people said those things because those feelings about whites came out of the racism they experienced from whites. They always called white people those things when they felt cheated, disrespected, and outright wronged.

After a few minutes, I let go of the incident, but not completely, and moved to a different place in my head. I started thinking about all I had accomplished since I ran away from Hilltop Drive. I was going to make the most of my new opportunity and let nothing get in the way and mess it up for me. Though everything seemed right and comfortable, my world was still incomplete.

I got up from my bed, opened the small top drawer on my desk, and pulled out a large envelope addressed to the State of New Jersey Adoption Registry. I slid back the chair, sat down, opened the envelope, and began to fill out the application inside.

Two weeks before I entered Lawrenceville, I called the adoption registry after being referred by someone I was talking to about finding my real family. I spoke with the director of the registry, a man named Jerry Giollio. I told him I wanted to find my biological family.

"How old are you?" he asked.

"Fifteen."

"You have to be eighteen," he said. "That's the law."

"I know, sir. But I don't live with my adoptive parents anymore."

I explained my situation to him, leaving out no details.

"Where were you born?" I was excited that he started asking questions. That meant he wanted to help me and would maybe help me.

"Montclair."

"What year?"

"1978."

"What was your last name?"

"My last name?"

"Yes. What was your name before you were adopted?"

"I don't know what my name was. My adoptive parents never told me."

"Do you have brothers and sisters?"

"I don't know."

"So you know nothing about your past?"

"No, sir. I only know when and where I was born."

Jerry told me that it didn't matter that I didn't know anything. He said that most people know very little about their pasts because adoption was designed to conceal information so that it was left up to the adoptive parents to tell the child or not about their past. He explained that any time a person was legally adopted in New Jersey, records of that adoption were kept at the registry. The documents were sealed. However, the registry had access to those records. He said he could look into them and write a short report about my adoption, but he couldn't give names and addresses. Once he did, he would need to get G and Myrtle to sign a release to conduct a search for my family because I was still a minor.

"If they agree, then the search will take about six months," he said. "Once we find your relatives, then we will contact them and ask if they want to meet you. If so, then we will set up a meeting."

"What if they say no?" my voice dropped.

"Then there's nothing we can do," he said. "You have to understand that people give up children for many different reasons. It becomes a secret sometimes. It's something they want to forget, keep in the past. Adoption is set up to protect the birth family's privacy. They may not want to meet you. So you have to be prepared for that possibility."

Fuck their privacy, I thought to myself. My birthright was more important than their privacy. They gave up their privacy when they brought me into this world. Their privacy didn't matter anymore because I was walking around feeling like a mystery and incomplete. That troubled me. My need to know what happened and where I came from outweighed their privacy.

I dismissed the possibility of being rejected by my biological family. I knew I wouldn't be able to rest if I didn't try to search for them, no matter what the outcome might be. So I filled out the request for a search and kept that fantasy of our reunion strong in my head.

I hadn't made any strong attachments to the people in my past. And I didn't expect to make any at Lawrenceville. My biological family members would be the only people I could make solid attachments with, I thought. When I finished the application, I dropped it in the mailbox the next morning. The waiting began again. So much of childhood is an unbearable waiting.

Of course, each day I spent at Lawrenceville, I learned something new. But my learning didn't take place just in the classroom. All my lessons didn't come just from books. Some lessons were good and others were bad. But I remembered something Mrs. Hughes told me: "Find the positive intent."

My first semester I read books like *The Great Gatsby* by F. Scott Fitzgerald, *Mrs. Dalloway* and *To The Lighthouse* by Virginia Woolf, *The Scarlet Letter* by Nathaniel Hawthorne, and *Pride and Prejudice* by Jane Austen. I approached all those stories with a bad attitude simply because they were books about white people and white culture. I didn't care to read about characters named Bingley, Hester Prynne, and Lady this or Sir William that. Where were the black people? Since there were no black people in those books, I thought there was nothing I could get out of them. So I sat back, resentful, and viewed white literature as odd, corny, bland, petty, and boring. Those rich, pretentious, uppity people didn't know shit about real struggle, I thought.

I came to the conclusion that my classes were all really about promoting whiteness and a celebration of it, but I read the books anyway. I yawned in class, fought sleep during discussions, and mocked the characters when I wrote papers on the books. But somehow I still came away with lessons about love, bigotry, class, wealth, and sin.

During one class we were finishing up with Henry David Thoreau's *Walden*. I got the gist of the story: a white man left modern society behind to find himself and some true meaning of life in the wilderness. Our class was analyzing a quote from the author: "I'd rather eat a fried rat with good relish."

Nasty, I thought. White people will eat anything, I said in my head.

There was a twenty-minute discussion over that one line. Other students broke out their neon highlighters and red pens. They jotted down ideas stemming from that one sentence. I sat there looking dumb.

"Any questions?" the English master asked.

I looked around the room waiting for somebody else to raise their hand. But everybody seemed to get the point but me. Troubled, I raised my hand.

"Miss Patton." The English master had a surprised look on his face. I hardly spoke in class or raised my hand. I answered only when I was called on.

"This guy is in the middle of nowhere, right?"

"That's correct," the teacher smiled. Everyone turned to look directly at me.

"There's just grass. Trees. Water. Animals. Right?"

"Yes," he nodded.

"And he's all alone out there, right?"

"That's right."

"Okay." I lifted my hands slowly in front of me. "I understand how he could have gotten the fried rat. But where did he get the relish?"

Everyone but me broke into laughter. I was serious. I wanted to know how that man made some relish to go along with his fried rat.

My teacher smiled and then gave me a deep stare. While my classmates continued giggling, he slid his glasses off his face and realized I wasn't joking.

"Miss Patton," he said gently, holding back his smile. "Relish means with happiness. He wasn't talking about Guldens relish, Heinz ketchup, or Grey Poupon mustard. No condiments, Miss Patton. Just happiness."

The laughter rose again. My first instinct was to curl up and feel like some ditz. But I found it funny too. So I laughed at myself. I found some power in being able to laugh at myself. I didn't try to pretend I knew things when I didn't. I learned how to ask questions when something didn't make sense. I wasn't ashamed to say that I didn't know the answer. I didn't use heavy and big dressed-up words. I knew what they meant, but I chose to speak in a way that everyone could understand. That was part of my twoness and double consciousness.

During one history class, I got into an intense debate with a boy named Gerald. The teacher threw out a question: Is the West guilty of crimes against other cultures around the world?

"That's a no-brainer," I said.

"Miss Patton," she nodded for me to continue.

"Just look at slavery. Hiroshima. Colonialism. Look at what happened to the Native Americans here."

"The West did many savage nations a lot of good," said Gerald.

"Savage?" I frowned.

"Yes, savage. The West was their saving grace. The West introduced civilization to those people. They would still be backward and unenlightened if it weren't for the West."

"So what do you call murder? Genocide? Stealing people's land? Apartheid? Slavery? Destroying entire cultures of people? You call that progress? You call that enlightened? You call that civilization? I call *that* savagery."

"The ends justified the means," he sneered. "They should be grateful for our help."

"Malcolm X said wherever the white man has gone, he has wreaked havoc and destruction," I quoted to Gerald looking him dead in his eyes.

"Malcolm X called white people devils. So how is he credible?"

"He called white people devils because they did devilish things," I defended.

"Radical bitch," he mumbled, but I still heard him.

"Faggot," I mumbled back. The teacher heard me.

"Miss Patton." She raised her voice to a cold and stern tone. "That is not an appropriate way to speak here at the Lawrenceville School. Excuse yourself from this classroom."

I didn't argue or defend myself. I closed my books, stuffed them into my backpack, rolled my eyes at Gerald and left.

That next day I was called to the school counselor's office. Scott Albert sat me down on the couch across from him. He showed me the canary, a pink slip that my history teacher had written up. A canary was given any time a student did something wrong. An eagle, which was green, was given occasionally when you did something good. Both types of slips were sent to your housemaster, the dean's office, and Scott Albert. So other people always knew when you did good and when you slipped up.

"You called him a faggot, Stacey?" Scotty said as he looked down at the canary in his hands.

"He called me a bitch. You don't call a black girl a bitch."

"So you call a white boy a faggot?"

"He shouldn't have disrespected me. Did he get a canary? Did anybody tell him he was wrong for calling me a bitch?"

Scotty didn't answer my question, but I could tell by the expression on his face that he knew I had a valid point. "Why did you call him a faggot?"

"I don't know. That's the first thing that came to my head."

"Did you call him a faggot because you think he's gay?" he asked me.

"No." I frowned.

"So why *faggot*, Stacey?"

"No specific reason. It was just a dirty name to call him. It was like calling him an asshole."

"So you weren't commenting on his sexuality?"

"No."

Scotty looked perplexed. He kept shifting in his seat and scratching his goatee.

"So do you call gay men faggots?"

"Of course not."

"But why Gerald?"

"Because he was acting weak," I answered.

"Weak?"

"Yes."

"So how do you equate weak with faggot?"

"Me calling him a faggot had nothing to do with his sexuality. That didn't even cross my mind when I said it."

If I thought Gerald was gay, I would have chosen something else dirty to say to him instead of faggot. *Faggot* was something I heard over and over again on the basketball court. Guys called each other faggots, bitches, and pussies all the time. If somebody missed an open basket, I heard, "You faggot! Get big! Play hard, you fuckin' pussy." It didn't mean they were gay. It meant they weren't being strong. They were scared little punks.

Eventually Scotty understood where I was coming from. He told me to use a better word the next time, something like *ignorant* or *simple-minded*. Derogatory terms like *faggot* could get me kicked out of Lawrenceville, he said. He promised to speak to Gerald about his choice of words as well.

He changed the subject. "How are you fitting in here at Lawrenceville, Stacey?"

"Fine." I shrugged.

"Are you sure?" His voice and the fact that he asked me again told me he didn't believe me. Scotty knew I was hiding my feelings.

"I'm happy and grateful to be here," I said. I did believe that because I was a scholarship kid and had been plucked from obscurity and given an opportunity of a lifetime, I had no right to complain about anything.

"Well, your housemaster and others don't seem to think so," he said.

"You don't associate with your peers. You spend most of your time in your room or in the field house playing basketball. Folks are afraid you're going to turn into a basketball."

"Why should they care?" I snapped. "I'm minding my own business. I'm not bothering anybody. Why can't they mind their business?"

"People think you have a chip on your shoulder," he said, massaging his knuckles.

"People? What people? A chip on my shoulder?"

"Yes."

"What does that look like, Scotty?" I was annoyed with him and those anonymous people.

"Looks like you don't want to let anybody in. You don't trust people. Looks like you're trying to repel the world."

"It's not a chip," I corrected him. "That's the wrong metaphor. It's the whole damn annoying world on my shoulders. Why can't people just let me be?"

"Because we see potential. Lots of potential. We see a great person behind those eyes and that big defensive wall you've built up around you. Nobody wants to hurt you here. We want you to grow. To be happy. To get the most out of your Lawrenceville experience."

"Well, if people would stop fuckin' with me, then I'd be fine," I grumbled.

"You want to tell me about it, Stacey?" He rested his back against the couch, tugged at his pants, and crossed his legs. He had given me an open invitation to share my frustrations.

I told Scotty that I felt alone in my dorm. Most nights I cried and rocked myself to sleep. Sometimes I didn't know why I was crying. My tears seemed to flow from some hidden place inside me. Maybe I was just backed up from all those years I wasn't allowed to cry. I told him I was tired of the other girls' curious questions about my black skin, black hair, and their attacks on my culture.

"'Why do you read black books all the time?' One girl asked me that the other day," I complained to Scotty.

"And what did you say back?"

"'Why do you read white books all the time?'"

"Good answer," he smiled.

"'Why do black people have nappy hair?'" I continued. "'How do you get it to stay in those Bob Marley braids?' I get called Tracy Chapman.

Tracy Chapman has dreadlocks! Bob Marley had dreadlocks! I have braids! There's a difference, Scotty. 'Why don't black people wash their hair every day? That's gross!' Black people don't have to wash their hair every day. It's different from white hair."

Scotty listened to me vent. It felt good just to say what was on my mind and be honest with him. Sometimes he nodded, assuring me that he understood my frustrations.

"Why would I want to associate with them? I'm supposed to understand, accept, and be sensitive to their differences, but they don't do that for me. We don't read black books at this school. How many black teachers are here? Four! Wow! How many black students? What? Thirty, maybe. Race does matter when you're on the other end of the spectrum, Scotty."

"Although I am a white man, I can assure you that I do know what it feels like to be different from everybody else," he said. "You have to develop positive ways to approach people when they offend you, Stacey."

From then on, once or sometimes twice a week, I sought refuge in Scott Albert's corner office on the second floor of Father's Building, the building we called Pop Hall. We talked about everything—sports, books, people I couldn't stand, people I admired, my fears, childhood memories, and hopes of finding my biological family. Sometimes we just sat for an hour and listened to Scotty's spaced-out music. I always walked out of his office having learned something new.

Scotty taught me that ignorance was everywhere and not specific to black or white people. He understood that I sometimes wanted to brand entire groups of people when one person pissed me off. He taught me the art of listening instead of being so quick to defend myself. Gradually I learned I didn't have to defend, justify, and explain myself all the time. Slowly Scotty and I began to take down my wall brick by brick.

THREE

People always say to be careful what you wish. Well, I did a lot of wishing when I was a child. And I must say that sometimes having just the dream is better than the reality. At least in the dream you have total control. People say what you want to hear. Everything makes sense. Everybody loves you. You write that perfect happy ending and live happily ever after. But sometimes that desire becomes a reality you wish never came to pass.

That March morning during my second semester at Lawrenceville began just as most days did. My alarm clock scared the hell out of me at seven. I lay there contemplating whether I wanted to skip class and pay the consequence of a Saturday night detention. I thought life shouldn't be so hard. I wanted to sleep my life away. I even thought about death. If I were dead, then I wouldn't have to go to class. If I were dead, then I wouldn't have to write papers. I would never have to pay bills.

I threw off the blankets before I allowed myself the chance to drift off into sleep again and miss Mr. Savoie's eight o'clock French class or even be late. Mr. Savoie was one of those teachers who shut his door just as the bell was ringing. If you weren't inside by the last chime, then you were locked out of class and given an absence for the day. My routine was the same: showered, brushed and flossed, changed outfits twice, sprayed some of that sweet-smelling African Pride oil on my braids, gathered my books, and sprinted across campus to Pop Hall before that last chime. Little did I know that my life was going to change that day.

I bumped into Scotty between classes. He had a nervous look on his face and some kind of worry in his eyes. He grabbed my arm before I could say hello.

"Come with me to my office," he said.

Oh, shit, I thought. What now? Who had I offended? Who felt threatened by me? Do they think the chip on my shoulder has gotten bigger? I did a quick inventory through my recent memories to see if there was some encounter or incident that I had forgotten. I came up with nothing. Still, I was worried. Scotty never stopped me in the hallway like that. Most times we had this sort of hidden language outside his office. I really didn't want other students to know I had problems and that I was in his office one or two times a week. So we'd say a casual hello in passing.

Scotty closed the door and took his spot on the couch across from me. He folded his hands and bowed his head like he was going to pray. But I knew that was his way of thinking of how to articulate his thoughts to me.

"Stacey, I've got good news and I've got bad news," he said. "Which do you want first?"

I thought about his question for a few seconds. Good news? Bad news? Something was good. Something was bad. I was hoping there'd be some middle ground between the two.

"It doesn't matter, Scotty," I shrugged. "If you tell me the good news first, I still gotta hear the bad news."

"Okay," he took a deep breath. "I'll tell you the good news first."

I leaned forward in my seat, anxious and ready.

"This morning I spoke with your Aunt Darlene Jones," he said.

I frowned and shook my head. "Scotty," I stopped him before he could go on. "I don't have an aunt named Darlene Jones."

He gave me a short smile. "Yes, you do," he said. "Darlene Jones is your biological mother's sister."

"Oh my God!" I almost screamed. "They found them! They found my family!" My face heated up. A warm chill ran down my neck and back. I felt like a floodgate of tears was going to burst through my eyeballs.

"Wait, there's more," he said as he took a piece of paper out of his shirt pocket. "You have another aunt. Her name is Trisha James. She lives in Trenton and works for Mayor Doug Palmer. You have an older brother named Steven, who is a marine. He is stationed in Italy and has been trying to search for you. You have an older sister named Stephanie who lives in Newark with your Aunt Darlene and your great-grandmother Serena Harrison. You also have a younger brother named Cecil who lives with his father and stepmother in Piscataway. They want to meet you."

I kept covering my mouth, fighting back tears, and trying to slow down my heart rate. I felt a headache coming on from all that happiness.

But in the midst of it, something hit me. And immediately a bad feeling descended over me before Scotty got the chance to tell me the bad news.

His voice and his eyes dropped. He folded the little piece of paper and put it back in his shirt pocket. I got quiet.

"Stacey, the bad news is that your mother is dead."

I felt cut up inside and a slow bleed beginning to drain me. I was suddenly bereft of life's meaning and worth. Everything that I had done in hopes of one day sharing it with my mother meant nothing. She was never going to share a birthday with me. She wouldn't be there for my graduation from high school or college. She would never cheer for me on the sidelines during a game. She wouldn't see me get married. She would never hold her grandchildren. There was nothing she could do for me and nothing I could ever do for her. Most of all, I'd never know if she loved me.

I had come to terms with but never accepted the fact that my mother gave me up for adoption. But I figured there was no use in being angry over it. I had promised myself that when I met her, I wouldn't ask her why she gave me away. I didn't want her to feel guilty. I just wanted us to move on. But the fact that she was dead made me feel abandoned to the greatest degree. When Scotty told me she was dead, I felt like I was doomed to be alone forever, with no one to protect me.

Scotty handed me a tissue, but I refused. What was the use of wiping them away? Many more were going to follow. Let the tears come, I thought. Let them dry and become salty tracks on my skin.

"How did she die?" I asked after nearly a half-hour of stopping and starting my crying.

"Suicide," he answered plainly. "She killed herself months after she gave you up for adoption."

How could she do that? Not only had she given me up, decided not to keep me, but also she completely robbed me of her by taking her life. Was I not important enough for her to live? Did she care nothing about me? Selfish! Was life really that bad for her?

"This is so unfair, Scotty," I whimpered. "It wasn't supposed to turn out this way."

I don't know if I would have been less disappointed or angry if my mother had died by accident or illness. I probably still would have felt cheated. But the fact that she took her own life made me feel torn. I had to remember that when I was a child, I wanted to kill myself. It had been an attempt to end my pain. Ending my pain through suicide would have been me asserting control and power over my powerlessness. So I understood wanting to die. But being on the opposite end of it was different. My mother had ended her pain by causing her own death. And death of any kind hurts only the people who are left behind.

I had to pull myself together. I had to be strong, like always. I knew that life was like some kind of card game. Sometimes the game wasn't fair and the cards were marked, but I still had to play. This was another messed-up hand for me. But I quickly pulled myself together.

"Well." I dragged my hand underneath my eyes and across my cheeks. I took in one hard sniff to clear my nose. "I have brothers and sisters. And aunts. And a great-grandmother." I tried to sound excited.

"Yes," Scotty said, still feeling my pain. "And they want to meet you. Your Aunt Darlene is waiting by the phone right now."

"She is?" I giggled.

Scotty jumped up. He reached for his cordless phone and dialed a number he had scratched on a notepad. I cleared my throat so I wouldn't sound like I had been crying. This was supposed to be a happy day. This was a new beginning, not a burial. Scotty handed me the phone.

"Hello," I said in a low and shy voice.

"Stacey," the shaky voice said my name. I had dreamed of hearing the voice of my mother for years. Since it was never going to happen, Aunt Darlene's voice had to suffice. "This is your auntie," she said, her voice breaking.

"I know," I smiled.

"Oh my God." I could hear her crying. "I knew you would find us. I always knew you would look for us. We never forgot about you, Stacey. Every night when I prayed, I always prayed for Steven, Stephanie, Cecil, and Stacey."

"I didn't know I had brothers and a sister," I said.

"You didn't know?" She sounded surprised.

"I didn't know anything. Nothing." What was my mother's name?"

"Robin," she said, like it was the most beautiful name she had ever known. At that moment it was the most beautiful name on earth to me. "Robin."

Aunt Darlene told me that the last time she saw me, I was two years old. After my mother killed herself, my great-grandmother, whom everyone called Nana, ordered my Aunt Trisha to get me out of foster care.

Nana thought that putting me up for adoption was the worst thing they could do. My Aunt Darlene and other Aunt Lana agreed, but Trisha didn't. She felt that the family was too dysfunctional for me to be brought back into it.

"So when will I meet you, Aunt Trisha, Aunt Lana, Nana, and my siblings?"

"Well, you won't meet Aunt Lana," she said,

"Why not?"

"She died last month. Your Aunt Lana adored you. She used to call you Boo-Boo Kitty."

I felt embarrassed. Why did adults come up with those weird names for kids? I hated the fact that she was dead, but I was relieved that no one would ever call me that name in public.

"How did she die?"

"She had AIDS," she said. "But it's something how when a person dies, God replaces them with a blessing. I just gave birth to your cousin Joshua. And now you're back with us. God took one and gave two."

Aunt Darlene told me to hold on. She clicked to the other line to call my Aunt Trisha. I couldn't believe that Trisha lived less than twenty minutes away and worked for the mayor of Trenton.

"Stacey," Aunt Darlene's voice came through the line again. "Your Aunt Trisha is on the line."

"Hello, Miss Stacey," Aunt Trisha said a southern preachy cadence.

"Hello, Aunt Trisha."

"Praise the Lord," she said. "So you don't live very far from me."

"No," I smiled. "Not far at all."

"I hear you're at a really exclusive prep school."

"Yes. Lawrenceville Prep," I said.

"You must be really bright," she said. "Your mother was very intelligent."

"I guess that's where I get it from."

"Tell us about your mother and father," Trisha said.

I didn't want to take the conversation there. Myrtle and G didn't matter anymore. Why did Aunt Trisha want to hear about them? I didn't ever want to tell them about my mean past with my adoptive parents.

"I don't live with them," I said. "I haven't lived with them since I was thirteen." I quickly changed the subject. "So I have a great-grandmother."

"Yes," Darlene said. "She drove me crazy all weekend. We got the letter from the Adoption Registry. Some man named Jerry Giollio. But that was on Friday. It was too late to call them, so we had to wait all weekend to call. Nana is so excited."

"Do you go to church, Stacey?" Aunt Trisha asked.

Who was thinking about church? Why was she asking? The missing pieces to my past were coming together.

"I used to," I said.

"Used to?" Her voice grew curious.

"I only went because I had to. I didn't go because I wanted to."

"Well, you need to develop a relationship with God."

It was a strange comment at the time, but I didn't read much into it. Most black people in my life always pointed to God for some reasoning. Everything was attributed to God. If good things happened, it was because of God. If bad things happened, it was because you didn't pray or have God in your life. But when I replay the conversation in my head again years later, her comment was foreshadowing what was to come. Aunt Trisha was telling me that I needed to have a relationship with God because God was all I would need for nurture and love. God would never abandon me. And God would never make me feel re-abandoned.

"Let's go see her," said Aunt Darlene.

Trisha said she would try to come. She had to shift her schedule around and find a way to get her daughters from school. Aunt Darlene said that she, Nana, and my sister would be at the school in one hour. When I hung up the phone, Scotty returned to his couch.

"How do you feel about all this?" he asked.

"I don't know, Scotty. I need to pinch myself to make sure I'm not dreaming. This is so weird. I can't believe it's happening. This has been my dream ever since I was four years old. But now that it's actually going to happen and I don't have to dream anymore . . ." I couldn't finish the sentence.

"In all my years working here at Lawrenceville, I've witnessed a lot of things. But this day I will never forget," he smiled.

I left Scotty and returned to my dorm to wait for my family. Everything was finally going to be all right. I could walk around and be less angry at the world, less cheated, less paranoid. I was going to feel complete and solved. That's what I thought. But I forgot to remind myself that adoption is always the result of a loss or tragedy, and rooted in the nature of adoption are secrets and lies. The person who always loses and is not let in on the secrets and the lies is the adopted child.

I sat there in the common room of Kirby House waiting for the missing pieces of my life to arrive. I figured it would be the last time during my childhood that I'd find myself waiting. Waiting is a real bitch. I guess that's why they call patience a virtue.

There was a short rain shower that came from nowhere. One moment it was soft like music; the next it whispered like catty women. Other times it got intense and darted through the trees surrounding my dorm. When it was over, the air smelled sweeter, the tree trunks were lit up, and the grass and leaves were a deeper green. I'm not saying that the rain was a sign. I just remember it because I paid close attention to every intricate detail of that day.

I even remember how Bucket, the ugliest and most foul-smelling dog I had ever encountered in life, staggered across the campus after the rainstorm. He looked confused as always, but he looked even more troubled because he had nothing to chase. When the sun was out, he spent hours chasing and barking at his shadow. I had heard that a group of seniors from the Haskell House had given the poor dog acid. That dog hadn't been right ever since.

I remember having a brief conversation with the cleaning woman as she emptied trash bags. She complained about how trifling some of those rich girls were. She said they had mistaken her for Florence on *The Jeffersons*.

"They take a shit," she sliced the air with a garbage tie. "They take a shit, and they don't flush the toilet." Her face tightened into a disgusted frown.

"Nasty heifers," I shook my head.

"They miss the garbage can and keep on walking," she complained.

"Like they didn't see that they missed, huh."

"Does it take that much energy to bend down and pick it up?"

"Nope," I answered.

"Does it take that much energy to flush the damn toilet?"

"Not at all."

"That's what they probably do at home," she said. "They don't have no home training."

I always had conversations like that with the housekeepers, custodians, and kitchen staff. They were all black. But the fact that I spoke with them, said "please" and "thank you," and "sir" and "ma'am" let them know that I respected them and didn't think I was better than them because I was one of those little preppies. They often rewarded me with double portions in the dining center or opened the gym for me after hours when I wanted to play ball. Many times I was offended and felt awkward at alumni or trustee functions where I was the only black student and the other blacks were all servants.

Mr. Rousseau slipped into the common room. He had no real expression on his face. He never did unless he was laughing or annoyed. I jumped to my feet, excited to tell him the news.

"Mr. Rousseau! Guess what?"

"I know," he slid off his glasses. "I knew before you did. Scott Albert told me everything," he said.

"So you know they're coming to see me?"

"Yes," he nodded.

I was confused by Mr. Rousseau's dull reaction. I thought he'd be jumping for joy. I thought he knew that I had been waiting my whole life for that day. My dream had come true!

"I know you probably can't think straight because all this has happened so fast." He sighed, like he was running out of breath. "But I'm going to be honest with you. I know they're your family, but you don't know anything about these people. So don't expect anything. Sometimes these things don't work out."

I didn't want to hear that.

He put his hand on my shoulder. "I don't want you to get your hopes so high that you end up crushed in the end. You've already been through so much in your life."

When I look back, I recall that Mr. Rousseau wasn't the only person who had forewarned me about expecting anything from my family. In fact, the people at Lawrenceville who cared most about me were skeptical. It's not that they weren't happy for me or that they didn't want things to work out. They just wanted me to be realistic and not set myself up for re-abandonment and more abuse. But I ignored them all. I let my fantasies and hopes rule. In my mind, rejection and a bad ending were not possibilities.

Nearly an hour passed. A whole confluence of emotions and thoughts fluctuated inside me. I kept hoping that the reunion would actually happen. I was afraid my family might turn off the wrong exit on the New Jersey Turnpike and get lost forever. I was afraid they might get run over by a tractor trailer. So many questions bounced around inside my head. What did they look like? Were they chocolate-colored like me? Did they have big Bette Davis eyes like mine? Did they have curly brown hair? How tall were they? Were they fat? Skinny? Attractive? Hard on the eyes? What would be their first impression of me? Would they like me?

The door opened.

Two very fair-skinned women, one almost pale white, walked through the door. They had green eyes. One woman had light brown hair. The other had long, stringy salt-and-pepper-colored hair like a white woman. Behind them were two younger fair-skinned teenage girls. They looked nothing like me.

I asked, "Do you want me to go upstairs and get someone for you?" I thought they had come for one of my dormmates.

"Stacey," the shorter woman said looking deep into my eyes like she had always known me.

As soon as she said my name, an elderly brown-skinned woman with curly hair and a teenage girl with the same complexion as me walked through the door. It was them.

"I'm your Aunt Darlene," she said. "This is your Aunt Trisha," she said, pointing to her sister. She turned her head. "That's your sister Stephanie and your great-grandmother, Serena."

Should I shake their hands? Should I hug them? Should I just stand there and look them over, as they did me? Should I cry? Should I give them a big Kool-Aid smile? Should I be mad at them? I had painted that first reunion moment in my head over and over again, but when it actually happened, it turned out different.

The old matriarch of a woman stepped forward and pulled me into her breasts. There was something about old black women and their big bosoms that I always found comforting. It was a place that felt safe, warm, nurturing, and overflowing with love. I felt like I could sleep, live, and die in that sacred place covering my great-grandmother's heart. Myrtle had never held me like that. But the churchwomen did. Sometimes they snatched me up out of nowhere. There was no use in my trying to resist or escape. Once my head was buried in their breasts, they rocked me and sometimes moaned spirituals. And then everything seemed all right.

"I'm yo' Nana," she said, struggling to get the words out of her throat. "I been prayin' fo' dis day since I last seened you. I axed Gawd not to lemme diie b'fo seein' this chile again." I felt her warm tears dripping on the side of my face. "The Lawd may not come when you want him. But he's always on time."

I had always heard preachers say that. But hearing my great-grandmother say it as she held me in her arms gave it a new meaning. But God was still simply a metaphor in her sentence.

Trisha, Darlene, Stephanie, and my cousins looked on unmoved. No tears. No smiles. Nothing but curiosity.

"Here," said Nana, handing me a battered photograph. "That's your mother." The warmth left her voice.

I reached for a chair because I felt like my legs were going to give out. It was a high school photo. She was eighteen. My mother had long, flow-ing dark hair with sienna brown highlights. She had a pointy nose just like mine. Same complexion. Same lips. And the exact same eyes. Those eyes looked like my own staring back at me. It was almost frightening. There was some kind of pain and sadness and emptiness that had gotten frozen by the flash the day that photo was taken. It was the same pain and sad-ness and emptiness I had seen in my own eyes for years.

"She looks like Robin," Darlene said.

"Yes, Lawd, she does." Nana stepped back from me to study my face. "Cut from the same cloth, I tell ya'. Look at dem eyes. Look like Robbie cut 'em out her own head and put 'em in this chile. Thought I never see eyes like dem on anutha walkin' soul. Ain't the Lawd sumpin'?"

"She don't look like her," Stephanie rang in, shaking her head hard.

I scanned the faces in the room. My eyes landed on my cousin Tammy's face. She was a prissy-looking bitch. Snotty. She stood off to the side looking like her shit didn't stink. Yes, that was my first impression of my cousin. It was right, and it still holds true to this day.

"I've seen you before," I said to her. She smirked. "What school do you go to?"

"Trenton High," she said.

"Tammy's an honor student," Aunt Trisha said, as if she was her daughter's agent.

"Are you on the debate team?" Tammy smirked again. Then the look on her face changed. It hit her: she had seen me before too.

"That's how I know you." I got excited. "I debated against you twice."

When I was a student at Ewing High, I was a member of the varsity debate team, the only freshman on the team that year. Tammy and I had competed in two Lincoln-Douglas tournaments. Twice we were in the same room with a timekeeper and a judge. The question for the first tournament was: "How can the United States government use foreign policy to reduce pollution worldwide?" The second question was: "Should the United States government curtail the First Amendment to protect certain citizens?" I would have never in a million lifetimes ever guessed that she and I had the same bloodline and genetic link.

"Who won?" Trisha's eyes turned to her daughter.

I crushed her both times. That season, I had lost only one match out of twelve, and I had captured the Mercer County Championship title.

"Oh, I don't remember who won," I lied. I felt awkward. I felt as if Trisha was pitting me against her daughter. I wasn't one to compete like that. The only competing I ever took seriously was on the basketball court.

"You know," Trisha paused, bringing my attention back to her, "we're a very dysfunctional family," she said. "We've been through a lot. So much dysfunction."

"Well, the past is the past. Can't change any of it. And we're all here together. Well, except for my brothers."

"You'll meet them soon," Darlene promised.

"What happened to your face?" Nana changed the subject. "You ain't have dem scars on your face when I last seened you."

I didn't want to go there with them. I didn't want to talk about G and Myrtle. I didn't want to talk about scars, beatings, youth shelters, and group homes. I never wanted to tell those stories. But everyone was standing there, silent and ready to lend me their ears. They wanted to know.

"My adoptive mother beat me with an extension cord when I was seven. She tore all the skin off the side of my face and then put peroxide on the open wounds. She lied to the police and told them I fell out of the car."

Darlene, Nana, and Stephanie looked horrified. Trisha looked guilty. Trisha parted her lips and put me on the spot again.

"Were you sexually abused?" she asked.

"Is that worse?" I asked.

"Were you sexually abused?" she repeated

Maybe Trisha had dismissed the fact that my adoptive mother beat the crap out of me as normal behavior. Besides, wasn't it normal for black people to beat the shit out of their kids and leave the scars to tell the story?

There was a short silence. I couldn't let my eyes connect with theirs. I wanted somebody to say something. I wanted lightning to strike.

"No," I lied. "No, I wasn't sexually abused. That didn't happen to me."

"DYFS told me you were in a good home," Trisha said in a defensive tone. "So I felt it was best not to tear you away from that. To bring you back into our dysfunction made no sense."

"Well," Nana coughed. "Lawd knows I ain't feel that way. Yeah, we had hard times. Lawd knows we done been through it all. The bad and the ugly. But you should have been with us. We your family. A chile should be with the family. I always said and I still say that givin' a chile away is the worst kind of sumpin' to do to them. They ain't neva gonna understand that kind of thang. We had hard times, yes. But you would have neva been mistreated like that. We ain't have much. We ain't have much of anythang but hard times. But we had love."

On that note, Trisha turned her wrist over to check the time on her watch. She said she had to get back to the office, the mayor needed her. She wrote her number on a piece of paper from her purse and told me to call her sometimes. Before she walked out the door, she asked me my adoptive parents' names. Why she wanted to know I had no idea, but I gave her their names anyway.

I'd discover weeks later that she called Myrtle and G and even visited their home that same evening. I'd never know the details of their conversation. Ultimately they'd have subsequent meetings together: dinners, parties, and church gatherings. She thanked them for raising me and told them they were good people.

Ain't that some shit?

I tried to rationalize why Trisha reached out to my adoptive parents. It didn't make sense at first. All those years, Myrtle had tortured me. They did not support me like good parents. The State of New Jersey had removed me from their home. They were deceitful and always put on the appearance of good church-going people with a clean home.

If I discovered that the people who were entrusted to take care of my sister's child had mistreated her the way I had been, I wouldn't want to go to their home and drink tea. I would never want to meet those people. I wouldn't want to touch their hands, hug them, or get to know them. I'd be ready to beat their ass if I ran into them on the street.

Guilt was the only explanation I could come up with. Trisha was the only family member who felt I should not have been brought back into the family after my mother's suicide. She claimed that she alone bore the burden of raising her own children and my mother's children. Perhaps she did feel overwhelmed by all that responsibility and did not want me adding to it. I do believe that she thought I was in a good home and being taken care of, but she couldn't accept the reality that it wasn't true. She was wrong. But it wasn't her fault. How was she to know what was really happening to me? Never once did I blame her or any of my biological family members for my bad adoption. There was no sense in pointing fingers and placing blame. We were together again, and that's all that mattered to me.

Trisha never asked me another question about my childhood. She just gave me lectures about God and prayer. She once told me that I needed to work on my relationship with God and my adoptive parents. She said they were my real family. And every time she introduced me to someone, she said, "This is Stacey, my sister's child."

I didn't get that woman! But I just knew I was going to make her accept me. I was going to make her love me. All I wanted from her was love and for her to share pieces of my mother with me. That's what I expected from all my family members.

But I was tapping a dry well. I was seeking life from walking corpses. The family endured so many problems: the murders of my grandparents, drug addiction, suicide, and fractured relationships. I was hoping to be loved by people who didn't have the capacity to love even themselves. Still, I thought I could beat the odds. Besides, I had always beaten odds. I could dig up bones. I could resuscitate hearts. I was Stacey Patton! Little did I know I was chasing ghosts.

FOUR

The night before graduation I sat quietly in a circle underneath a clear and crisp night sky with about ten of my dormitory mates. It was after midnight, and we had broken curfew, but none of us cared. For three or four years, and for some of us five, we had obeyed the rules, made the grades, and for the most part conformed to the traditions of our prep school experience. I watched a few girls smoke cigarettes and talk of their summer vacations before heading off to prestigious colleges that coming fall. We all laughed as we made fun of some of the weird students in our class, mocked our teachers, and relived the story of our senior prank.

Some of the boys had gotten their hands on thousands of goldfish and paper cups as well as keys to Pop Hall and Memorial Hall. Pop Hall was where the foreign languages and other humanities courses like philosophy and religion were taught. Memorial Hall was where English and history classes took place. Around 1:00 A.M. we all stole away from our dorms. The boys took Memorial Hall and the girls Pop Hall. We lined the entire hallways and steps with the cups before pouring water and goldfish into each.

"Oh, shit," I giggled when the job was done. "It's gonna take them hours to get all these cups off the floor."

The next morning, all the goldfish were still alive and swimming around in the cups.

"This is cruel!" yelled Ms. Townley, one of the English teachers. I stood at the opposite end of the Memorial hallway laughing devilishly. "Stacey Patton!" she screamed at me. "Clean this mess up!"

"It's a prank," I giggled. "Why are you getting so angry? You guys should have expected this."

A few of our teachers shook their heads and smiled, while others got upset over the fact that we used fish and those fish would probably die. I hadn't thought about that. Eventually they called the grounds crew to clean up the mess. And that's when I felt bad because all the grounds crew were older black men and women whom I had been friendly with. At that point, I decided to help.

After laughing and reminiscing for hours, we simply looked to the stars. It seemed like a melodramatic moment, but we all felt not only a sense of accomplishment but that life had placed us all in that institution for various reasons. And as girls, we had survived an old-boy school network. Somehow, though no one uttered it, we knew that we were expected to become extraordinary and elite women. Where would we go? What would happen to us? Who would marry first? Be the first to have a child? Which of us would be the wealthiest? Famous? A leader? Would any of us fail? Die before our time?

Morning came, brilliantly. It was sunny. Warm. Green. I believed that June day was made for my graduation. I took the good weather as a sign of optimism and good luck. When I looked out my dorm room window, I heard the birds as usual and could see cars creeping along Route 206. The smooth sidewalks had been neatly swept and washed by the grounds crew. New flowers that had been planted days before in strategic places stood upright and perfect. I could see hundreds of wooden chairs neatly lined and the commencement stage fully adorned with dormitory flags and a red carpet. The sounds of microphone checks and sporadic orchestra notes blared.

For three years, I had fantasized about graduation day. Before I even enrolled in Lawrenceville, I envisioned myself standing confidently among the best, the brightest, and the most talented. I went from a ward of the State of New Jersey to becoming a prep school graduate. I couldn't help but smile as I remembered Sister Lorraine's words: "You are not the cream of the crop. You'll never make it through a place like Lawrenceville." Sister Lorraine would never make it to eat her own words and witness my day of glory. She died from lung cancer a few months after I left the TRIAD Group Home.

Though I reveled in my sense of accomplishment, a big part of me was sad to leave the place I had called home for three years. Lawrenceville was a safe and comfortable world. There was so much color and life. It was also a bubble of privilege where many of us were shielded from the darker realities of life. That big black steel gate surrounding the campus kept out a great many of the forces and influences that affected other teens our age. For the first time in my life, I felt protected. Protected from Myrtle and her merciless whippings. Protected from her hurtful name-calling. Protected from the incompetence of the Division of Youth and Family Services and its social workers. Protected from being uprooted and sent from one foster home to the next. Lawrenceville represented stability, and I was about to leave it and move forward under the hypnosis of destiny. But I was scared.

My next move would be to Johns Hopkins University in Baltimore, Maryland. Folks told me how much of a great school it was. Hopkins was up there with the Ivy Leagues, everyone said. I had never lived outside New Jersey. All I knew about Baltimore was crabs, the Harbor, the Orioles, drugs, and homicide. I worried about how I would get along in a city where I knew no one. That previous January, I had applied for early decision because I did not want the anxiety of waiting for acceptance letters from other schools. I needed to know where I was going next. The basketball coach had assured me that I was a shoe-in with my grades and my 1490 SAT score along with the fact that I was black and female and had come from Lawrenceville. What mostly lured me to Johns Hopkins were the promises of the basketball coach.

"I see you coming here in the fall and playing right away for us. You are so quick. So talented," she said. "The way you slash and cut through the defense, I can't see very many players being able to guard you." More important, that coach knew about my family situation and the pain I had gone through. She looked me in my face and said, "Stacey, we are like a family here. I care about my players. We all look out for each other here. And we will be here for you."

I pulled my head out of the window and back into my room. The room itself was near empty. All that remained were a few boxes, the original furniture, my white lace dress, and matching open-toed sandals. There would be no caps or gowns for my high school graduation. It was Lawrenceville's tradition for the girls to wear white dresses and the boys to wear khaki pants, a blue blazer, white shirt, and red tie. The day before, I spent hours in Jan's Beauty Salon in Trenton getting my hair done. She even did my nails for free. It was the first time I wore nail polish. Myrtle had always forbidden me to wear any kind of makeup or nail polish.

"You ain't grown," she'd grumble. "When you get a house of your own and pay your own bills, you can do whatever you want. Then you'll be a woman. And when you become a woman, you can look like a woman. I don't care what you do with your hair, face, and nails. 'Til then you dress and look the way I say you can look."

I sat at my empty oak-colored desk and ran my hands slowly across the top. The nut-brown color of the desk reminded me of my great-grandmother's skin and how she'd always run her hands up and down her legs and arms as she talked to me. Nana's voice came to me.

"Any day now," she coughed, "the Lawd is gonna steal me away like a thief in the night."

"Ain't nobody gonna steal you, Nana," I heard myself tell her.

When I was a child, old people were like permanent fixtures, like knickknacks that were passed from one generation to the next. I didn't really pay much attention to them because I never expected to wake up one day and they'd be gone. Old people lived forever. They knew everything. Had seen everything. They held their families together even when they got to the point where they couldn't talk, feed themselves, or wipe their own backsides.

"'Joy dem wings. 'Joy dat sweet potato pie. May be the last time Nana cooks for you," she'd say. "Nobody gonna cook like that after I'm gone."

"Nana, why you always talkin' about dyin'?" I'd ask, as I'd sink my teeth into a juicy, crispy wing.

From the time I met Nana, she talked about her death. It got to the point where she annoyed me with that kind of talk. She'd cough real loud and say, "Oh, it's time. I feel the hands of the Lawd." She'd walk up the stairs and say she needed to find her ticket to get on that glory train. She'd get winded and then lay on her bed pretending it was a coffin. "Don't put no stockings on me. Put socks on my feet."

"Jesus Christ, Nana. Get a grip!" I'd shake my head and leave the house to go play basketball. I'd come back hours later, sweaty and stinking. "See, Nana. I told you you wasn't goin' nowhere."

Smiling as I thought of Nana, I turned full circle in my chair and studied my empty bed. I could see Nana sitting at the edge of her bed in a flowery housedress. I could hear her wheezing from emphysema.

"Don't smoke," she said. "You don't wanna end up like me when you get old. Gotta sleep with an oxygen tank next to your bed. Take it with you to the bathroom. Cook with it." She had such a sweet voice. She hardly ever called me by my first name. She called me "little one." I think she chose that name for me because I was the smallest of my siblings.

Memories of the past three years played across my mind in small clips. The good times. The bad times. The laughs. Lonely nights I cried myself to sleep. Virginia Woolf. Edith Wharton. Shakespeare. Toni Morrison. Ralph Ellison. F. Scott Fitzgerald. David Hume. Those were all writers that I'd never forget. There were teachers I promised to hold dear to my heart no matter what I did with my life. And there were one or two teachers that I vowed to forget. I remembered Dave, the skinny Chinese delivery guy who would trek in his banged-up blue minivan in the snow and rain just to deliver me some chicken wings and french fries.

My third form (sophomore) year flashed before me. I heard and saw Coach P. We were in the field house. He stood over me as he talked at me as he always did. I picked a spot on the floor of the basketball court. Diverting my eyes was my way of tuning people out or not allowing them to penetrate through me.

"Look at me, kid." He dipped his head down as if he was searching for my eyes. "You've got to learn how to look at people in the eyes when they're talking to you."

I gave him my eyes for a few seconds and then picked another spot on the floor as he continued his rant. Coach P was from Boston and had that funny accent to go with it. He had coached girls' basketball for decades, but he had never coached a player like me.

"You're like a rabbit on drugs," he said. "You're too quick even for yourself. You've got to slow down so your teammates can play with you."

"No, they've got to learn how to keep up," I mumbled back. "I don't wanna slow down. I'm trying to get stronger and faster so I can play college ball. These girls on this team aren't real basketball players. They play lacrosse and field hockey. They don't play like me. They're a bunch of slow white girls."

"You see," he raised his voice, "it's that attitude right there!"

"What?" I frowned at him. "It's true."

"No," he shook his head. "You have bad habits that you bring to the court. All that fancy dribbling. Running hook shots. All those tricks. This is not a playground. This is organized basketball. *Organized*," he stressed emphasis on the word. "I've told you over and over again about playing street basketball with those guys over in Trenton. They don't know the game."

"It's a different kind of game," I said. "It doesn't make yours any better and theirs any worse. It's a different culture of basketball. But you want to criticize it because you don't understand it. Or maybe you criticize it because you could never play like that. I understand street ball. I have fun. I can be free. I can improvise. This type of prep school ball is so white. It's slow. Mechanical. Boring!" I complained.

"S-Y-S-T-E-M," he said slowly and clearly for me.

Coach P didn't know that I had the utmost contempt for that word. It made my skin crawl. My blood boil.

"You have to learn how to play within the S-Y-S-T-E-M if you're going to become a great player. And this doesn't just apply to basketball. It applies to life, kid."

I hated the way he always called me kid. He never called the other players kid. He called them each by their names. He was affectionate with them. Patted them on their backs. And he never yelled at them. But I could never do anything right even when I did. The other players saw him as a father figure. I saw him as a white patriarch who liked his ego stroked.

"You're cocky," he said.

"Phht. Cocky? How am I cocky? I don't talk trash when I'm on the court."

"You don't have to," he said. "It shows in your body language. It shows in the way you play. You have no regard for those playing against you, even when it's your own teammates during practice."

"Am I supposed to have regard for an opponent? Coach, it's called the intimidation factor. It's supposed to show in my body language and in my game. What am I supposed to be—some kind of meek and humble player? Am I supposed to play like a nice little preppy girl?"

"You're arrogant."

"Why am I arrogant? Because I don't kiss anybody's ass? Because I don't kowtow? Because I'm confident and stubborn? If a white girl displays that kind of attitude, you call her brave and assertive and passionate. Let a black girl do it on or off the court, then you call her hostile, aggressive, or angry!"

"You're a hotdog," he got louder. "A show-off! Nobody likes a show-off!"

"I'm not a show-off. I just play with finesse. I do what I gotta do on the court to score and win. If I know I can get past somebody with a sharp and sweet move, then I'm gonna do it. If she looks stupid afterward, then that's her problem. She'll either step her game up and try to play with me, or she'll guard somebody else."

"You know, kid, you're like a lion in a cage. But I can't let you out until I tame you," he said.

I was disgusted with him. "How dare you refer to me as some kind of wild animal!" I yelled back at him. "Fuck you, redneck! Fuck you and your S-Y-S-T-E-M! Why don't you tame this . . ." I said shooting my middle finger up in his face before walking out of the gym.

Coach P suspended me from the team. One week later, my teammates had a vote. They too decided that I didn't fit into the S-Y-S-T-E-M.

Getting kicked off the basketball team was one of my angriest and lowest moments at Lawrenceville. It was embarrassing. I felt like a failure. People said I was kicked off the team because I was defiant. Had a chip on my shoulder. Couldn't be a team player. The way I saw it, the team couldn't play with me—somebody who was different and a nonconformist.

Coach P died that next summer from a heart attack while cutting his lawn. The following season, I played again with the same players and the same former assistant coach. I faced the same issues for the next two seasons. I never conformed. I didn't kiss ass. I got stronger. Faster. More defiant. I played my game. I brought everything that I had learned on the street courts of Trenton to that prep school court. I lived to make those girls look stupid when they tried to guard me. When I blocked their shots, I screamed right in their faces and walked away. I threw elbows. Knocked girls on their asses and didn't help them up. It was only on the court that I looked people in the eyes and dared them to stop me. I played with everything: my love for the game, my pain. my disappointments, my tenacity for life. Basketball helped me survive and gave me the will to keep going.

Sharon Dean was the female version of Coach P. She was a tiny white woman, and most of the students despised her. Her reddened face stared back at me in my head right alongside Coach P. Ms. Dean had been my English teacher twice. Most students who had her called her a "feminazi." She was also disliked because she had been behind the dismissal of some of our peers. During my senior year, Ms. Dean was my assistant soccer and track coach and also my housemaster. Throughout my entire career at Lawrenceville, I felt that she was wholly out to get me because I made her feel uncomfortable in her own skin.

One fall afternoon, I seated myself in the front seat row in the back of a twelve-passenger van with my other teammates. We were heading to a soccer match against Princeton High School. Two girls sat next to me, three in the seat behind us, and two in the last seat. The front passenger seat had been taken by another teammate who suffered from severe car-sickness. The second van in front of us was already full when Ms. Dean finally arrived. She peeked her head inside of the van searching for an empty seat. Glancing past my teammates, she planted her eyes on me.

"Stacey, move to the back of the van please," she said."

"Excuse me?" I said in a flippant tone as I removed my headphones. *I must not have heard her right*, I thought to myself.

"Move to the back of the van," she said again.

She hadn't stuttered. I did hear her right. I looked at the two girls sitting next to me, behind me, and all the way in the back. It didn't seem logical that I should be the one to get up and climb over all those players to take a seat in the back. I could still hear Donny Hathoway's smooth and soulful voice blaring through my headphones. He was singing about the ghetto.

"Why do I have to move? I was here before everybody else," I explained.

"Stacey," she huffed. "Don't give me a hard time. Just get up and move."

"Why can't you ask somebody else to move?"

"Just move, dammit!" shouted Mr. Hammond, a black man who had been my literature teacher and had taught me how to interpret Ralph Ellison's *Invisible Man.* I was shocked.

I thought about that invisible black man in Ellison's book as Mr. Hammond looked angrily at me through the rearview mirror. With my blaring eyes and closed mouth I recited the first paragraph of the book. I made him read those words through my eyes as I looked back at him, defiant and steadfast like a tree planted by waters. I am invisible. Not a spook like those who haunted Edgar Allan Poe; nor am I one of your Hollywood-movie ectoplasms. I am a girl of substance, of flesh and bone, fiber and liquids—and I might even be said to possess a mind. I am invisible, understand, simply because people refuse to see me. Like the bodiless heads you see sometimes in circus sideshows, it is as though I have been surrounded by mirrors of hard, distorting glass. When they approach me, they see only my surroundings, themselves, or figments of their imagination—indeed, everything and anything except me.

"Get up!" his thunderous voice rocked the van.

"My name is not Rosa Parks." I kept the pitch of my tone but added a bit of sassiness. "This is not 1954."

Mr. Hammond banged his hand on the middle of the steering wheel. "Stacey Patton. Move!"

A small hand gently tapped me from behind. "Stacey," she said, "I'll move. You can have my seat," she said as she moved herself and her bag to the back. I looked back at her blushed face. The whole scene had shaken her and my other teammates, though everyone sat silently. They all knew something was wrong with that scene. A part of me didn't want to move. I wanted to say, "Kelly, just stay there. Nobody is gonna give up their seat. Let Ms. Dean sit in the back!" But Kelly was trying to bring peace to the situation, so I got up and moved.

From that day forward, I lost respect for Mr. Hammond, though he would continue to be regarded and celebrated as one of Lawrenceville's greatest English masters. He would forever be an emblem for the school. I would continue to be courteous to him, but I put him on the same level as my adoptive father. He wasn't a man to me, and he was a sorry case for a black man. How could he let this white woman make me give up my seat and move to the back of the van? How could he yell at me and embarrass me the way he did? Would he have talked to my white teammates like that? Probably not. As I sat there at my desk recalling that scene, I got angry all over again. I wondered what would have happened if I had had the courage that Rosa Parks had and didn't give up my seat. I regretted moving. To this day, I regret moving.

My mind turned to brighter times. I began to think about all the people at Lawrenceville who nurtured me for three years. I smiled thinking about them. I thought of Mr. Savoie and his smooth demeanor. He was a tough French teacher who never allowed me to slip in class. He even kicked me out once for speaking in English. I didn't take it personally, though. Somehow I had to learn, even if it was the hard way. He and I would spend hours talking when there was no class. And he always called me by my French name—Fatu-Dominique. Monsieur Savoie was warm, gentle, funny, and brilliant.

Ms. Craddock (Moe) who worked in the library always had time for me. We'd spend hours together in her office talking about everything. Sometimes I was silent and just watched her work. I always made her laugh. She was like a mother I could go to after school and share the details of my day. She had a gentle way of keeping me in line. And eventually she even opened her home in Asbury Park to me and introduced me to her husband, Joe, who was like a cuddly Italian teddy bear. Moe made unbearable times easier for me. And just before graduation, she told me that I always had a home in Asbury Park. She was the person who taught me that it was okay to allow myself to be hugged and loved. It took some work, but she helped bring down my wall.

There was Leita Hamill who always found a place for me in a classroom conversation. She taught me that there was value in books written about white people and white experiences. F. Scott Fitzgerald's *The Great Gatsby*, Edith Wharton's *The Age of Innocence*, and even Virginia Woolf's *A Room of One's Own* offered some universal themes about the American experience despite the fact that black people were invisible in those novels. Those books could teach me a great deal about white American culture but also issues of gender, race, and class. It was in Mrs. Hamill's class where I finally realized that if I was going to get along in white society and become successful, I had to learn their literature, their ways, their humor, and their ideologies—not necessarily to celebrate them but to absorb them and then use them to my advantage even if was to turn it all against them one day, kind of like the spook who sat by the door.

My bare walls made the room feel suddenly cold. I tried to imagine it covered with all my posters again. Dr. Julius Erving dunking from the foul line in his tight 76ers uniform. Angela Davis lifting both her clenched fists to the sky after being freed from jail. Malcolm X with his sharp glasses, serious stare, and his chin resting on his hand. Huey Newton in his black leather jacket holding a large gun. What I loved most about those posters was each character's Afro. I wondered what I would look like with an Afro. It was so radical. So bold. So black. I felt I was born in the wrong decade. I wished I could have been a young woman of the sixties and seventies. To wear bell bottoms. Leather trench coats.

Platform shoes. Butterfly collar shirts. Listen to blaxploitation music. Watch *Superfly*, *Shaft*, and *Foxy Brown* in the theaters. To call people names like "Jive Turkey" and "Sucka." I think I would have fit in well during that era.

But there was I was, a child of the eighties and nineties about to graduate from one of the most prestigious institutions in the country. Lawrenceville had changed my life, and I had held true to my promise to myself. I did not become whitewashed. I did not lose my blackness. I still knew who I was. And there were many people, of all colors, at Lawrenceville who respected me for that. Whether it was folks in the library, cafeteria, field house, infirmary, or the classrooms, many people saw through my tough exterior and got to know me as an individual. They shared with me their wisdom, kindness, and love. They didn't judge me or try to break me. They let me be and celebrated my individuality. And like prophets, they looked me in my eyes and told me that I was destined to do great things.

Just about all my peers at Lawrenceville had no idea how I had come to the school. Perhaps I was altogether a mystery to them. A serious, angry, confrontational, hostile, radical black girl to some. And a funny, smart, giving, and energetic preppy to others. They never knew that I was a foster kid, a ward of the state. They never knew the real story behind my scars. When they asked me how I got the scars on my face, I told them I had an accident a long time ago. It wasn't completely a lie. I felt like destiny had accidentally placed me in the wrong home with Myrtle and G. As a result, I got those scars—lots of them.

My peers would never know that I didn't have parents supporting me. That I had been reunited with my biological family on that very campus. And they had no idea that I was not only going to be celebrating my graduation that day, but also being together for the first time in my life with my three siblings and my aunts. Seeing everyone together was going to be the perfect ending to my story—an epilogue to my childhood. I pictured myself scanning that sea of rich white faces and seeing my own flesh and blood. I would have to look a bit harder to find Aunt Darlene and Trisha's nearly white faces and green eyes in the crowd. Proud! Smiling! Cheerful! Maybe even crying. I imagined how they'd react when I walked across the stage to receive my diploma. That day was going to make everything all right.

The murders of my grandparents. My mother's suicide. Aunt Lana dying of AIDS. Aunt Trisha's cold and nasty demeanor and all her guilt. Aunt Darlene's drug addiction. Stephanie's anger at our mother. Cecil blaming himself for our mother's suicide. Steven's futile attempts to escape everything through jokes and laughter. And my scars. It would all fade away on that June afternoon. Brought together by me and my momentous occasion, my family would revel in my accomplishment and in love and redemption.

I would be that sign, that beacon of hope for our future. I would be the one to help us deal with our dark past and move beyond it. I would bring us together as a family despite our pain and dysfunction. My love for them would teach them to accept and love me. Nothing would break that bond. This was my hope. This was the same hope and dreams of the slaves who never tasted freedom. Love and time. Strength and hope. I think they knew that their descendants could find the power to heal despite the race's dark past. Despite the pain. The torture. The degradations. The whippings. The rapes. The lynchings. All that discrimination and disappointment. Despite the pain we've inflicted onto each other. Despite all our scars.

I looked petite and young in my white lace dress. I hated dresses because they made me feel vulnerable and unnatural. They made me aware of myself and of my femininity, especially since I constantly cast myself as strong and impenetrable. I was not a girly-girl by any stretch of the margin. If I had my way, I would have worn a slick white pants suit, matching white jacket, and a hat with a white feather.

Throughout the entire ceremony, I couldn't sit still. I saw everyone else I had invited, but there was no sign of my family. Maybe they were late. Perhaps they were sitting somewhere way in the back. I couldn't wait until the ceremony was over so I could hug them and take photos with them. I'd introduce them to everyone. I pictured myself gleefully saying, "This is my family." They weren't members of the Hearst, Penske, or Bunn families. They weren't rich or extraordinary. They would never become trustees or give millions of dollars to the school. But they were my family, and I would be proud of their presence.

The headmaster gave his speech. The valedictorian said her words. The awards were distributed. Diplomas handed out. The entire crowd stood and we all sang the school song:

Fight the good fight with all thy might;
Christ is thy Strength, and Christ thy Right;
Lay hold on life, and it shall be
Thy joy and crown eternally.

Run the straight race through God's good grace,
Lift up thine eyes, and seek His face;
Life with its way before us lies,
Christ is the Path, and Christ the Prize.

Cast care aside, upon thy Guide,
Lean, and His mercy will provide;
Lean, and the trusting soul shall prove
Christ is its Life, and Christ its Love.

Faint not nor fear, His arms are near,
He changeth not, and thou art dear.
Only believe, and thou shalt see
That Christ is all in all to thee.

The ceremony ended. I took photos. Smiled through my anxious feelings. I never stopped searching the crowd for my family. When the last chair was folded and placed onto the back of a utility truck, I looked around me and saw only roses and programs strewn about the lawn. They were soon collected, and only I was left there, alone and losing all hope. My family never showed up. I was devastated, but I would not allow myself to cry.

I looked up at the empty commencement stage with the flags draped above. In my mind's eye, I saw Aunt Trisha's image behind the podium. She was looking at me just as she had done two weeks earlier from a different stage. She had invited me to a debutante ball where she was the keynote speaker. She told me to wear a nice dress and to get my hair done because it was a high se ditty event.

"It gives me great pleasure to introduce a phenomenal woman. She works for the mayor of Trenton. Recipient of the Achievement Against the Odds Award from President George Bush. A brilliant attorney and speaker. Ms. Trisha James," said the announcer.

When Aunt Trisha took the stage, she received a roaring applause and ovation from the crowd. I couldn't get over how white she looked and how she and my mother had sprung from the same loins. Nobody in the room would have ever guessed that she and I were related.

"Before I begin my speech tonight," she paused as everyone took their seats again. "I'd like to introduce you all to someone in the audience."

My blood pressure suddenly spiked. I knew she was talking about me. She went on to tell the audience how I had been separated from the family. She also told them that I would be graduating from Lawrenceville and going off to college. The crowd received her description of me with oooohhhs and aaaaahhhs.

"Stacey, would you stand up," she said looking over to my table.

I clutched my cloth dinner napkin to keep my hands from shaking. My body got warm, and the entire room got dark except for her. I could feel people shifting in their seats to get a good look at me.

"Stacey," she removed her glasses off her pale face. "I want you to know that even though our family is dysfunctional, I love you. I love you because you are my niece, my sister's child, my flesh, my blood." The audience shot to their feet again and applauded.

It was all a show, I thought to myself, as her image disappeared from behind the podium. On the ride back to campus that night, Aunt Trisha asked me how it felt to hear her say those words to me in front of that big audience. "We could have been sitting on a broken curb in front of the 7-Eleven eating a hotdog," I said. "You could have looked me in my eyes, with nobody else around, and told me you loved me. I would have been happy."

My eyes moved away from the stage and then up to the sky. I whispered what I had once been told: adoption is always the result of a loss or tragedy. I looked to the ground and I whispered again, "Secrets and lies. Secrets and lies." I would always be the adopted child, and I would never be let in on the secrets or be given the truth. I began to wonder why my biological family ever showed up in the first place. They didn't intend to embrace me as a sister and niece. Perhaps they were curious. Maybe they just wanted to look me over and see how I turned out. I wanted happily ever after. I wanted love. Nurture. Blood and genetic ties. I honestly believed that those elements would make a difference. Were they not prerequisites of family? Of bonds? Of loyalty? Of love?

I felt abandoned again. That feeling seemed to be a constant refrain in my life. How would I learn to trust anyone? To open up? To allow myself to be vulnerable? To be loved? Would I ever stop treating people as suspects who would take advantage of me? Abandon me? Break my heart? Murder my soul?

The day after graduation arrived, and with it came the news that Nana had died. I hadn't expected her to last through the summer. For much of my senior year, she had been in and out of the hospital. I remembered all those days I heard her whisper prayers to the ceiling. She asked God to take her home soon. To end her pain. She had signed papers indicating that she didn't want to be resuscitated. I never got to say good-bye to her, and I didn't want to say good-bye. Nana was the only person in my family who fully greeted me with open arms and showed me that she loved me. And that, I wanted to keep alive. I shed no tears at her funeral. She looked years younger and peaceful, but the bad makeup job made her look like a different person. I was happy that she'd have no more physical or emotional pain or disappointment. Pain and disappointment had narrated her entire life. Nana was buried underneath a huge oak tree in a cemetery in Montclair, New Jersey. As they lowered her cheap blue casket covered with fresh flowers into the earth, I thought about my biological mother.

Would I ever be able to look at my mother's photo, her eyes and frozen half-smile, without crying? Would I ever stop being angry with her for her killing herself? For giving me up for adoption? For abandoning my siblings? Would I ever be able to enjoy my accomplishments and significant moments, even my birthdays, without being sad that she would never be there to witness them? Would I ever stop wishing for just a few minutes of life with her? Would I ever stop wondering if she loved me? Would that day come when my intense desire to dig her up from the ground and hug her bones finally end?

Perhaps she saw something in me and that's why she gave me up for adoption. Maybe she wanted to keep me from experiencing the same kind of dysfunction and pain that would befall my siblings. It would take years for me to realize that I had not come from my mother but through her into this world to serve a purpose. And I have to be grateful to her for the gift of my life. Unfortunately, I almost lost my life before learning this very valuable lesson.

Six weeks into my freshman year at Johns Hopkins University, I found myself lying in the emergency room at Union Memorial Hospital. A catheter was in my bladder and a tube of liquid charcoal in one nostril. I could feel the tube in the back of my throat, and throughout the entire night I kept vomiting the grainy black liquid. There was an IV in my arm, and wires were attached to my chest. It took four police officers and a phalanx of nurses and doctors to hold me down while they pumped nearly 200 pills from my stomach. But I didn't die. Life and something bigger than me kept me in the world.

I stayed at Johns Hopkins for another year despite the stigma attached to me. Just about everybody—teammates, coach, and friends—knew that I had tried to kill myself. Some knew why. Others didn't. Some treated me like I was fragile. Others treated me like an outcast. After my second year at Hopkins I transferred to NYU to finish my undergrad degree in a more diverse and friendly atmosphere. I always had angels around me, people who nurtured me and gave me strength when I wanted to lay down and die. And there were those from outside Johns Hopkins University who rallied around me to make me strong again.

"You have work to do, Stacey Patton!"

"There are great things ahead of you!"

"You are supposed to live!"

"Live, Stacey Patton! Live!"

Looking back on my childhood, I wish I had been more rebellious. Less obedient. Less deferential. Frankly, I wish I had literally killed my master. But perhaps I am alive today because the little girl understood that even in bondage, I had the power to preserve my humanity and shape my own identity. My courage and strength could not be limited by definitions of race, class, gender, or age. Once I escaped to freedom, I had to continue to unhinge myself from the grips of those who sought to determine my potential and possibilities. I defined what freedom meant for me. I decided to live!

ACKNOWLEDGMENTS

Thank you to all the members of my extended family. Thank you for the food, shelter, money, nurture, patience, prayers, time, faith, and love. I could not have survived to share this story without you!

P.T., I love you more than a billion watts of starlight!